World Religions in Education

Approaches to
Islam

Richard Tames
Deputy Organiser of Extramural Studies
at the School of Oriental and African Studies,
University of London

John Murray

World Religions in Education
Series Editor: Robert Jackson

Approaching World Religions
Robert Jackson (editor)

Approaches to Islam
Richard Tames

In preparation
Approaches to Christianity
Approaches to Judaism
Approaches to Hinduism

© Richard Tames 1982

First published 1982
by John Murray (Publishers) Ltd
50 Albemarle Street, London W1X 4BD

Typeset by Inforum Ltd, Portsmouth
Printed in Great Britain by
Richard Clay (The Chaucer Press) Ltd,
Bungay, Suffolk

British Library Cataloguing in Publication Data

Tames, Richard
   Approaches to Islam. – (World
   religions in education; 2)
   1. Islam
   I. Title   II. Jackson, Robert   III. Series
   297   BP45
                 ,T36
ISBN 0-7195-3914-5

Contents

Part Two   Islam in the Classroom

Appendices

Preface

This book has been written by a non-Muslim and it is assumed that it will be read mainly by non-Muslims. The title – *Approaches to Islam* – is deliberately indicative of the author's stance and of his sympathy with the view so cogently expressed by Khurram Murad of the Islamic Foundation: 'The only demand that Muslims can perhaps reasonably make is that those who claim to present Islam should do so "as it is" and not as they wish it to have been, to be compatible with their own theological positions' (*The Muslim World Book Review*, vol. 1, no 3, Spring 1981). This is what I have tried to do.

I would also endorse the view put forward by the author of 'Islam and the school' in *Education* (19 November 1976) with regard to the position of Muslims in Britain:

> Solutions will come, but not quickly and not easily. The experience of Jews in Britain may be more relevant to British Muslims than that of Muslims in Turkey or Egypt. But ultimately the responses must be Muslim and British. Neither Lahore nor non-Muslim Englishmen can dictate or determine what they shall be.
>
> Both for the host community . . . which prides itself upon its tolerance, and for Muslims working out their faith in a society which may be secular or Christian but is certainly not Islamic, the late twentieth century is going to be a period of challenge. It is not enough to know about Islam, it is far more important to meet and know Muslims.

In writing *Approaches to Islam* I have incurred many debts of gratitude – to colleagues at the School of Oriental and African Studies, from whose learning I have greatly benefited; to the World of Islam Festival Trust, whose generosity made possible an earlier publication on which the present book is partly based; to the members of the Shap Working Party on World Religions in Education, whose pedagogic good sense has enriched me; to Muslim friends, whose understanding has encouraged me; and to the editor of this series, Robert Jackson, and Ann Cochrane at John Murray.

Part One

Aspects of
Islam

1
What is Islam?

> Like all the other world faiths it overflows all definition because it is open at one
> end to the immeasurable greatness of the Divine and because also it relates itself at
> the other end to the immeasurable diversity of the human. (W.C. Smith, *Islam in
> Modern History*)[1]

Religion has been variously defined as man's response to the uncontrollable
forces of nature and his sense of the infinite, as a device for the enshrine-
ment of social values and as 'a disease of language'. In terms of human
behaviour it has been seen to involve the affirmation of specified doctrines,
the performance of acts of worship, the observance of codes of moral
conduct, and conscious association with groups and institutions designated
and recognised as religious.

Islam defies definition but its most fundamental characteristics may
certainly be delineated. The most significant of these is perhaps the inter-
penetration of the faith, as that term is narrowly conceived by the West, with
every other aspect of human existence. Islam acknowledges no separation
between the sacred and the secular, the realm of Caesar and the realm of
God. It is a religion, but it is also far more than the West usually understands
by that term. It is a *din*, a complete way of life.

> Morphologically 'Islam' is a verbal noun, the infinitive of a verb meaning 'to
> accept', 'to submit' or perhaps 'to surrender' . . . in contemporary theological
> language the word that most nearly renders its sense is 'commitment'. The verbal
> quality of the word should be emphasised; by its very form it conveys a feeling of
> action and ongoingness not of something that is once and for all finished and
> static. Hence, rather than 'commitment' it might still better be translated as
> 'committing' in order to underline the continued renewal and repetition of man's
> obeisance to his Creator that it implies. In its most basic meaning Islam is the name
> of a relationship between men and their Sovereign Lord in which men self-
> consciously and reverently commit, submit or surrender themselves anew with
> each moment to the highest reality they are capable of apprehending. (Charles J.
> Adams, *A Reader's Guide to the Great Religions*)[2]

As Bernard Lewis has warned:

> The word Islam is used with at least three different meanings. Islam means the
> religion taught by the prophet Muhammad . . . Islam is the subsequent develop-

ment of this religion through tradition and through the work of the great Muslim jurists and theologians . . . In the third meaning, Islam is the counterpart not of Christianity but rather of Christendom . . . not what Muslims believed or were expected to believe but what they actually did – in other words Islamic civilisation as known to us in history. (*Race and Color in Islam*)[3]

Ninian Smart has put a similar point in more homely terms:

Islam is, as it were, a sandwich. At the top is the theology and refined spirituality of the religious elite, at the bottom the local customs into which Islam integrates. In the middle is the world of characteristic Islam – the mosque, the Koran and the law. (*Background to the Long Search*)[4]

There is the Islam of the palace and the learned *ulema*, and the Islam of the village and the unlettered peasant. There is the Islam of formally prescribed worship, with its detailed rituals and precise verbal formulae, and there is the Islam of local customary practice, associated with the shrines of holy men or the commemoration of the dead or circumcision, return from the *hajj* or the opening of a new house or business, for which no prescribed ceremonies are available.

There is, in other words, Islam idealised, the religion of the theologian, Islam realised, the religion of the phenomenologist and Islam personalised, the religion of the believer.

Submission, in Islam, is symbolised by the insistent call to prayer, by the day-long fasts of the month of Ramadan, and by the obligations to give alms and to undertake, if practicable, the pilgrimage to Mecca. But Islam goes far beyond a mere acceptance of certain rituals and observances, doctrinal beliefs and ethical principles: it is enshrined in a complex and comprehensive code of law, governing every aspect of daily life, from debts to divorce; Islam likewise pervades and constrains every form of cultural expression, whether it be art, architecture or literature.

The essential assumptions of the Islamic world view may be summarised as follows:

(i) Man is the summit of God's Creation and can choose to conform to His ordinances, whereas the rest of Creation cannot. Man is theomorphic, sharing in the Divine attributes of Intelligence, Will and Speech. But man is also weak and forgetful. Through revelation's guidance he can seek to overcome his imperfection.

(ii) Conformity with God's will determines a man's destiny in this life and the next.

(iii) God has revealed to man the right way to live by means of His Prophets (twenty-eight are named in the Qur'an). Abraham proclaimed that there was one Creator God, who was to be worshipped. Moses enshrined the faith in law, but limited its application to one people. Jesus universalised God's Word; but the messenger was worshipped rather than the message. Muhammad, as the 'seal of the Prophets', set the record straight.

(iv) Islam as a set of beliefs is a restatement of what *God* has to say to man.

But Islam is also a form of society embodying and elaborating that restatement in action.

(v) The characteristic manifestation of Islam is, therefore, not doctrine but
law. Law is defined in the widest sense as a body of prescriptions for right
action in every sphere of life.

That the ideal and the reality have often been far apart many Muslims
would no doubt acknowledge. But this in no way invalidates the ideal:

> We believe in one thing but we do not practise it. Well, the encouraging aspect is,
> although we don't practise it, we don't repudiate these values! While, in other
> societies, even the established and cherished religious values are being challenged.
> But fortunately for us, even people who are deviating from the prescribed norms
> still keep on believing that their salvation lies in adhering to them, or returning to
> them. (Anwar ul Haqq, former Chief Justice of Pakistan)

Islam has also provided the social framework for a great culture for more
than a thousand years. As H.A.R. Gibb emphasised:

> The medieval Muslim society was above all a religious society. To religion it owed
> its existence, for the religion of Islam was its sole bond of union. To religion it
> owed its common language of intercourse, for Islam intervened to prevent the
> dissolution of Arabic into local dialects and imposed a knowledge of Arabic on
> Persians and Turks. To religion it owed its heritage of literature, for religion had
> supplied the incentive to those studies out of which Arabic literature (poetry alone
> excepted) arose. To religion it owed its social organisation and its laws, for Islam
> had built up a new legal system obliterating, at least in all the civilised lands, the old
> social organisations and social inequalities. To religion it owed its corporate
> feeling, for Islam gave to every believer the sense of common fellowship in its
> universal Brotherhood. Religion, in time, not only created the cultural back-
> ground and psychological orientation of Muslim society, but supplied for its
> members a philosophy of living and ordained even the least activities of their daily
> life. (Ibn Battuta, *Travels in Asia and Africa*)[5]

Carleton S. Coon has taken note of another highly significant consequence
of the bonds which grew out of Islam:

> It can truthfully be said that this was an economic unit, this vast Middle East and its
> neighbouring regions. It was not economics, however, that held it together . . .
> What held it together was the mutual confidence of human beings. Throughout
> its history only one force has been found which will furnish this kind of confidence
> among peoples far removed from each other, and that force is religion. (*Caravan*)[6]

The significance of Islam cannot be captured in an analogy or a metaphor.
To speak of a 'structure' or a 'framework' or even of a 'culture' or a 'world
view' is to fossilise a dynamic entity, to smother a living force in the ether of
rational classification. As W.C. Smith has stressed:

> To know Islam, as to know any religion, is not only to be apprised of, even
> carefully acquainted with, its institutions, patterns and history, but also to
> apprehend what these mean to those who have the faith.(W.C. Smith, op.cit.,p.16)

Islam is as much a religion of action as of faith, as much a religion of doing as of believing. Law provides the pattern for the realisation of man's ideal state, a state which it is within his capacity to reach. Evil is the result of man's ignorance, weakness and forgetfulness. Hence the characteristic stress in Islam on ritual and exhortation to sustain patterns of social expectations which will make 'Islamic' behaviour habitual. The religious duties imposed by Islam are believed by Muslims to convey clearly discernible psychological and social benefits, but they are undertaken not to ensure such benefits but because Allah has commanded them.

The self-image of Islam

What do Muslims believe to be the most fundamental features of their faith? Even a cursory survey of the proselytising literature produced by various organisations reveals a number of common themes and recurrent claims, supported by the same, frequently quoted, fragments from the Qur'an.

1 Islam is universal

Although proclaimed to the Arabs in Arabic, Islam is a religion for all mankind.

> 'We have not sent thee but as a mercy for all the nations.' (21:102)
> 'Islam is the only future hope of humanity and its victorious emergence out of the present ideological warfare is the only guarantee of man's salvation.'
> 'Islam based its system on the concept that all men form one community (umma) without distinction of race or colour, language or culture, history or religion.'

2 Islam is comprehensive

Islam is the basis of a complete way of life, not merely for the individual but for whole nations as well.

> Islam is not a mere creed, nor does it represent simply an edification of souls, or a refinement and training of human virtues, but is rather a harmonious whole that also includes a just economic system, a well-balanced social organisation, codes of civil, criminal as well as international law, a philosophical outlook upon life along with a system of physical instruction, all of these flowing down from the same fundamental creed . . . (K. Ahmad, *Islam: Basic Principles and Characteristics*)[7]

3 Islam is eternal

Islam is the one true religion because there has only ever been one true religion of Allah, revealed to man by successive prophets. Other apparent religions are therefore distortions, corruptions or in other ways derivative of the one true religion of Islam which was revealed through Muhammad in its final perfected form.

> Islam is not a novel religion that appeared in Arabia fourteen centuries ago, preached by the Prophet, Muhammad. It is the religion God made known on the

day when man first appeared on earth. (A.A.H. Mahmud,*Islam's Mission is a World Mission*)[8]

In every age, in every country and among every people, all God-knowing and truth-loving men have believed and lived this very religion. They were all Muslims, irrespective of the fact whether they called the way Islam or anything else. (A.A. Maududi, *Towards Understanding Islam*)[9]

4 Islam is dynamic

This is closely related to 3. The validity of Islam is not related to any one historical period or set of circumstances. It is entirely capable of meeting the demands of the modern age.

> The modern Islamic movement that is still gathering force derives its strength from the past and makes use of all the modern available resources with its gaze fixed on the future ahead, for it is fully capable of performing that great miracle which has once been already effected by Islam making man look higher and beyond animal pleasures with his feet planted firmly on the earth and with his gaze fixed beyond the heavens. (Muhammad Qutb, *Islam, the Misunderstood Religion*)[10]
>
> Islam presents an ideology which satisfies the demands of stability as well as of change. (K. Ahmad, op.cit.)
>
> It [Shari'a] is not based on the customs or traditions of any particular people and is not meant for any particular period of human history. It is based on the same principles of nature on which man has been created. And as that nature remains the same in all periods and under all circumstances, the law based on its unalloyed principles should also be applicable to every period and under all circumstances. (A.A. Maududi, op.cit.)

5 Islam is non-coercive

Muslims are concerned to refute the allegation that Islam achieved its conversions at the point of a sword. Discussions of Jihad often stress (a) the conditions that surround warfare 'in the way of Allah', notably the requirement that it should be defensive, and (b) that warfare is the 'lesser jihad', the 'greater jihad' being the struggle against self which takes place within each devout Muslim.

> 'And fight in the way of Allah against those who fight against you, and not aggressively; surely Allah does not love the aggressor.' (2:190)
>
> 'Let there be no compulsion in religion. The Right Path has surely been made distinct from the wrong . . .' (2:256)
>
> 'God will not change the condition of a people until they change what is in their hearts.' (13:11)

6 Islam is rational

Commentators stress that Islam is not anti-scientific, adducing the achievements of medieval Muslim scholars in support of this claim.

> 'O my Lord! Advance me in knowledge.' (20:114)

There is no trace of any conflict between science and their religious beliefs to be found in the minds of these great Muslim scientists. Nor did there exist any hostilities between them and the ruling authorities such as might have led to their suffering or burning alive. (Muhammad Qutb, op.cit.) ,

It [the Qur'an] contains nothing against reason, and nothing that can be proved wrong. None of its injunctions is unjust; nothing is misleading. (A.A. Maududi, op.cit.)

7   *Islam is realistic*

Muslim writers argue that Islam accepts human nature as it is and proclaims a *modus vivendi* which takes account of the qualities and appetites of man and woman. Polygamy and purdah are frequently defended in these terms:

'Say [to them]: By whose order have you forbidden (unto yourself) those amenities which God has created for His bondmen and those good things to eat and use [which He made for you].' (7:32)

No apology is needed for upholding this most balanced approach to social relationship between men and women. Through this institution [polygamy] Divine Guidance has steered a middle course between the two extremes that were devoid of rationality, decency and justice [i.e. celibacy and promiscuity]. (Muhammad Qutb, op.cit.)

8   *Islam is colour-blind*

This is, in part, a consequence of 1.

Long ago Islam freed humanity from all racial prejudices. It did not content itself with the presentation of a beautiful vision of equality above but in practice did also achieve an unprecedented state of equality between all people, black, white or red, declaring that none enjoyed any priority over the others except by virtue of piety. (Muhammad Qutb, op.cit.)

Discrimination based on colour, class, race or territory is unfounded and illusory. It is a remnant of the days of ignorance which chained men down to servitude . . . Islam gives a revolutionary concept of the unity of mankind. (K. Ahmad, op.cit.)

The human race began from one man: Adam. It was from him that the family of man grew and the human race multiplied. All human beings born in this world have descended from that earliest pair: Adam and Eve. (A.A. Maududi, op.cit.)

9   *Islam is harmonious*

Muslim writers emphasise that through Islam harmony can be achieved both for the individual and for society. Islam, it is argued, reconciles the conflicting claims of the individual and the nation, faith and science, the material and the spiritual, the terrestrial and the transcendent.

Thus Islam has a twofold objective in this regard: in the individual life, it aims at making a just and sufficient provision to each and every individual so as to enable him to lead a decent, clean life; and in the collective sphere, it arranges things in such a way that all the social forces of a community are directed towards the enhancement of progress and civilisation, in accordance with its basic outlook

upon life that aims at striking a balance between the units and the whole, between individuals and the community. (Muhammad Qutb, op.cit.)
One can achieve real peace of body and of mind only through submission and obedience to Allah. Such a life of obedience brings peace of the heart and establishes real peace in society at large. (K. Ahmad, op.cit.)
God has so formulated the Shari'a that harmony and equilibrium are established in the different fields of life and the sacrifice of others' rights is reduced to the barest minimum. (A.A. Maududi, op.cit.)

10 Islam is misunderstood

The view that Islam is widely misunderstood is often expressed. Some writers blame the heritage of the Crusades: other allege deliberate misrepresentation by adherents of other faiths and/or 'Western imperialists' who seek to downgrade Islam in the estimation of non-Muslims but also to subvert the faith of Muslims themselves, especially young ones. In such writings the tone is often strident, the language immoderate, and the use of evidence more vigorous than discriminating.

> Naturally the policy pursued by the British was one of deriding Islamic laws and principles, of exiling the sense of their sanctity from Muslims' hearts, and of painting Islam in the blackest of colours so as to make them look down upon it and in due course of time to discard it totally. They did all this in order to tighten up their imperialistic grip on this country . . .
> This Islam that we call upon our fellow men to adopt as their guide in life is not one and the same thing as that passed off under this name by some Muslim rulers of today's East. (Muhammad Qutb, op.cit.)

Sources

1 W.C. Smith, *Islam in Modern History* (Mentor, 1957), p.17.

2 Charles J. Adams (ed.), *A Reader's Guide to the Great Religions* (Free Press, 2nd edn, 1977), pp.407–88.

3 Bernard Lewis, *Race and Color in Islam* (Harper & Row, 1970), p.6.

4 Ninian Smart, *Background to the Long Search* (BBC, 1977), p.210.

5 Ibn Battuta, *Travels in Asia and Africa* (Routledge & Kegan Paul, 1929), pp.26–7.

6 Carleton S. Coon, *Caravan* (Holt, Rinehart & Winston, 1958).

7 K. Ahmad, *Islam: Basic Principles and Characteristics* (Leicester: Islamic Foundation).

8 A.A.H. Mahmud, *Islam's Mission is a World Mission* (Cairo: Higher Council for Islamic Affairs).

9 A.A.Maududi, *Towards Understanding Islam* (Lahore: Islamic Publications Limited).

10 Muhammad Qutb, *Islam, the Misunderstood Religion* (Lahore: Islamic Publications Limited).

Further Reading

General outlines of Islam

Muslim authors

Hammudah Abdalati, *Islam in Focus* (American Trust Publications, 1975). Exposition of beliefs and practices. Includes a chapter on 'Distortions about Islam', covering Jihad, Jesus and the position of women.

Khurshid Ahmad (ed.), *Islam: Its Meaning and Message* (Islamic Council of Europe, 1975). Anthology of extracts from prominent Muslim writers.

Manazir Ahsan, *Islam: Faith and Practice* (Islamic Foundation, 1977). Inexpensive, brief illustrated guide. Useful map and statistics.

Abd-al-Rahman Azzam, *The Eternal Message of Muhammad* (Quartet Books, 1979). Essays by an Egyptian diplomat; especially useful on international relations and Islam's world role.

Salem Azzam, *Islam and Contemporary Society* (Longman Islamic Council of Europe, 1982).

H.M. Balyuzi, *Muhammad and the Course of Islam* (George Ronald, 1976). Biography of the Prophet followed by an outline history of Islamic civilisation.

Ismail R. Al-Faruqi, *Islam* (Argus Communications, Niles, Illinois, 1979). Brief, well-produced outline with colour illustrations.

Muhammad Hamidullah, *Introduction to Islam* (MWH London Publishers, 1979). Detailed exposition of beliefs and practices. Text subdivided and well indexed for easy reference.

Mohammad Fadhel Jamali, *Letters on Islam: Written by a Father in Prison to his Son* (World of Islam Festival Trust, 1978). Essays by a former Iraqi Prime Minister.

Muhammad Zafrulla Khan, *Islam: Its Meaning for Modern Man* (Routledge & Kegan Paul, 1980). Detailed exposition of beliefs and practices written by a diplomat and leading member of the Ahmadiyya movement.

Abdel Haleem Mahmun, *The Creed of Islam* (World of Islam Festival Trust, 1978). Concise outline of beliefs by the Grand Sheikh Al-Azhar.

Abul Ala Maududi, *Towards Understanding Islam* (Islamic Foundation, 1973). Brief outline of the faith by influential Pakistani Muslim leader. Available in many editions in eighteen languages.

S.H. Nasr, *Ideals and Realities of Islam* (Allen & Unwin, 1967).

Cat Stevens, *Islam: My Religion* (Ta-Ha Publishers, 1981). Interview with an ex-pop singer.

Non-Muslim authors

Kenneth Cragg, *The House of Islam* (Wadsworth, 2nd edn, 1975). Elegant concise survey by leading Christian expert.

Caesar E. Farah, *Islam: Beliefs and Observances* (Barrai Educational Series, 1970). Fact-packed, concise historical survey.

Clifford Geertz, *Islam Observed: Religious Development in Morocco and Indonesia* (University of Chicago Press, 1968). Brilliantly written anthropological essay on the relation between faith and culture.

H.A.R. Gibb, *Islam* (OUP, 2nd edn, 1968) (formerly entitled *Mohammedanism*). Standard brief, scholarly outline.

Alfred Guillaume,*Islam* (Penguin, 2nd edn, 1956). Standard brief, scholarly outline.

Hava Lazarus Yafeh, *Some Religious Aspects of Islam* (EH Brill, 1981). Scholarly articles on such topics as festivals, Jerusalem, modern Muslim theology and the interaction of Judaism and Islam.

Bernard Lewis, *The World of Islam* (Thames & Hudson, 1976). Sumptuously illustrated 'coffee-table' book with the emphasis on history and culture.

Jean Mathe, *The Civilisation of Islam* (Minerva, Geneva, 1980). Well-illustrated general survey emphasising tradition and culture.

Folco Quilici, *Children of Allah* (Chartwell Books Inc., 1978). Superbly illustrated travelogue of the Muslim world.

D.S. Roberts,*Islam: A Westerner's Guide* (Kogan Page, 1981). Well-organised survey by a western architect working in the Middle East.

John B. Taylor, *Thinking About Islam* (Lutterworth, 1971). Brief illustrated outline aimed at upper secondary level.

A.S. Tritton,*Islam: Belief and Practices* (Hutchinson, 1951. Reprinted 1980 by Books for Libraries, Arno Press, New York). Scholarly outline; especially useful for chapters on sects and popular practices.

Charis Waddy, *The Muslim Mind* (Longman, 1976). Useful anthology of extracts from contemporary sources.

W.M. Watt, *What is Islam?* (Longman, 2nd edn, 1979). Scholarly analysis of the origins and development of Islamic doctrines and their role today.

The most comprehensive bibliography available is the on-going *Index Islamicus* compiled by Professor J.D. Pearson and published by Mansell. This gives details, under forty-three major subject-headings, of articles appearing in academic journals, papers given at international congresses and of the proceedings of learned societies.

There are two very useful quarterly publications which list and review recent and forthcoming publications on Islam and Muslim countries. *New Books Quarterly* is available from the Islamic Council of Europe, London, and *The Muslim World Book Review* is published by the Islamic Foundation, Leicester (see appendix 10 for addresses). For lively journalistic coverage of contemporary affairs see the monthly *Arabia: The Islamic World Review* (Islamic Press Agency Ltd). A major anthropological reference source is Richard V. Weekes (ed.), *Muslim Peoples: A World Ethnographic Survey* (Greenwood Press, 1978). Units 20–21 of the Open University's 'Inter-faculty Second Level Course' on 'Man's Religious Quest' cover *Islam and the Muslim* and are written by Kenneth Cragg. Illustrated and with questions and specimen answers.

2

Images and Perspectives

As Abdul Wahid Hamid has rightly declared, 'a rudimentary knowledge of Islam does not form part of the stock of information demanded of the educated in the West' (*The Muslim*, May 1972). The memoirs of an American oil company executive reveal the extent of this general ignorance:

> During our first week at the Aramco School on Long Island, questions were asked of us to ascertain our general knowledge about the Arab world . . . One of our members thought that Islam was a 'game of chance, similar to bridge'. Another said it was a 'mysterious sect founded in the South by the Ku Klux Klan' . . . The Prophet Muhammad was thought to be the man who 'wrote the Arabian Nights' . . . One of the more reasonable answers came from one of our men who said 'Muhammad had something to do with a mountain. He either went to the mountain or it came to him.' (Grant C. Butler, *Kings and Camels*)[1]

It would, however, be misleading for any teacher to assume that his pupils' minds are completely blank on the subject and, therefore, open and receptive to whatever information may be put before them. Opinions may be strongly held even when they are imperfectly articulated and based on minimal or distorted information. Consider, for instance, the following responses to the invitation 'Explain why you would or would not like to visit Saudi Arabia', from pupils in a comprehensive school near London.
In favour of a visit:
Second-year pupils (3)
'To see . . . if they have used their money on a worthwhile cause.'
'They just aren't realising that the oil will run out. Then they'll be back where they started. Also, they'll have to change their laws for a modern world. I think I'd like to visit but just for two or three weeks in a five-star hotel.'
Third-year pupils (3)
'It would be a change from school.' (All three respondents)
Fourth-year pupils (7)
'I would like to attend the public trials and whippings of people who have crimed [*sic*] . . . The food would be an experience, every evening having wine with the dinner.'
'Sometimes on films . . . you see camels and that kind of thing. I would like to know if it is really like that.'

'I, who lived there, remembered beaches and Roman aqueduct and fear of kidnapping.'

'Fascinating to find out how the rapid change from rags to riches has affected the people.'

'I would like to go . . . with a large armed force blow up the wogs and take over the oilfields and bring the economic situation under control so's to have more money to spend on arms to attack the Soviet Union. This would then possibly result in world peace and prosperity thus enabling the rich Western powers to help the smaller underdeveloped nations. I would also put the smelly arabs onto a world slave market.'

Against a visit:

Second-year pupils (11)

'If you stay out there too long you lose a lot of weight.'

'Israelis might launch an attack.'

'Expensive.'

'You need a bodyguard before you leave your home.'

'I have met the Saudi Arabian football team, when they came over to play they stayed in the same hotel as us. I didn't think much of them and if they're all like them I would hate to go over there.'

'As the country is a Muslim one the people have lives dominated by religion which I do not agree with.'

'They are very strict and put you in prison for drinking whisky.'

'They are always kidnapping people or they are fighting all the time.'

Third year pupils (8)

'I would not like the primitive traditional ways that they have.'

'It's such a restricted place to live, even to visit.'

'Because it's too barren and boring.'

'Their punishments are very severe.'

'The only good thing I can think of . . . is that they pay a lot of money in wages.'

'There are very strict religions which do not allow you to drink alcohol and certain animals are sacred.'

Fourth-year pupils (14)

'Because they have no freedom there.'

'The towns are dirty and smelly, the people are ill-mannered and unhelpful.'

'There is no middle class.'

'Women are treated as slaves.'

'I think the culture is wrong and the religion is wrong . . . We do not force Christianity onto Muslims that enter Britain, so why should they be able to push their religion on us?'

'They also have a lot of bandits out there in the desert . . .'

'Many people have slaves which you wouldn't think of nowadays.'

'Really I don't know what the country is like so I can't really comment on it but from what I hear in the papers and television it doesn't sound a very nice country to live in or visit.'

'The police and government are corrupt.'

'The only thing we need from Saudi Arabia is their money and their oil. Not the population.'

'The country is run by a bunch of oil-rich capitalist bastards who don't give a shit for the starving Bedouins and Tuaregs.'

These comments are both revealing and promising, largely because, although unprompted, they are couched in terms of value-judgements. Note, for instance, the assumption that Western culture is as much impera- tive as normative — 'they'll have to change their laws for a modern world'. Undoubtedly the views expressed above will need skilful handling if discus- sion is not to turn into confrontation or mere contemptuous dismissal of the point at issue. Role-playing and imaginative writing, which demand iden- tification with the object of hostility, may be useful preliminaries to debate. And debate should be directed to its proper function, serving as a stimulus to greater open-mindedness and a desire for further information and as a demonstration of the methods of civilised enquiry.

Teachers are not, of course, themselves immune from prejudice. Con- sider the following responses to a word-association test, based on the word 'Arab', offered by a group of second-year trainee teachers.

Words mentioned by at least 70 per cent of the group: camels, oil, tents, nomads, deserts.

Words mentioned by at least 45 per cent of the group: Muslim, mosque, sheikh, spice, bedouin, markets.

Words mentioned by 20 per cent or less of the group: sand, polygamy, Egypt, goats, palm trees, raids, Arabia, Hindu, mat-makers, blankets, greasy, anti-Jewish, T.E. Lawrence, sheeps' eyes, money, oasis, drought, heat, horses, dark skins.

The word 'Arab' may provoke a 'sheikh syndrome' but Islam itself also calls forth definite views, even amongst those who claim to know little about it. On a number of occasions I have asked groups of teachers to write down on a piece of paper three things they liked or admired about Islam and Muslims and three things they disliked or disapproved of. The following analysis of forty responses can be no more than indicative, because the sample is too small and too heavily biased towards female and primary school teachers to claim to be more than that. The results are, however, of interest, not least in suggesting priorities for further reading and reflection.

Achievements in art and architecture proved to be undoubtedly the most generally approved feature of Islamic culture, mentioned by half the sam- ple; a third mentioned close family ties, respect for the elderly and a sense of community responsibility. Respect for religion as such and a sense of devo- tion to its obligations was noted by about a quarter. Other facets of Islam that were approved included its high ideals (especially equality and brotherhood), its all-embracing character ('not just something for Sundays') and Muslims as examples of industriousness and hospitality. Food, festivals, the absence of alcohol, and a positive attitude towards education all received single commendations.

The list of dislikes was headed by what was seen as a repressive or restrictive attitude to women. No fewer than three-quarters of the respondents mentioned this and several others made a similar point in slightly different terms (for example 'patriarchalism', 'male domination'). Only three, however, referred explicitly to arranged marriages. The second most commonly expressed dislike, mentioned by a third, was 'fanaticism', or the associated ideas of 'intolerance' and 'rigidity'. A fifth of the sample referred to the strictness of traditional Islamic punishments. Two people alleged that Islam 'doesn't encourage people to think for themselves' and two referred to 'food and drink fetishisms'. Only one brought up the old charge of 'fatalism'.

A great deal of the responsibility for misunderstanding between Muslims and non-Muslims has been attributed to the mass media. But teachers must also be aware that academic writing is capable of arousing strong passions. Imagine, for example, Muslim reactions to *Hagarism: The Making of the Islamic World* by Patricia Crone and Michael Cook,[2] which advances what one reviewer, with masterly understatement, called a 'controversial' thesis – that Islam is the product, not of the divinely inspired utterances of a prophet, but of a lengthy process of ideological asset-stripping through which Christian, Jewish and Samaritan traditions were re-vamped to serve as the post-conquest rationalisation of Arab expansion and provide it with an institutional super-structure. As the authors disarmingly confess in their 'Preface', 'the account we have given of the origins of Islam is not one which any believing Muslim can accept' (p.vii); it is, in their own words, 'a book written by infidels for infidels' (p.viii). Asserting that 'there is no hard evidence for the existence of the Koran in any form before the last decade of the seventh century' (p.3) and that 'what purport to be accounts of religious events in the seventh century [that is Muslim historical sources] are utilisable only for the study of religious ideas in the eighth' (p.3), they proceed to construct an account of the origins of Islam by an intensive examination of contemporary non-Muslim sources. The argument is dense, based on great erudition (the 148 pages of text are supported by 81 pages of notes and references and a 21-page bibliography) and presented with considerable verve. Any brief summary must run the risk of caricature but the following points must suffice to indicate the general viewpoint of the authors:

(i) Muhammad is characterised as the appropriator of a Jewish messianic tradition which justifies an irredentist (and initially anti-Christian) Arab war of expansion to redeem Palestine. His prophetic status is subsequently magnified to authenticate a distinctive cultural identity for the Arab appropriators of the Fertile Crescent and the Sassanian empire.

(ii) 'Islamic civilisation may be defined as what was left after antiquity had been ground through a rabbinic mill' (p.104). Assisted by the conquered Syrians in the role of intellectual helots, the post-conquest Muslim elite re-work the wreckage of the cultures they have smashed to create a less than coherent, but quite distinctive, synthesis – Islam. Roman and other legal concepts and practices are repackaged and Islamised by manufacturing

Prophetic traditions to legitimate them. Greek philosophy, however, proves less amenable and more threatening and is, with difficulty, rejected. Iranian statecraft is likewise spurned. The result is 'a civilisation haunted by the desert and the ghetto' (p.106).

(iii) The result was, in the author's view, a 'profoundly dislocated' polity and culture.

Many readers may find *Hagarism* as unacceptable intellectually as a Muslim would theologically. But the book addresses itself to a major historical puzzle – the fact that 'Islamic civilisation is the outcome of a barbarian conquest of lands of very ancient cultural traditions. As such it is unique in history.' The authors seek to explain the phenomenon in terms of the cultural crises afflicting the conquered areas immediately prior to their 'pulverisation'. The analysis is complex but should prove thought-provoking even for those who can accept neither the authors' theory of the origins of Islam nor their characterisation of its subsequent 'intransigence'.

Hagarism is perhaps an extreme example of the 'Orientalist' scholarship which has been the subject of such spirited attack by Professor Edward Said. *Orientalism*[3] is an angry book. The author, Edward Said, is a Palestinian, educated in colonial Palestine and Egypt and currently (1981) Professor of English and Comparative Literature at Columbia University, New York. He traces the origins and development of 'Orientalism' as a 'style of discourse' evolved by an Anglo-French intellectual establishment, defining the terms in which the 'West' came to understand, as it came to control, the 'East', its 'cultural contestant', its 'other' in a most complete sense, the antithesis against which it could regard itself as the epitome of all that was 'rational, developed, humane, superior'. Said's wide-ranging survey encompasses the pioneers of Orientalist scholarship, such as Sir William Jones and Edward Lane, literary popularisers like Byron, Disraeli, Flaubert and Hugo, twentieth-century scholars such as Gibb and Lewis and even collective enterprises like the Cambridge History of Islam ('an intellectual failure by any standards other than those of Orientalism'). Said asserts that 'Orientalism' is characterised by four persisting conventions – that the West is inherently superior, that 'abstractions about the Orient, particularly those based on texts representing a 'classical' Oriental civilisation, are always preferable to direct evidence drawn from modern Oriental realities', that 'the Orient is eternal, uniform and incapable of defining itself' and that the Orient is to be feared and/or controlled. (Strategic motives, both in the narrow and specific, and a larger and more general sense, are seen to underpin the entire structure of the Orientalist enterprise.) Orientalists are vilified for their persistence in using stereotypes (for example 'the Arab mind', 'the Islamic mentality') long since discarded as racist crudities in other fields of study, and for their alleged predilection for pontificating in broad generalisations, vague metaphors and summative assertions, unsupported by evidence. In their treatment of Islam, Said argues, the Orientalists, bound by the philological origins of their discipline, approach it as a body of doctrines, not a way of life ('Islam is about texts, not about people');

diversity and conflict are obscured in the interests of producing a textually-based account of a phenomenon which has no particular location in time or space and is accessible and comprehensible only to Orientalists, but not to the ulema or the ordinary mass of Muslims. G.E. von Grünebaum, for instance, is accused of a 'virulent dislike of Islam' and of presenting it as 'a unitary phenomenon, unlike any other religion or civilisation ... anti-human, incapable of development, self-knowledge or objectivity, as well as uncreative, unscientific and authoritarian'. Only a few contemporary scholars (Berque, Rodinson, Geertz, Owen) escape general condemnation in such terms. What Said offers by way of critique, however, is complemented by no remedy or solution apart from allusions to the need to 'decolonialise' 'so-called area studies', a remedy couched in the same vague, metaphorical terms he abhors in others.

Given the heritage of propaganda and prejudice which has clouded the mutual perceptions of Muslim and non-Muslim it is scarcely surprising that each is likely to regard the other as holding views of his most cherished values which are grossly lacking in proportion and perspective. Some Christians, at least those without a professional knowledge of their faith, tend to regard it as ethically superior to Islam and seem to remain blithely indifferent to the complexities of the doctrine of the Trinity, which Muslims regard as theologically absurd. Muslims, on the other hand, are resentful of Western gibes about pork and polygamy and note the frequent failure of Westerners to respect religious values as such.

It is often difficult to convey to young sceptics just what it means to accept one's religion wholeheartedly. But it is very important to put across the idea that Muslims take their faith seriously, in other words that they are prepared to put up with a certain amount of inconvenience on its behalf.

It is also true that many young ex- or para-Christians find Muslims 'uncompromising' where their religion is concerned. But to use this adjective is to reveal that one has failed to make the imaginative leap into the mind of the believer. How can one compromise God's eternal Truth? Where there is no doubt there can be no compromise.

Those who argue for greater 'religious literacy', who desire that all children should be 'religiate', seem all too eager to assume that the critical, 'objective' approach to religion can be accepted by members of all faiths as a neutral meeting-ground and a firm basis for curriculum development. But the very notion of a critical study of religion, requiring the temporary suspension of value-commitments (or at least an attempt at this) has sprung from Western and, therefore, Christian, or perhaps post-Christian civilisation in the last two or three centuries. As W.C. Smith rather drily observed: 'To look for historical criticism of the Qur'an is rather like looking for a psychoanalysis of Jesus.' (*Islam in Modern History*, p.26.)

Consider, therefore, the following question from a university examining board's paper for its Diploma in Religious Knowledge. 'To what extent does the situation in Arabia previous to the time of Muhammad explain the emergence of Islam?' This question surely implies a historical cum sociological analysis of what one might call, to borrow the economists' jargon, the preconditions for religion's 'take-off into self-sustained growth'. But to the believer surely the 'emergence' of Islam (which to Muslim eyes had 'emerged' long before anyway) depends only on the Will of Allah, not necessarily incompatible with the terms of the other 'explanation' but a significant difference of emphasis.

To ask 'How far was Muhammad an original thinker?' is again to invite the indignation of the pious. If you believe that the Qur'an is the literal Word of God, the answer must be, not at all.

What is true of examination papers is also true of textbooks. Numerous textbooks on 'World Religions' have been published during the last decade or so. The results are not always what one would desire. Whether the fault lies in the superficiality of the author's knowledge of his subject or the virtual impossibility of presenting a balanced and accurate picture of a major religious tradition in the space of a few pages, the outcome can be a text loaded with questionable assertions and implicit value-judgements. The following examples – all taken from one chapter of a school text written by a well-known academic expert on comparative religions – may suffice to illustrate this point. The author declares, for instance, that 'He [i.e. Muhammad] is regarded . . . as intercessor for mankind and pleading for them on the day of judgement.' While it *is* true that generations of sophisticated Muslims have prayed for the Prophet's intercession, this is *not* in accordance with strictly orthodox belief which stresses that there are *no* intermediaries between man and God.

When dealing with the Qur'anic accounts of Heaven, the same author assures the reader that 'These descriptions are very much like those of the book of Revelation and *informed* Muslims do not take them literally. The descriptions of Paradise, with trees, streams, fruits, fountains, dark-eyed spirits, and so on, are all symbolical.' (My emphasis.) Yet Riadh El-Droubie – scarcely an 'uninformed Muslim' – asserts quite clearly that 'Heaven and Hell are believed by the Muslims to be actual places. Muslims also believe that their eternal life will be both spiritual and physical. It might differ from earthly life, yet it is not a purely imaginary existence.' (Introduction, *Basic Principles of Islam*.) The same author commits another doctrinal *faux pas* when he tells us that 'the most outstanding non-Muslim figure of the Qur'an is Jesus'. To a Muslim, of course, Jesus is one of the most revered of God's prophets and by no means a 'non-Muslim figure'.

Any author trying to produce a concise and comprehensive text which will prove comprehensible to secondary school children obviously faces great difficulties with regard to the concepts he chooses to present and the language he uses to explain them. But facile generalisation and short-hand phrases must be avoided. The statement (from the same author) that 'The emancipation of women and their security from easy divorce are still distant hopes for many Muslim women' is almost devoid of precise meaning and yet misleading in the overall impression that it gives. 'The emancipation of women' needs to be spelled out in concrete detail, giving due account to psychological and cultural as well as legal and political aspects (and also due credit to the rights of women which are enshrined in Islamic law). In referring to 'easy divorce' one needs to distinguish between the relative informality of the procedure and the infrequency with which it is invoked before a complex system of reconciliatory procedures have been exhausted. Likewise, one should beware of such vague referents as 'distant hopes' and 'many Muslim women'. The only generalisations that are worth making are about diversity.

One of the major problems raised by the comparative approach is that the teacher finds himself giving an encapsulated or foreshortened account of his subject matter. One effect of this is to present students with a series of distinct 'religions' as though each one was a totally coherent, autonomous and homogeneous 'system', whereas it might be more accurate to refer to 'religious traditions' each of which expresses certain central tenets through a wide variety of manifestations.

It would, therefore, be quite wrong to present Islam as a monolith, devoid of variety, either in the past or in the present. Historically, its development has been marked by the division between Sunnite and Shi'ite and by the complex sub-divisions which developed within and out of the Shi'ite community. There has also been a strong mystical tradition, chiefly, though not exclusively, associated with the Sufis. Nor has syncretism been absent, either at the individual level (e.g. the Mughal Emperor Akbar) or at the communal level (e.g. the Druzes of the Levant). In West Africa, South Asia and Indonesia, Islam has been obliged to come to terms with indigenous cultural traditions of great antiquity and strength. Its ability to absorb and transcend such diverse influences is the basis of its claim to be a 'world religion'.

Differences of perspective can have very direct practical implications, especially for education. For instance, a Muslim parent at a conference organised by the Muslim Teachers' Association at the Islamic Cultural Centre in April 1979 declared that 'Sex education and sex aids are for a society of people sick and disenchanted by their own promiscuity'. The Muslim Educational Trust in a 'Memorandum on the religious education of Muslim children in schools', submitted to the Secretary of State for Education in 1970, argued that:

> Indoctrination relates to the method of education . . . and not to its content. If authoritarian methods are adopted and teaching is done without giving adequate reasons, this would be indoctrination, whether this is done in the case of religious beliefs and practices, or in respect of scientific theories and concepts. There can be 'indoctrination' in the teaching of physics, biology, economics and sociology, as there can be in religious instruction.

The question of perspective can be illustrated with reference to an exchange of views which took place in 1975 on the question of single sex education raised in papers published by the Union of Muslim Organisations and the Religious and Cultural Panel of the Yorkshire Committee for Community Relations. In its issue of October 1975 *Education*, the periodical of the Association of Education Committees, devoted a leading article to the question of what it chose to call 'The sectarian threat to LEAs'. This drew forth a stinging rebuke from W. Owen Cole, the Convener of the YCCR Religious and Cultural Panel, couched in the following terms:

> The main point I would wish to make is that the opposition of Muslims to co-education is on religious grounds; that not all Muslims hold this view is beside the point. Because most Christians do not seem to be pacifists, this does not invalidate Roman Catholic objections to birth control or the Quaker peace witness as the consequences of religious belief. No matter what you say or think, understanding will only come through recognising that, for the Muslims this paper has in mind, this is a religious issue.
>
> Secondly, to denounce this view as a 'sectarian' travesty is to use highly emotive language, which betrays an intolerant attitude. Indeed I would argue that the whole tone of your piece was insensitive and even arrogant. Such a light dismissal of strongly held views, even if they are those of a minority, bodes ill for democracy.

In these circumstances it is encouraging to note that a recent Muslim publication gives vigorous endorsement to the role of education in promoting a better understanding of Islam.

> The Muslim community, the largest minority, is relatively new to Britain and the problems which they face do not stem from religious antagonism, or, generally speaking, racism, but rather from cultural differences and the aura of mystery and misconception associated with Islam. One of the advantages of bringing Islamic instruction into the schools would be to bring Islam into the open and to let people see Muslims as they are and thus erase the fantasy images projected on TV and in the press. (*The Muslim Guide*, Mustafa Yusuf McDermott and Muhammad Manazir Ahsan)[4]

Sources

1 Grant C. Butler, *Kings and Camels*, 1960, pp.16–17.
2 Patricia Crone and Michael Cook, *Hagarism: The Making of the Islamic World* (CUP, 1977).
3 Edward Said, *Orientalism* (Routledge & Kegan Paul, 1978).
4 Mustafa Yusuf McDermott and Muhammad Manazir Ahsan, *The Muslim Guide* (Islamic Foundation, 1980).

Further reading

The origins of current Western images of Islam are dealt with at length and with great scholarship in Norman Daniel, *Islam and the West, the Making of an Image* (Edinburgh University Press, 3rd edn, 1966) and *Islam, Europe and Empire* (Edinburgh University Press, 1966). For a more concise account of the same process see Maxime Rodinson's chapter on 'The Western Image and Western Studies of Islam' in J. Schacht and C.E. Bosworth, *The Legacy of*

Islam (OUP, 1974 pp.9–62). On specific aspects see Khalil I. Semaan (ed.), *Islam and the Medieval West: Aspects of Intercultural Relations* (State University of New York, 1980). The period from the Middle Ages to Thomas Carlyle's seminal lecture on Muhammad 'The Hero as Prophet' is covered in Byron Porter Smith, *Islam in English Literature* (Caravan Books, 2nd edn, 1977). Another important work on the same theme is Leila Ahmed, *Edward W. Lane: A Study of his Life and Work and of British Ideas of the Middle East in the 19th Century* (Longman, 1978). Lane produced the first English translation *from the Arabic* of the 'Arabian Nights' and wrote a classic ethnographic study of *The Manners and Customs of the Modern Egyptians* (1836) which is still a readable and valuable source of first-hand information (J.M. Dent, Everyman edition 1966). See also Katharine Sim, *Jean Louis Burckhardt: A Biography* (Quartet, 1981).

A wide-ranging study which places particular emphasis on popular literature and the cinema and considers some of the most recent developments in this field is Sari J. Nasir, *The Arabs and the English* (Longman, 2nd edn, 1979) (see especially chapter 6, 'New Encounter and Old Stereotypes'). Michael Adams and Christopher Mayhew, *Publish it Not . . .* (Longman, 1975), is a study of mass-media treatment of the Arab–Israeli conflict. Further illumination can be found in George N. Atiyeh (ed.), *Arab and American Cultures* (American Enterprise Institute for Public Policy Research, 1977) especially in William E. Leuchtenburg's essay on 'The American Perception of the Arab World'. An intriguing sidelight is thrown on the general theme of cultural interaction in E.L. Ranelagh, *The Past We Share: The Near Eastern Ancestry of Western Folk Literature* (Quartet, 1979), which includes a long section on 'The Arabian Nights'.

Travel writers have played a major part in shaping our image of the Muslim peoples. Robin Bidwell, *Travellers in Arabia* (Hamlyn, 1976) is a popular, attractively illustrated account which summarises the writings of such major figures as Burton, Palgrave, Doughty and Philby and reviews the impressions of many less celebrated ones. Peter Brent, *Far Arabia: Explorers of the Myth* (Quartet, 1979) covers much the same ground, and so does *Explorers of Arabia* by Zahra Freeth and Victor Winstone (Allen & Unwin, 1978).

Wilfred Thesiger is, perhaps, the last of this line and his account of journeys through the 'empty quarter' in *Arabian Sands* (Penguin, 1964) can truly be described as an epic tale of endurance. Of quite a different character is Jonathan Raban's quirky and immensely readable travelogue *Arabia Through the Looking Glass* (Fontana, 1980).

Other relevant studies include Sarah Searight, *The British in the Middle East* (Weidenfeld & Nicolson, 1969) and Denis Wright, *The English Amongst the Persians* (Heinemann, 1977).

Perhaps the most relevant work of all is Edward Said, *Covering Islam: How the Media and the Experts Determine How We See the Rest of the World* (Routledge & Kegan Paul, 1981). Said focuses on recent reporting of Islam, with special reference to the 'Death of a Princess' episode and the Iranian hostage crisis.

3
The Language of Faith

According to a distinguished American scholar, 'Serious study of Islam without acquaintance with Arabic is an absurdity' (Charles J. Adams, 'Islamic Religious Traditions').[1] It is therefore necessary that those of us who neither command any competence in Arabic nor are ever likely to do so should at least come to some appreciation of its importance.

First, we should note that the Qur'an, which Muslims regard as, quite literally, God's own speech, is in Arabic. And we should note that the Qur'an refers to itself as an Arabic Qur'an (42:4; 16:103; 26:195). As Cragg[2] has put it, 'The Qur'an is the glory of Arabic and Arabic the pride of the Qur'an'.

Second, we should be aware of the power and prestige of the Arabic language and poetry among the peoples of pre-Islamic Arabia and of the enduring significance of this cultural preference. According to Sir Hamilton Gibb, 'upon the Arab mind the impact of artistic speech is immediate; the words, passing through no filter of logic or reflection, which might weaken or deaden their effect, go straight to the head'. Something of the spirit of exultation induced by the Arabic language can be caught from these words of Al Tha'alibi (d.1038):

> Whoever loves the Prophet loves the Arabs, and whoever loves the Arab loves the Arabic language in which the best of books was revealed . . . Whomsoever God has guided to Islam believes that Muhammad is the best of Prophets . . . that the Arabs are the best of peoples . . . and that Arabic is the best of languages.

The great scholar al-Biruni (b.973) drew out some of the implications of the status of Arabic as a canonical and international language:

> Our religion and our empire are Arab . . . subject tribes have often joined together to give the state a non-Arab character. But they have not been able to achieve their aim, and as long as the call to prayer continues to echo in their ears five times a day, and the Qur'an in lucid Arabic is recited among the worshippers standing in rows behind the imam, and its refreshing message is preached in the mosques, they will needs submit, the bond of Islam will not be broken nor its fortresses vanquished. Branches of knowledge from all countries in the world have been translated into the tongue of the Arabs, embellished and made seductive, and the beauties of languages have infused their veins and arteries, despite the fact that each people considers its own language beautiful since it is accustomed to it and employs it in its

daily offices. I speak from experience for I was reared in a language in which it would be strange to see a branch of knowledge enshrined. Thence I passed to Arabic and Persian, and I am a guest in both languages, having made an effort to acquire them, but I would rather be insulted in Arabic than praised in Persian.

Third, we should be aware of the significance of Arabic as the core of traditional Muslim culture. Muslims, believing not only that the Qur'an was God's actual speech but that Arabic was an immortal language, safeguarded by God until the end of the world, began to study Arabic rigorously in terms of its grammar and phonology and to celebrate its power and charm both verbally, in poetry, and visually, in calligraphy.

Fourth, we should remember that Arabic has touched the lives and thoughts of all the Muslim peoples. As Titus Burckhardt has emphasised, 'decadent as they may have been, the great sedentary civilisations would have made short work of absorbing these hordes of Bedouin Arabs . . . But . . . it was the Arabs . . . who imposed on the sedentary peoples they conquered their forms of thought and expression by imposing their language upon them. (*Art of Islam: Language and Meaning*)[3] More than half of the vocabulary of Persian is Arabic and Arabic has supplied the script for Iran, Pakistan, Bangladesh and, until the 1920s, Turkey and its empire as well. It has moreover provided the Muslim world with a uniform theological and ethical vocabulary. Perhaps five-sixths of all Muslims do not speak Arabic as their mother tongue, but they revere it none the less.

Finally, we should bear in mind the significance of Arabic in the everyday practice of Islam. The 'shahadah' and 'Fatihah' must be the most frequently repeated words in human history. Muslims daily employ such verbal formulae as 'Bismillah' (In the name of God), 'Inshallah' (God willing) or 'Alhamduillah' (Thanks be to God) with respect to the most mundane acts and occurrences of everyday life. S.H. Nasr has argued that 'We cannot express our being in any way more directly than in speech . . . Islam makes it central in its rites, which revolve most of all around prayer.' Once the divine character of human speech is grasped many other features of Islam became much easier to appreciate – the importance of precision in reciting from the Qur'an, the emphasis in Muslim jurisprudence on the absolute letter of the law, and the special status accorded to Jews and Christians as ahl-al-Kitab (people of the book).

Sources

1 Charles J. Adams, 'Islamic Religious Traditions' in L. Binder (ed.), *The Study of the Middle East* (Wiley, 1976).

2 Kenneth Cragg, *The Event of the Qur'an* (Allen & Unwin, 1971), p.40.

3 Titus Burckhardt, *Art of Islam: Language and Meaning* (World of Islam Festival Trust, 1979), p.40.

4
Muhammad

To Muslims, Muhammad is not, as the textbooks would so often have it, 'the founder of the world's youngest religion', but rather the 'seal of the prophets', the last and greatest of God's messengers to man, who came to close the cycle of prophecy by restating, finally and clearly, the message of man's Creator and Judge. As Seyyed Hossein Nasr asserts, 'Islam is a religion based not on the personality of the founder but on Allah himself.' Hence profound Muslim resentment at the epithet 'Muhammadan' which implies worship of the Prophet and thus traduces the central tenet of their creed, the absolute Oneness of God.

Muslims insist that Muhammad was in no sense the author or composer of the Qur'an, which is God's own speech. Rather he was the illiterate vehicle through which God's revelation was conveyed to man. Muslims insist, moreover, that the Prophet was not, and never claimed to be, divine. He was an ordinary human being. But they also hold him to be al-Insan al-Kamil, the perfect man, the model to be imitated in all things, as husband or father, trader or soldier, diplomat, ruler or judge. As Charles J. Adams has observed, 'For the purposes of one interested in religion the place of Muhammad in the thinking and devotion of Muslims is of greater importance than the facts of his biography and personal development.' ('Islamic religious tradition'.)[1] Elsewhere the same authority has suggested that:

> The tendency throughout Muslim history has been toward an always greater idealisation, even romanticisation, of the Prophet. The trend culminates in the modernist biographies of Muhammad that portray him as the great hero of all history, the most profound thinker ever to have lived, and the perfect exemplar of all the virtues. This development testifies to the continuing and renewed significance of Muhammad for Islamic faith; for those who wish to understand the meaning of the Prophet to Muslims it is of little significance that the claims he made for himself are much more modest than those of his followers. (*A Readers' Guide to the Great Religions*)[2]

Ninian Smart in his companion volume to the BBC television series 'The Long Search' makes a similar point of contrast between the early Christian polemicists who portrayed the Prophet as a 'polygamous epileptic' and devout Muslims who see in him 'the culminating actor in the great drama of which God is author'.

In the years after his death Muhammad's sayings and doings were collected to form a body of traditions (*hadith*) which became a major source for Islamic law, second only to the Qur'an itself in authority. The author of the article on 'Islam' in the *International Encyclopaedia of the Social Sciences* asserts that 'Through the device of hadith, which contrasts strongly with the formalism and transcendentalism of the Qur'an, Muhammad is kept from becoming a dim historical figure; he emerges as a venerable, just but understandable human leader of his flock. In this way Islam maintains the principle of the strictest monotheism, while tempering it with a human touch . . .'

The classification and validation of hadith gave birth to the 'religious sciences' which came to form the core of higher learning in traditional Islam. (See, for instance, A. Guillaume, *The Traditions of Islam* Khayats, 1966.)

In approaching the study of the life of the Prophet, non-Muslims should perhaps bear in mind W.M. Watt's assertion that 'Of all the world's great men none has been so much maligned as Muhammad' and his warning that 'It is clear that those of Muhammad's actions which are disapproved by the modern West were not the object of the *moral* criticism of his contemporaries. They criticised some of his acts, but their motives were superstitious prejudice or fear of the consequences.' (W.M. Watt, *Muhammad: Prophet and Statesman*.)[3]

Muhammad's Life: a summary

c. 570   Birth in Mecca of Muhammad, son of the merchant Abdallah and Amina, both from the Meccan tribe of Quraish. Muhammad's father dies before his birth.

576   Death of Amina. Muhammad is brought up first in the house of his grandfather, the guardian of the Ka'ba, and later by his uncle, Abu Talib, who takes him on journeys in the caravan trade.

595   At the age of twenty-five he marries Khadija, a rich widow and his only wife until her death. Among their children is Fatima, who is to become the wife of the fourth Caliph Ali.

605   The traditional date of the eighth of the ten reconstructions of the Ka'ba.

610   Muhammad retires to a cave on Mount Hira for meditation and has his first vision. He confides this secret to Khadija and a few close friends.

613   Finally convinced of his mission, Muhammad begins to preach openly and proclaims the existence of one single God to whom people owe complete submission.

615   Emigration to Abyssinia of Muslims being persecuted in Mecca.

616	Conversion of Muhammad's opponent, 'Omar ibn al-Khattab, to Islam.
619	Death of Muhammad's wife, Khadija, and of his uncle, Abu Talib.
620	Muhammad marries the widow Sauda and celebrates his betrothal to Aisha, the 17-year-old daughter of his rich relative, Abu Bakr, one of his first converts. Muhammad has the vision of the miraculous Night Journey to Jerusalem.
622	Persecution increases. On 20 September Muhammad secretly leaves Mecca and travels with Abu Bakr to Medina. This (*hijra*) is regarded – in accordance with Caliph Omar's ruling – as the beginning of the Muslim Era. The Muslim lunar calendar starts from 622.
624	Defeat of the Meccans at Badr in January. Muhammad then embarks on a series of wars and raids. The *qibla*, the direction to which Muslims turn in praying, is changed from Jerusalem to Mecca.
627	The Meccans besiege Medina in vain.
628	Truce between the Meccans and Muhammad.
629	Muhammad, at the head of his Medinan followers, peacefully enters Mecca where they perform acts of communal reverence before the Black Stone.
630	Considering his forces sufficiently strong, Muhammad marches on Mecca and conquers it. He destroys all the idols, leaving only the Black Stone intact, and proclaims Mecca as Islam's sacred city.
630–32	Muhammad devotes his energies to the problems of government, introduces a new calendar and battles against the superstitions widespread among the Arab population.
632	Muhammad dies in Medina on 7 June. Abu Bakr is elected as the first Caliph.

Hadith transmitted by Bukhari

The Messenger of Allah, peace and blessings of Allah be on him, has said:
'Worship Allah as if you see Him; if you do not see Him, know that He sees you.'
'None of you has faith unless he loves for his brother what he loves for himself.'
'When a person is drowsy during his prayers, let him go to sleep until he knows what he recites.'
'The prophets leave knowledge as their inheritance. The learned ones inherit this great fortune.'
'There is no disease for which Allah has not sent a cure.'

'Whoever builds a mosque, desiring Allah's pleasure, Allah builds for him the like of it in paradise.'

'Say part of your prayers at home so your houses do not become like graves.'

'Say Allah's name and eat with your right hand and eat from near you.'

'Charity is incumbent on each person every day. Charity is assisting anyone, lifting provisions, saying a good word, every step one takes walking to prayer is charity; showing the way is charity.'

'He who does not give up uttering lies and acting according to them, Allah has no need of his giving up food and drink.'

'Modesty is part of faith.'

'Marriage is incumbent on all who possess the ability, it keeps the eye cast down and keeps a man chaste; he who cannot should take to fasting which will cool his passion.'

'No one eats better food than that which he eats from the work of his own hands.'

'May Allah have mercy on the man who is generous when he buys, sells, and asks his due.'

'Visit the sick, feed the hungry and free the captives.'

'It is charity for any Muslim who plants a tree or cultivates land which provides food for a bird, animal or man.'

'Believers are like the parts of a building to one another – each part supporting the others.'

'Every drink that intoxicates is prohibited.'

'There are two blessings which most people misuse – health and leisure.'

'The young should say "Salaam" to the old, the passer-by to the one sitting and the small group to the large one.'

'Whoever believes in Allah and the next world, should not harm his neighbour and should honour his guest.'

'The best Islam is that you feed the poor and offer salutations to those you know and those you do not know.'

'The best Jihad is to speak the truth before a tyrant.'

'The best of you is he who has learnt the Qur'an and then taught it.'

'None of you has faith unless I am dearer to him than his father, and his son and all mankind.'

'Be careful of your duty to Allah and be fair and just to your children.'

'One who tries to help the widow and the poor is like a warrior in the way of Allah.'

Sources

1 Charles J. Adams, 'Islamic religious tradition' in L. Binder (ed.), *The Study of the Middle East* (Wiley, 1976).

2 *A Reader's Guide to the Great Religions* (Free Press, 2nd edn, 1977), p.414.

3 W.M. Watt, *Muhammad: Prophet and Statesman* (OUP, 1961), pp.231–3.

Further reading

Maulana Muhammad Ali, *A Manual of Hadith* (Curzon Press/Humanities Press, 2nd edn, 1978).

Sayyid Amir Ali, *The Spirit of Islam* (Christopher's Revised edn 1922 and many others). Written as a riposte to what the author considered to be the generally calumnious view presented by Western biographers.

Tor Andrae, *Mohammad, the Man and his Faith* (Allen & Unwin, 1936). Classic biography stressing the psychology of the Prophet's vocation.

Zakaria Bashier, *The Meccan Crucible* (FOSIS, 1978). 'Care has been taken that the book should express a Muslim point of view . . .' This readable account of the life of the Prophet up to the Hijra combines narrative and analysis (e.g. of the nature of prophethood and revelation and of the Meccan setting). The author argues that pre-Islamic Arabia was not characterised by total immorality and explains the intricacies and significance of tribal politics. Useful table of the first fifty converts.

H.A.L. Craig, *Bilal* (Quartet Books, 1977). Narrative of the Prophet's life told through the eyes of the black Abyssinian slave who became the first muezzin in Islam. Superb colour photographs from the film 'Mohammad – Messenger of God', for which the author wrote the screenplay.

A. Rahman I. Doi, *Introduction to the Hadith* (Arewa, 1981).

A. Guillaume (trans.), *Life of Muhammad* (OUP, 1955). English version of Ibn Ishaq's *Sirat Rasul Allah*, one of the earliest full length biographies of the Prophet. The author was born (85 AH) and grew up in Medina. An invaluable source of anecdotal detail.

Zafrullah Khan, *Muhammad: Seal of the Prophets* (Routledge & Kegan Paul, 1980). Narrative biography stressing Muhammad's role as exemplar. The author, a judge and former foreign minister of Pakistan, is a member of the Ahmadiyyah.

Afzalur Rahman, *Muhammad: Blessing for Mankind* (Muslim Schools Trust, 1979). Brief narrative followed by detailed exposition of Muhammad's role as exemplar of moral virtues, commander, ruler, judge, legislator, educator and benefactor of humanity.

Afzalur Rahman, *Muhammad as Military Leader* (Muslim Schools Trust, 1980). Detailed account not only of tactics but also of Islamic teachings on war and peace.

Maxime Rodinson, *Mohammad* (Penguin, 1973). Stylish scholarly biography with useful 'Explanatory table of Arabic words and names of individuals and ethnic groups'. The author, a French Jewish Marxist, shows a self-conscious awareness of the problems of objectivity and commitment throughout (see especially pages 215–19) and notes, 'Muslims have every right not to read the book . . . but if they do so, they must expect to find things put forward there which are blasphemous to them.'

Maxime Rodinson, 'A critical survey of modern studies on Muhammad' in Merlin L. Swartz (ed.), *Studies on Islam* (OUP, 1981).

James E. Royster, 'The study of Muhammad: A survey of approaches from the perspective of the history and phenomenology of religion' (*Muslim World* LXII, 1972, pp.49–70).

Ziauddin Sardar, *Muhammad: Aspects of his Biography* (The Islamic Foundation, 1978). Engagingly written brief biography with thirty-six maps and photographs. Suitable for upper secondary readers.

Ruth Warren, *Muhammad: Prophet of Islam* (Franklin Watts, 1965). Written for school-age readers. Three chapters on the Prophet's significance and legacy.

W. Montgomery Watt, *Muhammad at Mecca* (OUP, 1953), *Muhammad at Medina* (OUP, 1956). Standard scholarly biography in which 'special attention is paid to the economic and sociological background and the relation of this to the religious conceptions of the Qur'an'.

W. Montgomery Watt, *Muhammad: Prophet and Statesman* (OUP, 1961). According to the author this is 'essentially an abridgement' of his two-volume work, 'the chief difference is that chronological order is more closely followed'.

Antonie Wessels, *A Modern Arabic Biography of Muhammad* (E.J. Brill, Leiden, 1972) is a study of Muhammad Husayn Haykal's *Hayat Muhammad* (The Life of Muhammad) (Maktabah al-Nahdah al-Misriyah, Cairo, 5th impression, 1952) which is probably the most widely read and influential biography in any Islamic language.

5
The Qur'an

The Qur'an is the heart of Islam. Muslims believe it to be the literal, uncreated Word of God. It is inimitable and untranslatable, an object of veneration and the basis of human understanding of the universe and man's place in it. Albert C. Moore has summarised its significance thus:

> The Qur'an is the one central miracle of Islam and this miracle of the Divine Word is actualised again and again, not in visual and material form but verbally in recitation . . . Its phrases are repeated in cantillations at the mosque, in teaching and memorisation at the mosque school and in the prayers of believers. The book provides the basis for the study of Muslim theology and law. At the popular level its texts may be regarded as talismans . . . and in the sphere of art it has conferred something of its religious power on the Muslim art of calligraphy. (*Iconography of Religions: An Introduction*)[1]

The meaning of the Qur'an cannot be divorced from its impact. As M.M. Mujeeb has emphasised:

> We must look to the Qur'an for the stimulus to spiritual experience. It is only through such experience and not through clever interpretation, that we can give it genuine significance. (*Studies in Islam, V*)[2]
>
> The verses of the Qur'an are not only utterances which transmit thoughts; they are also, in a sense, beings, powers, talismans. The soul of the Muslim is as it were woven out of sacred formulae; in these he works, in these he rests, in these he lives, in these he dies. (F. Schuon, *Understanding Islam*)[3]

Sufis assert the 'hidden meaning' of the Qur'an. Seyyed Hossein Nasr refers to an inner dimension which no amount of literal and philological analysis can reveal.

Muslims emphasise the comprehensive nature of the Qur'an. On one occasion the Libyan leader Colonel Gadafi described Jean-Paul Sartre as 'a lost man' because the Qur'an already contained all the answers to his questions, and indeed, to all significant questions, 'Arab unity, socialism, inheritance rights, the place of women in society . . . the destruction of our planet following the intervention of the atom bomb. It's all there for anyone willing to read it.'

Muslims believe that previous revelations have been corrupted intentionally or otherwise, but that the Qur'an, God's final message to Man, is exactly the same in its present version as it was in the time of the Prophet and that it is the foremost duty of each generation of Muslims to pass it on, word perfect, to the next. Hence its central importance in traditional Islamic education, which insisted on the exact memorisation of each detail of phrasing and emphasis. Hence also the fact that Pakistan's 1973 constitution makes it a crime, punishable by law, to publish an edition of the Qur'an with a printing error in it.

Modern Western thought is sceptical of the powers of human memory. Contemporary educational practice tends to discount it as a skill. It is essential, therefore, to stress that in pre-Islamic Arabia poets and geneologists were both renowned and relied upon for the performance of prodigious feats of memory. These traditional skills were harnessed to the cause of Islam and, although portions of the Prophet's revelation were written down during his lifetime, it was not until a large number of those who had memorised the Qur'an were killed in battle in the 'wars of apostasy' which followed Muhammad's death, that the Caliph Umar ordered the compilation of a definitive written edition, a task which was completed under his successor, Uthman. In this connection it is also worth noting M. Hamidullah's assertion that 'the Prophet recited every year in the month of Ramadan, in the presence of the angel Gabriel, the portion of the Qur'an till then revealed, and that in the last year of his life, Gabriel asked him to recite the whole of it twice. The Prophet concluded thereupon that he was going soon to depart this life.' (*Introduction to Islam*.)[4]

A number of English versions of the Qur'an are available, but the titles of the Arberry (*The Koran Interpreted*), and Pickthall (*The Meaning of the Glorious Koran*) versions show their implicit acceptance of the Muslim view that it cannot be translated. To read the Qur'an for devotional purposes and with true understanding a Muslim must read it in Arabic, which is not the native language of some five-sixths of the world's Muslim community. As Hitti notes:

> The style of the Koran is God's style . . . This is basically what constitutes the 'miraculous character' of the Koran . . . if all men and jinns were to collaborate they could not produce its like (17.90). The Prophet was authorised to challenge his critics to produce something comparable (10.39). The challenge was taken up by more than one stylist in Arabic literature – with a predictable conclusion. The relevance of Muhammad's illiteracy to this argument becomes obvious. (*Islam – A Way of Life*)[5]

The problem of translation should be emphasised. Comparison of any two versions of a particular passage will reveal significant differences in word choice, word order and rhythm. This will underline the problem of precise meaning, which is critical, and of emotional impact, which is no less important.

Consider, for example, the following differences between the Arberry (A) and the Dawood (D) translations of Sura 55 (The All-Merciful):
(i) He has taught him the Explanation (A)
  . . . taught him articulate speech (D)

(ii)   His too are the ships that run, raised up in the sea like landmarks (A)
       His are the ships that sail like banners (or mountains) upon the ocean
       (D)

(iii) All that dwells upon the earth is perishing, yet still abides the Face of thy
       Lord, majestic, splendid (A)
       All who live on earth are doomed to die. But the face of your Lord will
       abide forever, in all its majesty and glory (D)

Pickthall wrote of the Qur'an, 'that inimitable symphony, the very sounds of
which move men to tears and ecstasy', whereas Carlyle, the first European to
produce a sympathetic account of Muhammad, referred to it as 'as tedious a
piece of reading as I ever undertook, a wearisome, confused jumble . . .
nothing but a sense of duty could carry any European through the Koran'.
Pickthall read Arabic, Carlyle did not.

The awe in which the Qur'an is held by Muslims is well illustrated by the
following quotation:

> They will never suffer the Koran to touch the ground, if they can help it; and if it
> chance at any time to fall they check themselves for it and with haste and concern
> recover it again and kiss it, and put it to their forehead in token of profound
> respect . . . They think they cannot prize the Koran enough and there cannot be
> too much care in preserving it. Nay, I have known many that could not read one
> little of it, to carry some part of it always about them esteeming it as a charm to
> preserve them from hurt and danger . . . They have so great a veneration and
> esteem for the Koran, that they will not suffer a scrap of clean paper to lie on the
> ground, but take it up and kiss it, and then put it into some hole or cranny, because
> on such the name of God is or may be written . . . (Joseph Pitt of Exeter, 1678)

The Qur'an in a Muslim home is invariably kept up on a shelf out of harm's
way, and usually wrapped up against dust and damp. Muslims refrain from
eating, drinking, or making a noise while it is being read aloud.

The Qur'an is not a long book – about two-thirds the length of the New
Testament – but Ninian Smart has warned us that it is structurally diffuse
'Those who look to read it like a novel, hoping for drama and plot, are going
to be disappointed. It is more like an anthology, but an anthology by one
author.' There are ecstatic passages, proclaiming the nature of God and His
creation, there are narratives, which recount the teachings and trials of
earlier prophets, there are passionate refutations of pagans and sceptics and
detailed juridical regulations for the ordering of the Muslim community,
for the Qur'an is a book of *Hidayah*, a Guidance for man, and as such its
authority is final.

Beginners might find the Qur'an easier to read 'back to front' (ignoring
the conventional arrangement of suras which has placed them, with the
exception of the first, in more or less descending order of length), starting
with the short, lyrical Meccan utterances, and ending with the longer,
Medinan pronouncements which deal with the complex, practical issues
which faced Muhammad as the leader of the newly founded Muslim community. J.B. Taylor in *Thinking About Islam*[8] suggests the following sequence
where time (or power of concentration) is limited: Suras 86, 74, 82, 84, 93,
101, 112.

The Qur'an cannot, in any strict sense, be translated (see the article by A.L. Tibawi reviewing Muslim opinion on this subject, 'Is the Qur'an translatable?').[7] But it can be rendered into other languages. Of the English versions, J.M. Rodwell's *The Koran*[8] is rather stilted and its chapters have been rearranged according to his view of Qur'anic chronology. Marmaduke Pickthall's *The Meaning of the Glorious Koran*[9] is approved by many Muslims, the translator himself being an English convert. N.J. Dawood's *The Koran*[10] rearranges the chapters for literary effect and has some useful notes. A.J. Arberry's *The Koran Interpreted*[11] represents a major attempt to convey something of the poetic force of the original. A. Yusuf Ali's *The Holy Qur'an, Text, Translation and Commentary*[12] and Muhammad Ali's *The Holy Qur'an*[13] provide an introduction to the great tradition of *tafsir* (Qur'anic exegesis).

Sources

1 Albert C. Moore, *Iconography of Religions: An Introduction* (SCM Press, 1973).

2 M.M. Mujeeb, *Studies in Islam, V* (Delhi, 1970).

3 F. Schuon, *Understanding Islam* (Allen & Unwin, 1976), p.60.

4 M. Hamidullah, *Introduction to Islam* (MWH London Publishers, 1979).

5 P. Hitti, *Islam − A Way of Life* (OUP, 1968).

6 J.B. Taylor, *Thinking About Islam* (Lutterworth Press, 1971).

7 A.L. Tibawi, 'Is the Qur'an translatable?', in *Muslim World LII*, (1962), p.4ff.

8 J.M. Rodwell, *The Koran* (J.M. Dent & Sons, Everyman series, 1909).

9 Marmaduke Pickthall, *The Meaning of the Glorious Koran* (Mentor, 1953).

10 N.J. Dawood, *The Koran* (Penguin, 1959).

11 A.J. Arberry, *The Koran Interpreted* (OUP, 1964).

12 A. Yusuf Ali, *The Holy Qur'an, Test, Translation and Commentary* (Ashraf, Lahore, 3rd edn, 1938).

13 Muhammad Ali, *The Holy Qur'an* (Ahmadiyyah Anjuman Isha' at Islam, 1951).

Further reading

John Burton, *The Collection of the Qur'an* (CUP, 1977). Controversial scholarly account of the process of scriptural compilation.

Kenneth Cragg, *The Event of the Qur'an: Islam in its Scripture* (Allen & Unwin, 1971). An examination of the physical and cultural environment in which the Qur'an was received and an attempt to answer the basic question, What happened in the Qur'an?

Kenneth Cragg, *The Mind of the Qur'an: Chapters in Reflection* (Allen & Unwin, 1973). An examination of the ways in which the Qur'an has been studied and interpreted.

A. Rahman I. Doi, *Introduction to the Qur'an* (Arewa, 1981).

Helmut Gatje, *The Qur'an and its Exegesis: Selected Texts with Classical and Modern Muslim Interpretations* (Routledge & Kegan Paul, 1976). 'The book shows the teachings of the Qur'an and the views of later commentators on such topics as revelation, Allah, Muhammad, angels and jinn, eschatology and Muslim beliefs and duties. It also shows the Qur'anic view of other religious communities . . . There are chapters on mystical, philosophical and Shi'ite Qur'anic exegesis, and a chapter on polygamy as an example of modern Muslim exposition.'

Thomas Ballantine Irving, Khurshid Ahmad and Muhammad Manazir Ahsan, *The Qur'an: Basic Teachings* (The Islamic Foundation, 1979). An anthology of Qur'anic passages arranged thematically to cover the Qur'an itself, basic principles of doctrine, prophets, duties and morality, society and the state.

Martin Lings and Yasin Hamid Safadi, *The Qur'an* (World of Islam Publishing Company, 1976). Illustrated catalogue of an exhibition of Qur'an manuscripts. Much detailed information on calligraphy, design, buildings, etc.

Sayyid Qutb, *In the Shade of the Qur'an*, Vol. 30 (MWH London Publishers, 1979). Detailed commentary on suras 78–114.

W.M. Watt, *Bell's Introduction to the Qur'an* (Edinburgh University Press, 1970). Concise, scholarly guide-book dealing with the history, structure and style of the text as well as its teachings and their interpretation.

W.M. Watt, *Companion to the Qur'an* (Allen & Unwin, 1967). Detailed, chapter by chapter commentary, based on the Arberry translation.

6
The Pillars of Islam

The topics of belief, prayer, fasting, almsgiving (*zakat*) and pilgrimage (*hajj*) provide a ready-made framework for teaching about Islam, and several schemes of work in Part Two of this book are planned around these five pillars of the faith. The first pillar is the *Shahada*, the profession of faith: 'There is no God but God, and Muhammad is the Prophet of God.' Initiation into the faith involves the recitation of the *Shahada* in the presence of believing Muslims, and the same words are whispered by Muslim parents into the ears of newborn babies.

The pillars of prayer, fasting, almsgiving and pilgrimage are dealt with in Chapters 7, 8 and 9.

7

Prayer and Zakat

Prayer

'Seek help in patience and prayer. This is indeed hard except to those who are humble, who bear in mind that they shall meet their Lord and that they are to return to Him' (2:45–6).

A Muslim should perform an act of worship five times a day, each occasion consisting of a set cycle of words and ritual gestures (*rakat*) as follows:

Fajr (between dawn and sunrise) – two rakat
Zuhr (noon till mid-afternoon – four rakat
'Asr (mid-afternoon to sunset) – four rakat
Maghrib (between sunset and darkness) – three rakat
'Isha (before retiring) – four rakat

These are the prescribed (*Fard*) prayers. Additional prayers are recommended as following the *Sunna* (words and deeds of the Prophet). Personal prayers (*du'a*), whether of praise, thanks or supplication, may be added in the worshipper's own language afterwards.

Prayers may be combined under pressure of time and shortened to two rakat while travelling, but prayers missed should be made up later. Women are exempted during menstruation and confinement.

Prayer is not for the benefit of God, whose glory and authority are complete without the praise or obedience of men. Prayer is for the benefit of man. Children are to be encouraged to pray as soon as they can and are obliged to do so after puberty.

The Qur'an refers to prayer variously as *salat* (inclination), *du'a* (appeal), *dhikr* (remembering), *tasbih* (glorification) and *Imabah* (returning, attachment). Regular prayer is held both to develop humility, an awareness of God's presence and mercy, and a willingness to submit to His will, ('Establish regular prayer, for prayer restraineth from shameful and unjust deeds . . .') (29:45) and to develop an ability to avoid undue immersion in the affairs of the world, to the detriment of the spiritual concerns ('whom neither merchandise nor traffic diverts from the remembrance of Allah and the observance of prayer') (24:37–9).

Non-Muslims may regard the time spent in prayer as burdensome.

Muhammad Zafrullah Khan comments:

> 'It is a matter of comparative values. All five services taken together do not take up more . . . time than a person in the West is apt to spend watching television. In the eyes of a Muslim, a diversion such as television, or the formalities attendant upon ceremonial dinner . . . has little value, whereas participation in congregational worship is nutriment for the soul'. (*Islam: Its Meaning for Modern Man*)[1]

Prayer is also an expression of brotherhood among believers. This is especially clear in the case of the congregational Friday prayer; but each act of worship also ends with the worshipper turning to those on either side of him and saying 'Peace be on you, and God's Mercy'.

The sense of solidarity is reinforced by the knowledge that Muslims everywhere, each day, are repeating the same words and gestures, praying in the manner prescribed by the Prophet, and focusing their devotions on Mecca, his birth-place and the scene of his first revelations and triumph.

When praying, the worshipper, if male, should be covered at least from navel to knee. The head may be bare or not. Shoes are always removed. Women should expose only the face and hands.

Worshippers are summoned to prayer by a call (*adhan*) issued by a *muezzin* from a minaret (nowadays this is often tape-recorded). Prayer must be a conscious act, and is invalid unless the worshipper has made a statement of his intention (*niyyah*) to offer his worship.

Prayer is preceded by an act of ablution (*wadhu*) involving the thorough washing of hands, mouth, nostrils, face, arms, head, ears, neck and feet (in that strict order). This preparation need only be repeated between prayers if the worshipper has slept, bled, vomited or performed any toilet function. (A full bath should be taken after sexual intercourse and menstruation.) Where water is scarce or unavailable, or, in case of sickness, may do harm, a dry cleansing using earth or sand (*tayammum*) may be substituted. Ablution cleanses the worshipper of substances which are, in religious terms, polluting (bodily excretions, blood, pus, wine) and also symbolises a spiritual cleansing. In practical terms it contributes to maintaining a high standard of personal hygiene. 'Cleanliness is half of the faith' is a saying attributed to the Prophet. Prayers should be offered in a clean and quiet place, not necessarily a mosque, but preferably in the company of other Muslims.

Prayer begins with a proclamation of God's greatness – *Allahu Akbar* – and this phrase is proclaimed by the imam to signal the changes of posture whose cycle constitutes a rakat. This is followed by the recitation of *al-Fatiha*, the opening sura of the Qur'an, which is a plea for guidance and serves as 'the heart and soul of the service'. The rest of the prayer reiterates themes of praise and submission. For the most part the words of prayer are uttered inaudibly.

Prayers are made in Arabic, regardless of the language of the worshipper, because God chose to reveal the Qur'an in Arabic and prayer is a collective and social act, the use of Arabic emphasising the universality of Islam. Any Muslim anywhere can join in the service with perfect competence and know himself 'at home' among fellow-Muslims. Du'a, being a purely private communication, may be in the vernacular.

The four basic postures of prayer are: standing (*qiyam*) – right hand clasped lightly above left wrist, the hands held just above the waist (Malikites, and Shi'ites leave the hands hanging loose by the thighs); bowing (*ruku*) – hands placed above the knees; prostrating (*sujud*) – forehead and nose touch the floor, fingers spread and elbows raised; sitting (*julus*) – legs folded beneath the body. Al-Ghazzali explained the symbolism of prostration as 'the highest degree of submission, for the dearest of your members, which is your face, gets hold of the humblest thing, which is the dust . . .' Sick persons are permitted to pray sitting or even lying down. Travellers in motion are likewise permitted to pray sitting down.

It is recommended that whenever two or more Muslims are together they offer their prayers together. An imam, preferably a mature male of pious character with a sound knowledge of the Qur'an and Sunna, should lead the prayers (but in no sense does he act as an intermediary), the other worshippers praying, shoulder to shoulder but not touching, in ranks behind him, women forming parallel rows behind the men. Rows are formed in sequence of arrival, there being no place for human precedence. Late arrivals take their cue from the imam and join in worship at the stage it has reached. On Fridays all adult males should make their second prayer at the congregational mosque, where there will also be a sermon in the local language. This will usually involve a discussion of the application of Qur'anic teaching to a daily problem followed by ritual blessings and praise. Women are not obligated to attend Friday congregational prayers at the mosque.

In conclusion it should be stressed that the Muslims' worship is not limited to formal acts of prayer. Every action of daily life, when consciously performed in accordance with the dictates of the Qur'an and the Sunna of the Prophet, is an act of worship. The repeated invocation *Bismillah* is indicative of this outlook. (Worship, in Islam, is *ibadah*, a word derived from the same root as *abd*, slave.)

This larger conception of worship does not, however, minimise the significance of prayer:

> . . . absolutely misconceived is the view of those who are given to laxity . . . with regard to the obligatory acts of worship and imagine that . . . the basis of true faith is merely purity of heart, goodness of intention and soundness of conduct . . . deliberate disregard of ritual obligations is destructive of the very foundations of religion . . . The prayers . . . serve to distinguish the ones who do really have faith . . . from those who are content with lip-service. So important indeed is prayer that the Prophet has said, 'Salat is the pillar of the Islamic religion and whosoever abandons it, demolishes the very pillar of religion.' (Mustafa Ahmad al-Zarqa, 'The Islamic concept of worship')[2]

Zakat

It is obligatory upon all Muslims to make over a certain proportion of their wealth in alms (*zakat*) to be used for charitable purposes – such as the relief of the destitute, orphans, slaves, prisoners, debtors and travellers. It may also be used to pay for those engaged in its collection and to support those who have committed themselves to the 'way of Allah' (for example students of the religious sciences). New converts to Islam may also benefit from zakat (9:60). (The Prophet specifically excluded himself and his family from benefit.)

Those in receipt of zakat should feel no shame or obligation. The Qur'an stresses that the poor have a just claim on the wealth of the well-to-do (51:19). Practical acknowledgment of this right should serve to diminish envy in the community of believers. Recipients should not accept more zakat than they need. Those who refuse charity are warned of the consequences in the Qur'an (3:180).

The rate at which zakat must be paid became the subject of complex regulation. One-fortieth of annual disposable income is a rough rule of thumb, but there are detailed rules covering different amounts payable on crops, minerals, livestock, and so on. Zakat is not chargeable on wealth used for daily living (e.g. houses, furniture, clothes). Allowance must be made not only for the owner's needs but also for those of any person dependent upon him.

Zakat is payable by all Muslims, regardless of age or sex, and is also payable on the estate of a deceased person, even before creditors are satisfied; in this sense zakat is like a debt to God.

Zakat is not a tax. Some commentators have referred to it as a sort of loan to God which will be repaid many times over. Others speak of it as a 'purification' of one's wealth, because zakat means 'that which purifies'. Maududi warns that 'when we pay in the name of Allah, we shall neither expect nor demand any worldly gains from the beneficiaries nor aim at making our names as philanthropists'. Zakat rather embodies the Muslim's willingness to curb selfishness, to cultivate the spirit of sacrifice and to care for others. Muslims regard the institution of zakat as a distinctive step forward for mankind, elevating charity from a matter of individual choice to one of collective duty. Rightly considered, zakat is an expression of worship, and it is frequently mentioned in the Qur'an in the same verse as an injunction to prayer (2:277; 31:1–5).

The payment of zakat does not mean that the Muslim should not also make free-will offerings (*sadaqat*), which are recommended for the relief of the needy and as a means of expiating offences.

Sources

1 Muhammad Zafrullah Khan, *Islam: Its Meaning for Modern Man* (Routledge & Kegan Paul, Zudedu, 1980).

2 Mustafa Ahmad al-Zarqa, 'The Islamic concept of worship', in Khurshid
   Ahmad (ed.), *Islam – Its Meaning and Message* (Islamic Council of Europe,
   1975).

Further reading

Prayer

Qur'an (4:45–9, 100–104; 5:5–9; 17:80–84).
E.E. Calverley, *Worship in Islam* (Luzac, 1957).
C.E. Padwick, *Muslim Devotions* (SPCK, 1961).
M.Z Khan, *Islam: Its Meaning for Modern Man* (Routledge & Kegan Paul,
2nd edn, 1980). Contains a selection of prayers for specific occasions
(pp.107–11).
M.Z.A. Souidan, *Prayer in Islam: Hygienic, Preventive and Curative* (S.O.P.
Press, Cairo, 1976). Discusses the medical value of ablution and the postures
and breathing associated with prayer.
Khalil Ahmad Hamidi, *A Hand Book of Islamic Prayers* (Islamic Publications,
Lahore, 2nd edn, 1978). A wide-ranging anthology.
Afzalur Rahman, *Prayer: Its Significance and Benefits* (The Muslim Schools
Trust, 1979). Detailed study, emphasising the spiritual and social implica-
tions of regular devotion.

Zakat

K. Ahmad (ed.), *Studies in Islamic Economics* (Islamic Foundation, 1980).
Syed Nawab Haider Naqvi, *Ethics and Economics: An Islamic Synthesis* (Islamic
Foundation, 1981).

8
Fasting and Food

Fasting

During Ramadan, the ninth month of the Islamic calendar, during which the Qur'an was first revealed, Muslims are obliged to fast from dawn until dusk (signified by one's being able to distinguish a black thread from a white one).

Fasting (*saum*) means abstention from food and drink, smoking and sexual activity. Because of the physiological demands that it makes, fasting can never be reduced to the level of a formality. The object is mastery of the urges which sustain life and procreate it.

Fasting is not incumbent upon the sick, the very old and very young, and women who are pregnant or have infant children to feed. In certain circumstances, soldiers and travellers are also exempt. The sick and the traveller should make up the days they have missed when they are able to do so.

The act of fasting is accompanied by a particular emphasis on personal devotions. Many Muslims will spend long hours during Ramadan in prayer or reading the Qur'an. It has been referred to as a time of 'spiritual stock-taking'. Even before Islam, Arabs used the month of Ramadan to settle disputes and debts and do good turns for their neighbours. Islam incorporated this tradition and gave it fuller meaning. During the nights of Ramadan Muslims are enjoined to perform a special salat, known as *tarawih*, which is at least as long as all the others of the day combined. Ideally, it should involve the recitation of the entire Qur'an by the time the month has ended.

Fasting is believed to convey singular benefits on those who practise it: an ability to curb (but not deny) bodily desires and habitual self-indulgences and to develop will-power; an awareness of the privations of the poor. It is recommended that those who can afford it should feed a poor neighbour.

Fasting is not regarded as an act of penance or atonement but as a discipline and prompt to charity. Its purpose is not asceticism but action.

Because all Muslims are fasting together during Ramadan the experience reinforces the collective sense of belonging to a community. Even Muslims who neglect their prayers are generally inclined to keep the fast. They are certainly subject to strong public disapproval if they do not. This sense of belonging is reaffirmed in the joyous feast of Eid ul-Fitr which marks the ending of the month of self-restraint.

Food

The flesh of the pig, in any form, is forbidden (*haram*) to Muslims. Hence any food which contains lard, be it biscuits or ice-cream, is also forbidden. Carnivorous animals, rodents and reptiles are also forbidden to Muslims.

A Muslim cannot consume the flesh of animals or birds which have not been slaughtered in the approved ritual fashion. (5:3) 'Kosher' meat (meat slaughtered by a Jewish *shochet* or butcher) is acceptable. The animal is killed with the invocation of God's name (*Bismillah*) in token of recognition that the life of a created thing is taken only to serve man's need for sustenance. The meat from a ritually killed animal is called *halal*. Note that meat products such as steak and kidney pies, corned beef, and oxtail soup are forbidden both because the meat from which they are made is not *halal* and because such products may contain pork fat as an ingredient.

Alcohol is forbidden to Muslims in any form (5.90–91; 2:219). This includes its use in cooking or for medical purposes, unless there is positively no other substitute. A tradition reports that when Tariq ibn Suwayed protested to the Prophet that he made alcohol to be used as a medicine Muhammed replied, 'It is not medicine, it is a disease.' A Muslim should not offer alcohol to a non-Muslim guest, nor sell it if he owns a shop or restaurant.

Muslims believe that alcohol not only leads to addiction and waste and an inability to perform one's duties towards one's family and the community, but also, because it diminishes a man's control over his faculties, damages his ability to relate to God through prayer.

Further reading

Qur'an II: 183–7.
Chapter 3 of G.E. von Grünebaum, *Muhammadan Festivals* (Curzon Press, 1976), contains a discussion of various aspects of fasting and includes two lengthy first-hand accounts of Ramadan (from Elden Clutter in 1926 and H. St J. Philby in 1918).

9

Hajj

> Lo! The first Sanctuary appointed for mankind was that at Mecca, a blessed place, a guidance to the peoples . . . (Qur'an 3:96)

Hajj is the name given to the pilgrimage to Mecca which is incumbent upon each Muslim once in his lifetime, provided he can afford to undertake the journey and does not endanger either his health or his family by doing so. The word 'hajj' literally means 'to set out for a definite purpose'. It is performed during the second week of the twelfth month of the Islamic calendar, Dhull-Hijja.

The main stages of the hajj are as follows:

(i) The pilgrim dons *ihram*, two white sheets of seamless cloth. (There is no prescribed dress for women but they must go unveiled.) This symbolises purity, renunciation and the equality of believers whose rank can no longer be distinguished by dress.

(ii) The pilgrim enters the *haram*, the sacred area around Mecca, forbidden to non-Muslims, within which living things are protected from violence.

(iii) The pilgrim enters the Great Mosque and walks seven times around the Ka'ba, the lifelong focus of his prayers, which Muslims regard as the oldest functioning shrine for the worship of the one true God.

(iv) The pilgrim performs the sa'y – running seven times between the hills of Safa and Marwah, re-enacting the search of Hagar, wife of Abraham, for water for her infant son, Ishmael. This ritual expresses respect for maternal love, and gratitude to God, who made the sacred spring of Zam Zam appear for Hagar's relief.

(v) The pilgrim journeys to Mina, five miles east of Mecca, to spend the night in prayer and meditation.

(vi) The pilgrim goes to the plain of Arafat to perform the rite of *wuquf* ('standing'), the supreme experience of the hajj; starting when the sun passes the meridian, the pilgrims pray and meditate until just before sunset. (Muslims believe that Adam and Eve, separated after their fall from Paradise, were reunited at Arafat by God's grace.)

(vii) After spending the night at Muzdalifah, the pilgrim proceeds to Mina just before daybreak and here he spends three nights, stoning three pillars symbolic of devils (who tempted Abraham not to sacrifice his son) and sacrificing an animal as a gesture of renunciation and thanksgiving, and his commemoration of the poor and of Abraham, who was willing to sacrifice his son, Ishmael. This sacrifice is also part of a worldwide celebration which unites Muslims everywhere in the common rite of Eid ul-Adha.

Pilgrims interpret the hajj to themselves in a variety of ways – 'The purpose . . . is to clean the heart', 'a rehearsal for Resurrection Day', 'you go to please God, not yourself', 'democracy in love – under God'. Some have stressed the arduousness of the journey and the climate – 'the spirit of hajj is the spirit of total sacrifice: sacrifice of personal comforts, worldly pleasures, acquisition of wealth, companionship of relatives and friends, varieties of dress and personal appearances, pride relating to birth, national origin, accomplishments, work or social status . . .' The Qur'an itself says, 'And proclaim the Pilgrimage among men: they will come to thee on foot and on every kind of camel, lean on account of journeys through deep and distant mountain highways, so that they may witness the benefits [provided] for them and celebrate the name of Allah during the appointed days.' But more frequently it is the intensity of the emotional experience which endures. Malcolm X, the American black Muslim, recorded in his *Autobiography* that 'They were of all colours, from blue-eyed blondes to black-skinned Africans. But we were all participating in the same ritual, displaying a spirit of unity and brotherhood that my experiences in America had led me to believe never could exist between the white and the non-white.'

According to Abdullah Naseef, Vice Rector of King Abdul Aziz University:

> The Hajj is a practical application of all the pillars of Islam and some of its major ethical principles. It is a manifestation of the belief in the unity of Allah . . . The Hajj demonstrates Islam's abhorrence of all forms of social distinction . . . It embodies certain characteristics of Zakat as the sacrifice is for the poor . . . It also contains some aspects of fasting since the pilgrims must refrain from sexual activities . . . Finally, like Salat, the Hajj is a continuous immersion of oneself in the presence of Allah.

Bernard Lewis has emphasised the historical importance of the hajj in continually re-unifying the Muslim world:

> If the pilgrim was a merchant, he might combine his pilgrimage with a business trip . . . If he was a scholar, he might take advantage of the opportunity to attend courses, meet colleagues and buy books . . . In order to facilitate the pilgrimage . . . it was necessary to maintain a suitable network of communications between Muslim countries . . . The pilgrimage gave rise to a rich travel literature . . . All this helped to develop among Muslims the feeling of belonging to a single vast whole. This awareness was reinforced by the participation in the ritual and ceremony of the pilgrimage. *(The World of Islam)*[1]

The article on Islam in The International Encyclopaedia of the Social Sciences makes an intriguing comparison:

> . . . the social function of the pilgrimage has been to serve as a journey to a common hearth fire from which the pilgrims could carry back the renewed and

restored flame of faith to their own communities. In this sense, the pilgrimage may be looked on as the counterpart of the fast, for while the fast solidifies the bonds that hold together each community by a common sacrifice, the pilgrimage allows the members of the élites of widely different regions and groups to engage in a spiritual intercourse which strengthens the ties between the various communities of Islam.

The organisation of the hajj is an immense administrative task for the Saudi authorities, food, shelter, transport, interpreting and the prevention of disease are only a few of the major problems. Congestion is another. Almost two million pilgrims must be accommodated in a valley less than two kilometres wide. Yet the capacity of the Great Mosque is only 75,000. Modern technology has, therefore, been pressed to the service of ancient ritual and the Saudi government allocates some $280 million a year to the Ministry of Pilgrimage and Religious Endowments to enable it to cope with the logistics of the hajj and to subsidise pilgrims' outlays on food, travel and accommodation. The new King Abdul Aziz International Airport at Jeddah is the largest in the world and its specially-designed Hajj terminal, covering 370 acres, can handle ten 747 Jumbo jets simultaneously. There is evidence that the situation is nearing breaking-point, though the Saudi authorities would be loath in the extreme to place any limit on numbers. Nevertheless, an article in the *Financial Times* (21 March 1977) commented that 'huge Saudi revenue to subsidise the hajj, good weather, TV publicity (since 1974), better road and transport systems, lack of war and relatively increasing prosperity or lower travel costs in the less-developed countries . . . have all combined to make the last three pilgrimages dangerously large'.

It should be noted that in 1975 an interdisciplinary Hajj Research Centre was established at King Abdul Aziz University to solve the problems of pilgrimage in the fifteenth century of Islam.

Statistics

Non-Saudi pilgrims:

1927	90,764	1957	209,197
1932	25,291	1962	199,038
1937	59,577	1967	318,507
1942	62,590	1972	645,182
1947	75,614	1977	739,319
1952	149,841		

Although the numbers fluctuate considerably from year to year, the overall trend is clearly upwards.

Breakdown of pilgrims by country of origin, 1977:

Meccans	178,360	Nigeria	104,577
Other Saudis	213,769	Pakistan	47,591
Non-Saudi residents	496,141	Sudan	32,353

Algeria	53,230	Syria	24,829
Egypt	30,951	Turkey	91,497
India	21,113	Yemen	79,347
Indonesia	35,703		
Iran	36,942	United Kingdom	1,309
Iraq	34,909	France	642
Jordan	14,211	Spain	52
Libya	20,770	Yugoslavia	1,115
Morocco	22,674	American countries	473
		Total	1,627,589

Sources

1 Bernard Lewis, *The World of Islam* (Thames & Hudson, 1976).

Further reading

Short personal accounts of the hajj can be found in Sherrat and Hawkins, *Gods and Men* (Blackie, 1972), pp.89–90; J. Kritzeck, *Anthology of Islamic Literature* (Pelican, 1964), pp.226–32; and Riadh El-Droubie and Edward Hulmes, *Islam* (Longman, 1980), pp.48–58. Longer accounts are given in A. Kamal, *The Sacred Journey* (Allen & Unwin, 1961); Idries Shah, *Destination Mecca* (Octagon, 1957); Hussein Yoshio Hirashima, *The Road to Holy Mecca* (Kodansha, 1972); and Saida Niller Khalifa, *The Fifth Pillar* (Exposition Press, 1977). Technical aspects are dealt with in Ghazy Abdul Wahed Makky, *Mecca: The Pilgrimage City: A Study of Pilgrim Accommodation* (Croom Helm, 1978) and Z. Sardar and M.A. Zaki Badawi, *Hajj Studies*, Vol. 1 (Croom Helm, 1978). A descriptive analysis of the rituals of the hajj can be found in G.E. von Grünebaum, *Muhammadan Festivals* (Curzon Press, 1976). There are also a number of superbly illustrated 'coffee-table' books. Mohamed Amin, *Pilgrimage to Mecca* (Macdonald & Jane's, 1978), is the most sumptuously illustrated and most expensive. Photographs by Mohamed Amin accompany the text of Desmond Stewart's *Mecca* (Newsweek, 1980) which presents Islam in terms of the city and the hajj, as does Emel Esin, *Mecca the Blessed, Madinah the Radiant* (Elek, 1963). D.E. Long, *The Hajj Today* (State University of New York, 1979) is a definitive survey, covering religious and administrative aspects and evaluating the impact of the pilgrimage on Saudi Arabia itself. Hamza Kaidi, *Mecca and Medinah Today* (Les éditions j.a., 1980) is a practical pilgrimage handbook which also gives a detailed account of the rites and invocations involved.

10
Shari'a

As a number of scholars have observed, law, rather than theological speculation, is the characteristic manifestation of the Muslim faith: no doubt
because what God has revealed is not His character but His will and what He
requires of man is not his understanding but his submission (Islam).
Derived from four major sources (Qur'an, *hadith, qiyas* (Analogy) and *ijma*
(Consensus)), it was elaborated into four major schools which evolved in the
second and third centuries of the Muslim era (Hanafi, Maliki, Shafii, Hanbali). It is less important that students should attempt to master any of the
technicalities of Islamic jurisprudence than that they should be aware of its
range and subtlety.

In Western law an act is either lawful or not. Whether it is decent, pious or
in good taste is irrelevant. In Muslim law this is not so and the *shari'a* assigns
any act to one of five categories:

obligatory (*fard*) e.g. prayer;
commendable (*sunna*) e.g. hospitality;
allowed (*halal*) e.g. kindness to animals;
discouraged (*makruh*) e.g. divorce;
forbidden (*haram*) e.g. drinking alcohol.

In Islam, law and morality are coterminous, whereas in Western liberal
democracies they overlap but do not coincide. In Islam, sin is a consequence
of transgression, rather than a spiritual condition which man cannot resolve
for himself. Muslims believe strongly in the ideal of a moral society buttres-
sed by laws stringently enforced. Law is a means of protecting what is valued
and worthy of respect – one's wealth (hence the severity of punishments
for theft), one's health (hence capital punishment for rape and murder), one's
mind (hence the prohibition of alcohol), one's honour (hence the prohibition of extra-marital sex and the severe penalties against slander), and one's
religion (hence the obligation to undertake *jihad* when the practice of Islam
is under attack).

As J. Schacht has emphasised:

> Islamic law is the totality of God's commands that regulate the life of every Muslim
> in all its aspects; it comprises on an equal footing ordinances regarding worship
> and ritual, as well as political and (in the narrow sense) legal rules, details of toilet,

formulas of greeting, table-manners and sick-room conversation. Islamic law is the typical manifestation of the Islamic way of life, the core and kernel of Islam itself. (*The Legacy of Islam*)[1]

In practice, however, the application of the shari'a was most closely related to religious and domestic matters, while commercial, criminal and constitutional affairs often fell outside its strict control. The role of the *ulema* as formulators and interpreters of the law should be made clear, because the shari'a has been largely the creation of legalistically-minded intellectuals rather than the evolved product of changing social circumstances.

Sources

1 J. Schacht,*The Legacy of Islam* (OUP, 1974), p.392.

Further reading

For traditional Islamic law see: Isam Ghanem, *Outlines of Islamic Jurisprudence* (Express Printing Services, Dubai, 2nd edn, 1981), a concise survey of history and principles; N.J. Coulson, *A History of Islamic Law* (Edinburgh University Press, 1957), especially chapters 4, 5 and 6; J. Schacht, *An Introduction to Islamic Law* (Oxford, 1964) and 'Law and justice', chapter 4 of Part VIII of the *Cambridge History of Islam Vol. 2*. An extract from al-Shafii can be found in McNeill and Waldman, *The Islamic World* (OUP, 1973).

On the contemporary situation, with special emphasis on family law, the Indian sub-continent and the legal situation of Muslims in Britain, see David Pearl, *A Textbook on Muslim Law* (Croom Helm, 1979). For a vigorous defence of the contemporary relevance of shari'a see A. Rahman I Doi, *Shari'a in the 1500 Century of Hijra: Problems and Prospects* (Ta-Ha, 1981).

11
Subdivisions
in Islam

Muslim spokesmen everywhere proclaim the solidarity of the *umma*. Yet few non-Muslims can be unaware that the Islamic aspect of recent events in Iran has revealed itself in terms of a particular style and tradition. In secular matters, at least, the distinction between Sunnite and Shi'ite does seem to have definite consequences. Nor is this surprising, since the origins of Shi'ism were primarily political. Christianity grew up persecuted by the State and was only subsequently, and with difficulty, accommodated to it. But Islam, as a complete way of life ordained by God, was both State and religion from its very birth. Hence the pattern identified by Bernard Lewis as recurrent in the history of Islam, 'whenever a grievance or a conflict of interests created a faction in Islam, its doctrines were a theology, its instrument a sect, its agent a missionary, its leader usually a Messiah or his representative'. (*The Arabs in History*.)[1]

Shi'a is short for Shiat Ali, the party or faction of Ali. Ali, the cousin and son-in-law of the Prophet, was the fourth Caliph and, according to the Shi'a, the first to have succeeded rightfully to the authority of the Prophet. Whereas the Sunni (followers of the Sunna, the way of the Prophet), who constitute some ninety per cent of all Muslims, hold that the Caliphate could be held by any pious Muslim who commanded the approval of the community's spiritual leaders, the Shi'ites regard the succession as only belonging rightfully to descendants of the Prophet's blood-line through Ali. The history of Shi'ism is very complex and only a few significant points can, therefore, be noted here:

1 Ali's authority was challenged both by Mu'awiya (who became the fifth Caliph and inaugurated the Umayyad dynasty) and by the Kharijites (seceders), a fundamentalist group who rejected Ali's political compromise with Mu'awiya after the battle of Siffin and were eventually to be responsible for his death. When Mu'awiya died, Ali's son Hussein tried to challenge Umayyad power but was killed at Kerbala in 681, an event which is commemorated annually in the emotional rituals of the 10th of Muharram. Ali and Hussein are regarded as martyrs and the theme of opposition and suffering in the name of justice and righteousness has become central to the Shi'ite outlook, which has historically taken on the character of a religion of the oppressed.

2   Shi'ites believe in a kind of apostolic succession of *imams*, starting with Ali. The majority recognise twelve imams ('Twelver' Shi'ism has been the state religion of Iran since the sixteenth century) culminating in Muhammad al Muntazar (the awaited one) who did not die but remains hidden, destined to re-emerge and purify the world. The other main branch is represented by the Isma'ilis (Seveners) who recognise Isma'il, rather than his brother, Musa al-Kazim, as the rightful heir to the sixth imam, and hold that the Qur'an has an esoteric, inner meaning, secretly transmitted to Ali and by him through the line of Isma'ili imams. The Isma'ilis gave rise to the brilliant Fatimid dynasty which proclaimed its Caliphate over North Africa in the tenth century, founded Al-Azhar university and later gave rise to the notorious sect of Assassins. Revived in the nineteenth century, the Isma'ilis now constitute a worldwide and well-organised community under the leadership of their present (forty-ninth) imam, better known as the Aga Khan.

3   Of the other tendencies which arose out of Shi'ism the Druzes and Alawites may be mentioned on the grounds of their contemporary political significance and peculiar doctrinal tenets. The Druzes are an important factor in current Lebanese politics and Ninian Smart has remarked, with them 'we have come right to the edge of Islamic orthodoxy if not beyond. No longer is Islam seen as universal and outward looking but rather as cloaking a secret, elitist, religious revelation' (*Background to the Long Search*).[2] The Druzes, who are a closed sect, regard the Fatimid Caliph Hakim (996–1021) as an incarnation of God. The Alawites, by contrast, elevate Ali to divine status. President Assad of Syria is an Alawite turned Sunni Muslim and Alawites enjoy a great influence in his regime.

4   Some scholars have drawn a contrast between Sunni Islam, with its emphasis on uncompromising monotheism and its adherence to the Shari'a, and Shi'ism, with its esotericism and emotional rituals, in terms of a parallel contrast between Judaism and Christianity, especially in its Mediterranean form, perceiving in Shi'ism such elements as the cults of a holy family, a symbolic sacrifice and a second coming.

Sources

1   Bernard Lewis, *The Arab in History* (Hutchinson, 5th edn, 1970), p.99.
2   Ninian Smart, *Background to the Long Search* (BBC, 1977), p.212.

Further reading

A.J. Arberry (ed.), *Religion in the Middle East* (CUP, 2 vols, 1969). Synthesis of recent scholarly research; especially useful on sectarian divisions.
William C. Chittick, *A Shi'ite Anthology* (Muhammadi Trust, 1980). Anthology of the teachings of the Shi'ite imams on the Unity of God, the Ruler and Society and the Spiritual Life.

S.H.M. Jafri, *The Origins and Early Development of Shi'a Islam* (Longman, 1979).
Allamah Tabataba'i, *Shi'ite Islam* (Allen & Unwin, 1975).

Sub-divisions in Islam

	Origins	Distinctive Beliefs and Ritual	Historical Importance	Current Distribution
Kharijites	Discontented tribesmen dispute Ali's authority CE656.	Militant puritan emphasis on jihad and asceticism. Egalitarian opposition to Arab aristocracy.	Assassinated Ali CE661. Antagonised early Umayyads. Declined into antagonistic factions.	Scattered small communities in Algeria, Tunisia (especially Berber areas), Tanzania and Oman.
Shi'a Twelvers (Imami)	Movement (Shi'a = faction) to restore caliphate to Ali and his line. Recognise twelve imams etc. to CE873 when twelfth imam disappeared at Samarra – await return of 'hidden imam'.	Imam regarded as charismatic and infallible leader. First ten days of Muharram as major festival. Non-literal interpretation of Qur'an. Tombs of imams (especially Hussein) and Karbala as major shrines. Salvation through messianic return of Mahdi.	Attracted many non-Arab converts excluded from power. Anti-establishment revolts. State religion of Iran since 16th century.	Iran (majority of population), Iraq (*c*.50%), Lebanon (*c*.20%), India and Pakistan (*c*.8%).
Seveners (Isma'ili)		Recognised imams ending with Isma'il. Mobilised social discontent. Evolved esoteric faith for initiates.	Established Fatimid caliphate in N. Africa 909–1171. Assassins flourished 12th & 13th centuries. Re-emerged under Aga Khan in 19th century.	India and East Africa.

	Origins	Distinctive Beliefs and Ritual	Historical Importance	Current Distribution
Zaidi	Recognise only first four imams.	Apart from refusal to accept caliph's legitimacy, virtually Sunni.	Conquered Yemen in 9th century. Zaidi imams reigned until 1962.	
Alawi	= 'worshippers of Ali' – offshoot of Isma'ili missionary activity.	Extreme syncreticism – include pagan and Christian elements.	Survive as withdrawn minority.	Syria (*c*. 10%).
Druze	Established by Darazi, 11th century Isma'ili missionary.	Fatimid Al-Hakim (d.1021) as hidden imam. Monogamy. Transmigration of souls.	Evolved very distinctive doctrine and social structure.	Lebanon and Syria (*c*. ¼ million) (total).
Bahai	Established in 1844 by the Bab, a Persian teacher of religion, and developed by his disciple Bahaullah (1817–92).	Claims to be fulfilment of all previous religions. The Bahai faith should now be regarded as a separate world religion in its own right, representing a movement to find a common amalgam of faiths.	Persecuted – spread to Levant, USA and Europe.	Bahai communities in 139 countries (*c*. ½ million in Iran).
Ahmadiyya	Established in 1889 by Hazrat Mirza Ghulam Ahmad (1835–1908) to re-affirm Islam in the face of Western dominance.	Founder claimed to be Messiah mentioned in Biblical and Qur'anic prophecies.	Vigorous proselytising movement. Founder's claim to prophethood rejected by orthodox Muslims.	World-wide, but especially in Africa and Indonesia.

12

Sufism

> The ideal and morally perfect man should be of East Persian derivation, Arabic in faith, of Iraqi education, a Hebrew in astuteness, a disciple of Christ in conduct, as pious as a Greek monk, a Greek in the individual sciences, an Indian in the interpretation of all mysteries, but lastly and especially a Sufi in his whole spiritual life. (Ikhwan as-Safa) (ninth century)

The mystical tradition in Islam is usually referred to as Sufism, a word derived from the rough woollen robes (*suf* in Arabic) worn by early Muslim ascetics. Sufis are those who have set themselves to experience intimate closeness with God. Out of their experiences an elaborate system of mystical theory and practice has been developed. Originating in the spiritual activities of an elite of devotees, Sufism came, as other expressions of the faith lost their vitality, to embrace a mass following from at least the fifth Islamic century onwards, recruiting members into brotherhoods, many of which were linked with craft and charitable organisations and each of which followed a particular *tariqa* (path) in its search for Haqiqa, the inward, divine reality. Perhaps the most famous of these is the Maulawi (better known under its Turkish name Mevlevi) tariqa founded by Jalal al-Din Rumi (1207–73), perhaps the greatest mystical poet of Islam. The most characteristic feature of Mevlevi devotions is the whirling dance performed as an accompaniment to their *dhikr* (invocation or remembrance of God's name). Other famous orders include the Qadiri, Tijani, Suhrawardi, Shadhili, Chrishti and Naqshbandi.

There has usually been some tension between the mystics and the guardians of more formalistic expressions of Islam. When Al-Hallaj (d.922) proclaimed in ecstasy 'I am the Truth' he was promptly executed for his presumption. And in more recent times Sufi practices have been attacked by reformers as corrupt and degenerate. On the other hand Sufism has attracted a considerable body of interest among Western intellectuals and continues to impart a distinctive character to the popular Islam of such areas as Pakistan and North Africa. The Sufi brotherhoods are also a major force behind the continuing rapid spread of Islam in sub-Saharan Africa.

Modern Sufi writers tend to assert the orthodox nature of Sufism in Islam. Seyyed Hossein Nasr asserts that it 'has its roots in the Qur'an'.

William Stoddart declares bluntly that 'One cannot be a Benedictine without being a Christian, or a Sufi without being a Muslim. There is no Sufism without Islam' (*Sufism: The Mystical Doctrines and Methods of Islam*).[1] The same author elaborates his argument as follows:

> The only difference between spirituality (or mysticism) and religion in the ordinary sense, is that spirituality envisages as its main end the attaining of sanctity (or the embarking on the path that leads to sanctity) even in this life here and now. All spiritual methods are orientated towards this end. This is what the mystical or initiatic path is all about.
>
> To embark on a spiritual path, a rite of initiation is indispensable . . . In Sufism the aspirant receives the rite of initiation from Sufi master (shaikh or murshid) who, in turn, has received it, at the beginning of his spiritual career, from his shaikh . . . and so on back to the Prophet himself who, by Divine Grace, initiated the first Sufis.
>
> The name 'Sufi' did not exist in the time of the Prophet, but the reality did. The Prophet conferred this rite (and gave the corresponding counsels) to only some of his Companions; they in turn passed it on, and in this way, up to the present day, the rite, in unbroken succession, is still passed on. (op.cit., p.54)

The American anthropologist, Clifford Geertz, has in his characteristically detached way observed that Sufism,

> as an historical reality, consists of a series of different and even contradictory experiments . . . in bringing orthodox Islam into effective relationship with the world, rendering it accessible to its adherents and its adherents accessible to it. In the Middle East, this seems mainly to have meant reconciling Arabian pantheism with Koranic legalism; in Indonesia, restating Indian illuminationism in Arabic phrases; in West Africa, defining sacrifice, possession, exorcism and curing as Muslim rituals.

A more empathetic explanation of the appeal of Sufism can be gained from Al-Ghazali (d.1111) who gives an account of his own involvement in the mystic quest:

> Then I turned my attention to the Way of the Sufis. I knew that it could not be traversed to the end without both doctrine and practice, and that the gist of the doctrine lies in overcoming the appetites of the flesh and getting rid of its evil dispositions and vile qualities, so that the heart may be cleared of all but God: and the means of clearing it is *Dhikr Allah* i.e. commemoration of God and concentration of every thought upon Him. Now, the doctrine was easier to me than the practice, so I began by learning their doctrine from the books and sayings of their Shaykhs, until I acquired as much of their way as it is possible to acquire by learning and hearing, and saw plainly that what is most peculiar to them cannot be learned, but can only be reached by immediate experience and ecstasy and inward transformation . . .

Sufism is a search for God. It requires discipline and commitment, training and effort under the guidance of a spiritual master. It represents the 'greater jihad', the struggle against selfishness which alone can liberate the heart to move towards God and, therefore, the realisation of true selfhood. God is Unity and Transcendence and the temporal world is merely contingent and chaotic; but, although the Sufi must strive for detachment from everyday cares, his commitment need not involve rejection of the world, merely a continuing awareness that one must not be trapped by it. As the hajj is an outward journey towards God, so the tariqa of the Sufi is an inward journey towards God. Rumi put the point very elegantly:

> Though the roads are various, the goal is one. Do you not see that there are many roads to the Ka'ba? For some the road is from Rum, for some from Syria, for some from Persia, for some from China, for some by sea from India and Yemen. So if you consider the roads, the variety is great and the divergence infinite: but when you consider the goal, they are all of one accord . . . Now the literalists take the Holy Mosque to be that Ka'ba to which people repair. Lovers, however, and the elect of God, take the Holy Mosque to mean union with God.

Sufism is not, however, for initiates alone. Sufi sages have long been regarded as profound sources of wisdom:

> A man said to Ibrahim Ibn Adhan, 'O Abu Ishaw I would like you to accept this cloak from me to cover you.' 'If you are rich,' he replied, 'I will accept it, but if you are poor, I will not.' 'I am rich,' said the man. 'How much have you?' asked Ibrahim. 'I have 2,000,' said the man. 'Would you like to have 4,000?' asked Ibrahim. 'Yes,' said the man. 'Then you are poor,' said Ibrahim, 'and I will not take it.'

> Someone complained to a Sufi sage that the stories which he gave out were interpreted in one way by some people, and in other ways by others.
> 'That is precisely their value,' he said. 'Surely you would not think much of even a cup out of which you could drink milk but not water or a plate from which you could eat meat but not fruit? A cup and a plate are limited containers. How much more capable should language be to provide nutrition? The question is not "How many ways can I understand this and why can I not see it in only one way?" The question is rather "Can this individual profit from what he is finding out in the tales?" '

Sources

1 William Stoddard, *Sufism: The Mystical Doctrines and Methods of Islam* (Thorsons, 1976).

Further reading

A.J. Arberry, *Sufism* (Allen & Unwin, 1950).
Laleh Bakhtiar, *Sufi: Expressions of the Mystic Quest* (Thames & Hudson, 1976). Superbly illustrated exposition of esoteric symbolism, 'the most sacred of Sufi sciences'.
Titus Burckhardt, *Introduction to Sufi Doctrine* (Thorsons, 1976). Exposition of Islamic metaphysics.
Shems Friedlander, *Submission: Sayings of the Prophet Muhammad* (Wildwood House, 1977). Contains numerous black and white photographs of dervish practices.

Martin Lings, *What is Sufism?* (Allen & Unwin, 1975). Concise authoritative survey by an adherent.

Martin Lings, *A Sufi Saint of the 20th Century* (Allen & Unwin, 1971). Biography of the Algerian shaikh Ahmad al-Alaw (1869–1934). Useful descriptions of doctrines and practices.

S.H. Nasr, *Sufi Essays* (Allen & Unwin, 1972). Attempts to relate Sufism to contemporary problems.

R.A. Nicholson, *Rumi: Poet and Mystic* (Allen & Unwin, 1978). Translated poems of a celebrated mystic.

R.A. Nicholson, *The Mystics of Islam* (Routledge & Kegan Paul, 1975). Classic sketch written in 1914.

Annemarie Schimmel, *Mystical Dimensions of Islam* (University of North Carolina Press, 1975). Magisterial scholarly survey. Erudite and comprehensive bibliography.

Frithof Schuon, *Understanding Islam* (Allen & Unwin, 1963). Exposition of Islam which regards Sufism as its kernel.

Idries Shah, *The Sufis* (Cape, 1964). Essays by the best-known populariser of this subject.

Idries Shah, *Thinkers of the East* (Penguin, 1974), *Tales of the Dervishes* (Panther, 1973), *Caravan of Dreams* (Quartet, 1973). Anthologies of Sufi teaching stories.

Margaret Smith, *The Sufi Path of Love* (Luzac, 1954). An anthology of the writings of Sufis and their interpreters.

J.S. Trimingham, *The Sufi Orders in Islam* (Oxford, 1971). Standard scholarly study.

Mir Valiuddin, *Contemplative Disciplines in Sufism* (East–West Publications, 1980). According to one Muslim reviewer, 'Every page of this little book is strewn with pearls beyond compare.'

W.M. Watt, *Muslim Intellectual: A Study of Al-Ghazali* (Edinburgh University Press, 1963). Biography of a famous academic theologian turned mystic.

13
Islam and
Christianity

Ninian Smart has written of the relationship between Islam and Christianity that 'each is too close for comfort to the other, yet too different for its peculiar excellences to meet the eye'. In the medieval period Islam was seen more as a physical than as an intellectual threat and Muhammad was vilified not so much as the founder of a different religion but as the lascivious progenitor of a hideously successful Christian heresy. Not until after the Renaissance, when more accurate translations of the Qur'an became available and the crusading spirit began to wane, did Islam begin to be evaluated in its own right rather than as a fulfilment of prophecies prefiguring the last days. As European knowledge increased, however, so did European power, and by the nineteenth century Islam was perceived no longer as a threat but as a prime cause of the backwardness of conquered societies and doomed to inevitable extinction. The 'Islamic revival' of recent years has been accompanied by a revival of the image of Islam as threatening and mysterious; crusading propaganda still seems to supply a framework for popular perceptions as reflected in the mass media.

In these circumstances it may be as well to bear in mind W.M. Watt's view: 'It must be realised that much of our fathers' belief in the superiority of Christianity was a belief in the superiority of European material culture, and that simply as religions Christianity and Islam are roughly on an equal footing, that is to say, that Islam, just as much as Christianity, has a 'gospel' for the modern world.' (*Islamic Revelation in the Modern World.*)[1]

This is not a view to win ready and universal acceptance. The stance taken by the Bishop of Guildford in his pamphlet on Christian–Muslim relations – 'A New Threshold' – was tartly criticised in a *Church Times* editorial which, having paid tribute to his sincerity, learning and orthodoxy, nevertheless concluded that:

> The Bishop's prolonged attempts to play down the fundamental theological differences between Cross and Crescent really carry little, if any, conviction. Christians have a duty to convert Mohammedans from the error of their beliefs to the truth of Christ. Kindness and charity towards non-Christians is one thing. Readiness to accept their religion as on a par with Christianity is quite another. (*Church Times*, 6 February 1976)

Muslims and Christians do share the belief that God is the creator and sustainer of a coherent universe in which He has revealed Himself to man, who is endowed with moral responsibility for his actions, and has the duty of worship and the privilege of petition. Both religions also acknowledge their membership of a common 'Abrahamic' tradition, venerate Jerusalem and enjoin the practice of weekly congregational prayer.

'Vatican II' stated its conception of the common ground between the two faiths in the following terms:

> Upon the Moslems too the Church looks with esteem. They adore one God, living and enduring, merciful and all-powerful, Maker of heaven and earth and Speaker to men. They strive to submit wholeheartedly even to his inscrutable decrees, just as did Abraham, with whom the Islamic faith is pleased to associate itself. Though they do not acknowledge Jesus as God, they revere Him as a prophet. They also honour Mary, his virgin mother; at times they call on her, too, with devotion. In addition, they await the day of judgement when God will give each man his due after raising him up. Consequently, they prize the moral life, and give worship to God especially through prayer, almsgiving and fasting. Although in the course of the centuries many quarrels and hostilities have arisen between Christians and Moslems, this most sacred Synod urges all to forget the past and to strive sincerely for mutual understanding on behalf of all mankind, let them make common cause of safeguarding and fostering social justice, moral values, peace and freedom. (Declaration on the Relationship of the Church to Non-Christian Religions, *Nostra Aetate*, Article 3, Vatican II)

A. Guillaume, *Islam*,[2] sets out an interesting comparison between Christian and Islamic beliefs by analysing the Apostles' Creed from the Qur'anic point of view. An abbreviated, tabular version of this approach appears in Sherrat and Hawkins, *Gods and Men*[3]. These authors note that:

> The differences are perhaps more apparent to the Muslim than to the Christian. Islam tends to be thought of by Muslims as a correction of Judaism and Christianity. For this reason the differences tend to lie more in what Islam rejects as false rather than what it asserts as true.

Thus Muslims reject both the doctrine of the Trinity (God is One absolutely, nothing may be 'associated' with Him) and the divinity of Christ (Jesus was sinless but human). But they do accept the Day of Judgement, the forgiveness of sins, and the resurrection of the body.

It is also important to remember that Muslims and Christians encounter one another in Britain in a multi-faith situation. This no doubt creates some complications of its own. Some Muslims feel, for instance, that Hindus and Buddhists are treated more sympathetically than they are, perhaps because there is no past history of antagonism. But the multi-faith situation does open up interesting new possibilities as well.

Reporting on a 'trialogue' organised by Christians, Muslims and Jews in St John's Wood, London, David Goldberg noted that the experience had been

> surprising for Christians, illuminating for Jews and reassuring for Muslims . . .
> surprising for Christians, because it has shaken up their assumptions about the

special relationship between Judaism and Christianity, with Islam as the outsider
... the religious thought-processes of Judaism and Islam have more in common
than those of Judaism and Christianity. Christianity derives its inspiration from an
individual, Judaism and Islam derive theirs from two holy books ... Christianity,
with its emphasis on Faith, takes a different path from Judaism and Islam, with
their allegiance to Law. ('Christians, Muslims and Jews join a unique venture' *The
Times*, 24 January 1981)

In reviewing his experience of Islam at the sixth-form level, Roy Robinson[4] has confessed that:

We found it impossible to avoid making constant comparisons between the concepts of Islam and our understanding of religion as seen from within Protestant
Christianity ... Christians cannot help but be prejudiced, making inevitable
comparisons with the life of Christ to the detriment of the Prophet of Islam. It
does not really help to acknowledge that such comparisons are invalid ...

It is, of course, inevitable that one will use familiar categories and concepts as tools for the analysis of a different religious tradition, but it would
be absurd to assume that one cannot learn to handle new concepts derived
from that religious tradition or to use the old ones with greater subtlety and
precision. One must also strive to achieve an awareness that familiar
categories and concerns may simply not have the same significance when
considered in a different context. Thus the Qur'an explicitly denies both the
incarnation and the crucifixion, matters of central importance to Christianity, but does so almost in passing (53:19–22; 4:154ff). And Muslims have
little interest in being told, in the words of one eminent authority, that Islam
has a 'defective conception of sin', or that in presenting their faith to others
they should give first priority to those aspects which non-Muslims hold to be
'problematic' (the status of women, Shari'a punishments, etc.). Rather do
they wish to ensure that their religion is approached in terms which make
some sort of sense to those who subscribe to it. The objective of study is not
so much to find out what the faith of another means to oneself but what it
means to him.

It may, however, be illuminating to reflect on what Muslims may think
about Christianity and Christians in contemporary Britain. Undoubtedly
attitudes will vary, not least with the incidence of such factors as their degree
of knowledge of both Islam and Christianity and the extent of their personal
acquaintance with Christians. Nevertheless it would probably be true to say
that many of the older generation would regard Christians as being very lax
in their religious observances and in any case in error with regard to the true
teachings of Jesus. Younger Muslims would probably have some more or
less indirect experience of Christian worship via school or television, but
they are unlikely to have much systematic knowledge of Christian beliefs.

The teacher who does find himself drawn into a situation in which overt
comparisons are being drawn between Christianity and Islam can at least try
to ensure that the comparisons being made are consistent, for instance that
Christian ideals are compared with Muslim ideals, Christian practices with
Muslim practices. To contrast, for example, the Christian ideal of marriage

with the actual treatment accorded to some Muslim wives would be not only misleading but also intellectually illegitimate. It may also be helpful in such circumstances to underline not so much what the two faiths share theologically but what they both endorse in terms of ethics and what areas are open to common endeavour for both Christians and Muslims (for example action in the field of community relations, concern to secure the position of religion in education, and maintenance of buildings for worship, and so on).

At the risk of understatement it may be said in conclusion that inter-faith dialogue requires qualities of intellect and maturity which are unlikely to be found in the average secondary school classroom, although it is one very important place in which a contribution to the development of such qualities may be made. What school-age pupils need first and foremost is accurate knowledge, empathetically presented as worthy of their careful and serious consideration. This may be a preliminary to more sophisticated endeavours, but it is also a worthwhile enterprise in itself.

Sources

1 W.M. Watt, *Islamic Revelation in the Modern World* (Edinburgh University Press, 1969), p.5.

2 A. Guillaume, *Islam* (Pelican, 2nd edn, 1956).

3 Sherrat and Hawkins, *Gods and Men* (Blackie, 1972).

4 Roy Robinson in *Perspectives on World Religions*, Robert Jackson (ed.), (SOAS, 1978), chapter IX.

Further reading

Robert Betts, *Christians in the Arab East* (John Knox Press, Atlanta, 1978). Scholarly survey, emphasising the current situation.
David Brown, *A New Threshold: Guidelines for the Churches in their Relations with Muslim Communities* (British Council of Churches, 1976).
Kenneth Cragg, *The Call of the Minaret* (OUP, 1956). Interpretation of contemporary Islam with the emphasis on Christian–Muslim relations.
Kenneth Cragg, *The Dome and the Rock* (SPCK, 1964). Essays comparing Muslim and Christian views of social and theological issues.
Rudolf Frieling, *Christianity and Islam: A Battle for the True Image of Man* (Floris Books, 1978). An account of the origins of Islam by an author who 'can only regard it as tragic through Muhammad's imperfect encounter with Christianity he did not understand its essential mysteries'.
S. Joseph and B.L.K. Pillsbury, *Muslim–Christian Conflicts: Economic, Social and Political Origins* (Dawson, 1979). A series of case studies.
Don M. McCurry (ed.), *The Gospel and Islam: A 1978 Compendium* (Missions Advanced Research and Communication Center, Monrovia, California,

1979). Bulky survey of evangelisation efforts and techniques in Muslim countries. Also includes useful surveys of the comparative status of Christianity and Islam in various regions and countries.

Geoffrey Parrinder, *Jesus in the Qur'an* (Sheldon Press, 1976).

Muhammad Ata Ur-Rahim, *Jesus: Prophet of Islam* (Diwan Press, 1977), 'shows us how the "true" Christian teaching was diverted, or one might say derailed, by a powerful Pauline explosion'.

Annemarie Schimmel and Abduljayad Falaturi, *We Believe in One God: The Experience of God in Christianity and Islam* (Burnes & Oates, 1979). Scholarly essays by Muslims and Christians.

Secretarius Pro Non-Christianus, *Guidelines for a Dialogue between Muslims and Christians* (Edizion Ancora, Rome, 1969). 'We are not trying to fix definite formulae for such a dialogue but rather to define the spirit in which it should take place.'

W.C. Smith, *On Understanding Islam* (Mouton, 1981).

J. Spencer Trimingham, *Christianity among the Arabs in Pre-Islamic Times* (Longman, 1979). Scholarly study.

W.M. Watt, *Islamic Revelation in the Modern World* (Edinburgh University Press 1969). 'Not a direct comparison of Islamic and Christian thought, but an attempt to relate both to the secular or rather neutral world-view associated with the scientific outlook.'

For a useful survey of periodical articles see Abstract no. 4, March 1981, 'European Muslims and Christian–Muslim Relations', published by the Centre for the Study of Islam and Christian–Muslim Relations, Selly Oak Colleges, Birmingham.

14
Expansion
and Empires

Muhammad's sudden death in 632 faced the Muslim community with a major crisis. Deprived of his towering leadership, would the tribal confederations split up into feuding and anarchy? Would his moral political revolution be subverted? Meeting hurriedly, the elders of the Muslim community decided to elect Abu Bakr, one of the Prophet's oldest converts, as his 'Khalifa' (Caliph) or 'successor'. It was made clear, however, that the Caliph succeeded only to the temporal role of the Prophet, as governor of the *umma*, the community of the faithful. He could claim no powers of revelation and Umar, the second Caliph, made plain that the era of prophecy had ended, saying, 'If there are any among you who worshipped Muhammad, he is dead. But if it is God you worship, He lives for ever.' From its inception in the year of Muhammad's death to its demise in 1924 the Caliphate has been a key institution in the development of the Islamic umma, and the continuing struggles to define its powers in theory and in practice have shaped much of the internal political history of the Islamic world.

Islam had proclaimed the brotherhood of all Muslims. Raiding, feuding and stealing – the traditional occupations of the bedouin – were forbidden among Muslims. The restless energies of the nomads were, therefore, turned outwards from the Arabian peninsula and Islam was thus launched upon a remarkable century of expansion. Armed with the conviction that death in battle against the unbeliever would bring instant admission to Paradise, the Muslim armies swept north and then spread east and west. Exhausted by a quarter-century of bloody warfare, the Byzantine and Persian empires were capable of only the feeblest resistance, and, in many cases, their subjects welcomed the Muslims as liberators from oppressive imperial rule. Damascus, capital of the Byzantine province of Syria, was captured in 635, Ctesiphon, capital of the Sassanian empire, in 637, and Alexandria, capital of Byzantine Egypt, in 642.

The fact that the Arabs had been Islamised meant that they came as teachers not as learners, capable of resisting cultural, especially Christian, absorption. Islam established the framework within which cultural borrowing took place. That Muslim civilisation was hardly, if at all, influenced by Greek art, drama, poetry, mythology, historiography, and political life and thought clearly shows how deeply Islam had affected its adherents. But, as Bernard Lewis has emphasised, the fact that Islam gave its adherents such a sense of self-sufficiency and equanimity enabled it to display a remarkable degree of tolerance and great powers of assimilation.

The assassination of Ali, Muhammad's son-in-law, in 661, brought to an end the line of Rashidin or 'rightly guided caliphs' who had all been close personal companions of the Prophet. The caliphate passed into the hands of Mu'awiya, governor of Syria. A shrewd statesman, Mu'awiya represented the Umayyads, an aristocratic branch of Quraish, early enemies of the Prophet and late converts to the faith. Breaking away from the theocratic simplicity of his predecessors, he remodelled the Islamic State on Byzantine lines, dissolving the old tribal basis of the army, creating a navy, appointing officials on the basis of their competence rather than their piety and making Damascus his capital. Whatever misgivings or opposition these changes may have aroused, they did not check the avalanche of conquest which rolled on east and west, thrusting Muslim armies into Central Asia and gobbling up the Berber kingdoms of the North African coast-lands.

In 711 a Muslim army crossed into Spain. Brushing aside the crumbling Visigothic kingdom, the invaders had taken control of almost the entire peninsula within three years. Not until 732, exactly a century after the Prophet's death, were Muslim forces brought to a decisive defeat in the west, at Tours, just south of Paris. Twenty years later, at the farthest frontier of the Islamic world, a Muslim army met and defeated a Chinese punitive expedition on the borders of the T'ang empire. Thwarted at Tours in the west, the Muslims triumphed in the valley of the Talas river, and claimed Central Asia for Islam. From prisoners captured at this battle, they learned the secrets of manufacturing both silk and paper. Over the course of the next five centuries knowledge of these techniques gradually percolated through to Western Europe.

In 750 the fourteenth Umayyad caliph was ousted. As Lewis has observed:

> It was a revolution in the history of Islam, as important a turning point as the French and Russian Revolutions in the history of the West. It came about not as the result of a palace conspiracy or *coup d'état* but by the action of an extensive and successful revolutionary propaganda and organisation, representing and expressing the dissatisfactions of important elements of the population with the previous regime and built up over a long period of time.

The new dynasty, the 'Abbasids, who were descended from the Prophet's uncle, Al-abbas, shifted their capital from Damascus to the purpose-built city of Baghdad. This change in the centre of gravity of the Islamic world gave new prominence to Persian influences in many fields, from courtly etiquette to textile design. The court became less Arab, less secular and less accessible to the ordinary Muslim.

By the tenth century the political unity of the Islamic empire had begun to fragment under the impact of the ambitions of local rulers in the provinces and warlord usurpation at the centre, aggravated by sectarian divisions. The Buyid conquest of Iraq reduced the Abbasid Caliph to a cipher. In Spain an autonomous caliphate was established by descendants of the Umayyad line (925). In North Africa yet another caliphate was set up by the Shi'ite Fatimids (909) who claimed descent from the Prophet's daughter Fatima and founded a new capital for themselves at Cairo.

The tide of conquest rolled forward again in the following century with armed incursions into Western Africa, and Northern India. At the same time the Abbasid caliphate fell effectively under the control of Turkish invaders, the Seljuks, who briefly reinvigorated it – thus, in effect, provoking the Crusades. Seen against this general background, the Crusades assume the perspective of local and temporary reverses in a general trend of expansion. The chivalrous and statesmanlike Salah-al-Din (Saladin) not only recaptured Jerusalem from the Christians but also reunited Egypt and Syria under firm rule, if only briefly.

Intellectual activity, meanwhile, continued with undiminished vigour.

Medieval Islam seems, however, to have remained largely indifferent to Europe. Only one personal account by a named traveller seems to have survived (the record of a tenth-century diplomatic mission from Spain to Otto I) and only one Latin work is known to have been translated into Arabic. Rome itself was regarded as remote and barbaric, and even after the Crusades Islamic writers failed to distinguish between the various types of Westerners, all of whom were lumped together as 'Franks'.

In 1248 the Mongol hordes of Hülegü, grandson of Chingis Khan, struck deep into the heart of Islam. The last Abbasid caliph was murdered and the glittering imperial capital of Baghdad was virtually wiped off the face of the earth. The psychological shock was tremendous but short-lived. In 1260 the Mongols were checked in Palestine by an army of Mamluks, slave soldiers who had established themselves as a military oligarchy in Egypt. Cairo henceforth supplanted Baghdad as the hub of the Islamic world, and its university of Al-Azhar became the foremost seat of Muslim learning.

As Lewis has observed, 'Most scholars would now agree that the harmful effects of the Mongol conquests were not as great, as lasting or even as extensive as was once thought'. Iraq and northern Persia were badly affected but most other areas were either never troubled or were subject only to the most distant suzerainty. And the Mongols, once converted, became great patrons of culture. In the full perspective of history the steppes gave to Islam much needed infusions of invigorating new leadership – Seljuks, Mamluks, Mongols and Ottomans. Historians have seen them as the human basis of the military resurgence of the sixteenth century. They brought with them not only traditions of courage and military skill but also techniques of statecraft and patterns of institutionalisation adapted from Chinese and Byzantine examples.

If the Islamic empire was no more than a political fiction by the four-teenth century the Muslim world yet retained the substance of cultural unity. Bonds of trade and law, language and learning were kept alive by thousands of travelling scholars, judges, merchants and pilgrims. A civilisation consists of shared experiences and shared meanings. For the Muslim world these were supplied by Islam – by the five daily prayers, the fast of Ramadan, the rites of the Hajj, the charitable hospices for merchants and travelling scholars and the Arabic language of the Qur'an.

The history of Europe from the fifteenth century onwards is a history of widening intellectual horizons – the Renaissance and the Reformation, the Scientific Revolution and the Age of Enlightenment crowd upon each other's heels. For Islam almost the reverse is true. Experimental science fell into decay and disrepute. Even theology lost its speculative dimension and degenerated into mere rote learning and the uncritical accumulation of references to the authorities of the past. The period between medieval and modern times was not without significant achievements but these were political and artistic rather than intellectual or technological. In the wake of the Mongol storm three great empires arose – the Ottoman, the Safavid and the Mughal. Marshall Hodgson has called these 'the gunpowder empires' because, as McNeill and Waldman have observed, 'Each ruler's reach was defined, in large part, by the time required to transport siege guns to distant parts; because he could usually not afford to be away from his capital for an entire year lest someone usurp power during his absence, three to four months travel time from the capital fairly well defined the limits of these states.'

Each of these empires centred on a court of surpassing grandeur, dazzling to the eyes of European visitors. Each bestowed lavish patronage upon the arts and, in architecture and miniature painting especially, gave birth to works of art of enduring significance. Each passed through a century or two of self-confidence and military ascendancy to enter upon a longer period of stagnation which would finally be terminated by more or less violent dismemberment at Western hands.

Of these three empires, the Ottoman was not only the earliest to emerge but also the longest to survive. It expanded from an obscure thirteenth-century kindgom in north-west Anatolia to embrace by 1500 the heartland and capital city of the former Byzantine empire. The height of its glory was attained under Selim I, 'the Grim' (1512–1520) and Sulaiman II, 'the Magnificent' (1520–1566), who conquered Egypt, Syria, Iraq, the coastlands of North Africa and the Red Sea, the island of Rhodes and the Balkans as far as the Hungarian plain. In 1634, Blount, an English traveller, was still moved to declare, 'He who would behold these times in their greatest glory could not find a better scene than in Turkey'. Proximity to Europe made the Ottoman empire an integral part of its diplomacy. Religious loyalties usually appear to have been overridden by pragmatic considerations of power and profit. The Ottomans twice laid siege to Vienna (1529 and 1683) but were unable to operate effectively so far from their Anatolian base. By the eighteenth century prolonged inflation, military conservatism and political corruption had forced the Ottoman Empire onto the defensive. The Treaty of Karlowitz (1699) under which for the first time the empire ceded conquered territory, marked a major turning-point. Sporadic and largely successful attempts at reform were made throughout the nineteenth century but the fate of the Empire was sealed by defeat in the First World War.

In Persia the Safavid empire endured from 1500 until 1722. Militarily it was based on an elite of Turkish tribesmen but administrative power was effectively in the hands of Persian judges and bureaucrats. The regime reached its apogee under Shah Abbas (1587–1629) who not only put down internal feuds and instituted much needed reforms in the political structure of the State, but also embellished the city of Isfahan with unrivalled splendour.

In 1526 Sulaiman the Magnificent laid the foundations of Ottoman power in the Balkans by annihilating a Hungarian force at the battle of Mohacs. In the same year, but at the other end of the Muslim world, the Mongol-descended Babur took the first decisive step towards the establishment of Mughal power in India, securing local supremacy with a victory at Panipat outside Delhi. His grandson, Akbar, doubled the area of his inheritance to take in all but the extreme south of the subcontinent. A contemporary of Shah Abbas and strongly influenced by Persian culture, he imitated his northern rival by building a splendid capital at Fatepur Sikri but abandoned it after fifteen years in preference for the rural idyll of newly conquered Kashmir. Whereas the Safavids and Ottomans owed their decline to mutually destructive border wars and Russian pressure, Mughal power was gradually eroded by internal disintegration. The French and then the British intervened to fill the vacuum thus created, though the fiction of Mughal suzerainty was maintained until 1857.

Further reading

C.E. Bosworth, *The Islamic Dynasties* (Edinburgh University Press, 1962).
Marshall G.S. Hodgson, *The Venture of Islam* (University of Chicago Press, 3 vols, 1974) is a *tour de force*.
For a more concise survey, written from the Muslim point of view, see A. Ezzati, *An Introduction to the History of the Spread of Islam* (News and Media Ltd, second revised edn, 1978). See also W.C. Brice, *An Historical Atlas of Islam* (E.J. Brill, 1981).

Table of dates

The Muslim dating AH (Anno Hegirae: 'in the year of the Hijra') begins on 16 July 622 (AD), when Muhammad emigrated from Mecca to Medina. A Muslim year consists of 12 lunar months, and each therefore 'recedes' approximately 11 days each solar year. The Muslim calendar thus gains about three years every century on the Christian calendar. The Muslim year 1400 began on November 21, 1979 (see Appendix 6).

AH		AD
52 years before H.	Birth of the Prophet	570
27 years before H.	Marriage with Khadijah	*c*.595
12/13 years before H.	First experience of the Qur'an	609–10
7 years before H.	First Muslims find refuge in Ethiopia	615
3 years before H.	Death of Khadijah and of Abu Talib, Muhammad's protector	619
–	The Hijra	622
2	Muhammad's victory at Badr	624
3	Muhammad's reverse at Uhud	625
8	Conquest of Mecca and consolidation of Islam	630
11	Death of Muhammad	632
13	Death of Abu Bakr, the first Caliph	634
13/15	Capture of Damascus and Jerusalem	636/637
18/19	Conquest of Egypt and Persia	639/40
23	Murder of 'Umar, the second Caliph	644
29	Canon of the Qur'an established	*c*.650
35	Murder of 'Uthman, the third Caliph	656
40	Assassination of 'Ali, the fourth Caliph	661
41/132	The Umayyad Caliphate	661–750
50	Foundation of Qairawan, Tunisia	670
61	Massacre of Karbala and death of Husain	680
71/72	Construction of the Dome of the Rock, Jerusalem, and of the Al-Aqsa Mosque	690/91
92	Construction of the Great Mosque at Damascus	710
92	Muslims under Tariq cross from Morocco into Spain	711
94	Entry into Indus Valley, capture of Multan	713
94	Taking of Cordoba, Spain	713
95	Capture of Samarqand	714
110	Death of Hasan al-Basri, earliest Sufi	728
114	Battle of Tours: Turn of the tide of Islam in France	732
132	Rise of the 'Abbasid Caliphate	750
145	Foundation of Baghdad by Caliph Al-Mansur	762
148	Imam of the Seveners goes into 'hiddenness'	765
150	Death of Abu Hanifah, great early legist	767
179	Death of Malik Ibn Anas, founder of the second School of Law	795
193	Death of Harun al-Rashid of the 'Abbasid 'golden age'	809
204	Death of Abu 'Abdallah al-Shafi'i, founder of the third School of Law	820
212	Caliph Al-Ma'mun's official proclamation of the Mu'tazilite doctrine of the Qur'an	827

AH		AD
241	Death of Ahmad ibn Hanbal, Founder of the fourth School of Law	855
256	Death of Al-Bukhari, the great traditionalist	870
264	Imam of the Twelvers goes into 'hiddenness'	878
297	Rise of the Fatimids in North Africa	909
345	Seljuq Turks Islamicise	956
356	Fatimids in Egypt: Cairo founded	966
358	Foundation of Al-Azhar, Cairo	969
492	Crusaders capture Jerusalem	1099
564	Accession to power of Salah al-Din (Saladin)	1169
616–21	Mongol devastation of Transoxiana and Khurasan	1219–24
657	Sack of Baghdad by the Mongols and fall of the 'Abbasid Caliphate	1258
659	Mamluks halt the Mongols in Palestine	1260
859	Ottoman Turks capture Constantinople	1453
897	Fall of Granada: end of Muslim Spain	1492
923	Salim I conquers Egypt and carries the last titular 'Abbasid Caliph to Istanbul	1517
927–74	Sulaiman the Magnificent, greatest of the Ottomans	1520–66
971	Akbar, greatest of the Mughals, comes to power	1563
1119	Death of Aurangzeb, decline of Mughal India	1707
1213	Napoleon in Egypt	1798
1218	Wahhabism victories in Mecca and Medina	1803–4
1246	French occupation of Algeria	1830
1265	Death of Muhammad 'Ali, founder of modern Egypt	1849
1274	Indian rebellion (or the Indian Mutiny)	1857
1286	Suez Canal completed	1869
1298	British occupation of Egypt: French occupation of Tunis	1881
1300	Rise of the Ahmadiyyah movement in Indian Islam	1883
1316	Death of Sayyid Ahmad Khan, Indian Muslim reformer and founder of Aligarh College	1898
1320	Qasim Amin pioneers Egyptian feminism	1902
1323	Death of Muhammad Abduh, first of the Arab 'modernists'	1905
1323	Rise of Ibn Sa'ud	1905
1325	'Young Turks' in Istanbul and new 'liberalism'	1908

AH		AD
1330 f.	Beginnings of oil-prospecting in Persia	1910–11
1342	Abolition of the Caliphate and secularisation of Turkey under Atatürk	1924
1347	Founding of the Muslim Brotherhood by Hasan al-Banna	1928
1364	Independence of Syria and the Lebanon	1945
1366	Partition of India and creation of Pakistan	1947
1366	UN vote partitioning Palestine and creation of the State of Israel	1947
1371	Egyptian Revolution: rise of Nasser	1952
1386	Israeli occupation of Jerusalem, West Jordan and Sinai	1967
1391	East Pakistan leaves West Pakistan and becomes Bangladesh	1971
1393	Organisation of Petroleum Exporting countries (OPEC) quadruples oil price. Arab–Israeli War	1973
1395	Civil war breaks out in Lebanon	1975
1396	World of Islam Festival in Britain	1976
1397	First Muslim World Education Conference. General Zia takes power in Pakistan	1977
1398	Marxist coup in Afghanistan	1978
1399	Pahlevi dynasty overthrown in Iran	1979
1400	Armed attack on the Great Mosque at Mecca	
1400	Iran–Iraq war breaks out 'Death of a Princess' TV film	1980
1401	Assassination of President Sadat	1981

15
Islam in
Africa

The first account of Muslims in sub-Saharan Africa was written by the Spaniard Al-Bakri, around 1060. By that time Islam had probably been established as a minority faith within the West African empire of Ghana for about a century. The city-states of the East Coast were Islamised in about the thirteenth century, and in the fourteenth century Sufi teachers began the conversion of Nubia. At first Islam was the ghetto religion of immigrant traders but quite soon they won special privileges, such as exemption from prostration before local rulers, a tribute perhaps to their spiritual self-confidence or a recognition of their prestigious associations with a dynamic, powerful and sophisticated culture. Over the course of centuries Muslims came to serve as royal ministers and diplomats and even to take over such traditionally 'religious' functions as divination, cursing, interpreting dreams and praying for divine favour. The spread of Islamic education provided African rulers with a pool of literate men who could record the collection of taxes, legal decisions and diplomatic correspondence. Islam was spread by the influence of this elite as well as by the example of ubiquitous Muslim traders. Conversions were aided by the fact that acceptance into the faith depended neither on prior literacy nor on catechetical knowledge. The risks of dilution and doctrinal contamination were therefore ever present (for example Ibn Battuta's attitude to fourteenth-century Mali). Many 'converts' continued to observe pagan practices and failed to observe the exclusivist claims of their new faith. In Mali the *qadis* went so far as to prostrate themselves before their ruler. In some areas Islam disappeared altogether. But in others its influence was extended by ambitious chieftains anxious to legitimise wars of conquest as *jihads*. Significant centres of Islamic scholarship developed in Gao, Djenne and Timbuktu.

Everywhere the maintenance of a proper understanding of the faith depended upon the existence of adequate links with the Islamic heartlands through mechanisms such as trade, the *hajj* and correspondence in Arabic. Islam remained mostly a religion of the trading towns. But although few rulers tried to enforce Islamic laws throughout their empires, they gradually influenced local laws and customs. The close link between Islam and urbanism also implied that whenever trade and the cities that depended on it declined, Islam would lose ground. The force of traditional religions also remained strong and in turn prompted successive waves of Islamic reformism. The most important of these was associated with the Hausa jihads of Uthman dan Fodio (1754–1817), and the proselytising activities of religious orders such as the Qadiriyya initiated a wave of Islamisation which, further strengthened by the reaction against Christian missionary endeavours, has given the faith a broader and deeper social base than it had ever previously achieved.

Islam today claims more than 50 million followers in sub-Saharan Africa, two-thirds of them in West Africa, notably in Northern Nigeria. Mauritania, Senegal, Guinea, Mali and Niger are mainly Muslim. In the east the Sudan and the Somali Republic are likewise predominantly Muslim, while Tanzania and Ethiopia have substantial Muslim minorities. The influence of Islam can be seen throughout Africa in terms of architecture, rites of passage, family law and education. In many states Islamic sentiment is also a powerful political factor.

Further reading

E.W. Bovill, *The Golden Trade of the Moors* (Oxford, 1968). An absorbing account of trans-Saharan commerce.

Said Hamdun and Noel King, *Ibu Battuta in Black Africa* (Rex Collins, 1975).

M. Hiskett, *The Sword of Truth: The Life and Times of Shehu Usuman Dan Fodio* (OUP, 1973).

I.M. Lewis (ed.), *Islam in Tropical Africa* (OUP, 1966).

I.M. Lewis, 'Africa South of the Sahara' in J. Schacht and C.E. Bosworth, *The Legacy of Islam* (Oxford, 2nd edn, 1974).

J. Spencer Trimingham, *A History of Islam in West Africa* (Oxford, 1962) and *The Influence of Islam upon Africa* (Longman, 2nd edn, 1980). A standard academic analysis, covering the differing characteristics of Islam in different parts of the continent, the relationship between religious and cultural change and daily life. The author also considers recent developments and the international context. Useful bibliography.

Cambridge History of Islam, vol. II, Part VII, chapters 5 and 6.

A number of titles in Heinemann's African Writers series are also relevant, including: Tayeb Salih, *The Wedding of Zein*; Len Ortzen, *North African Writing*; Jan Knappert, *Myths and Legends of the Swahili*; Chakykh Hamidou Kane, *Ambiguous Adventure*.

16
Islam in
South-East Asia

There are more than 130 million Muslims in South-East Asia. The great majority of them live in Indonesia, the most populous Muslim nation in the world. The political implications of Islam in South-East Asia are profound. Indonesia is not an 'Islamic State'. Sukarno bequeathed it a syncretic ideology which attempts to blend together the archipelago's different cultural traditions. In Malaysia some 6 million Muslim Malays face an almost equal number of non-Muslim Chinese. The Malays dominate the apparatus of the State and the army; the Chinese dominate the commercial life of the country. In a country where ethnic and occupational cleavages are reinforced by religious and cultural ones, where the phrase to describe conversion to Islam literally means 'to become a Malay' (masuk Malayu), tensions are bound to result. In the Philippines a Muslim minority of 2 million perceives itself as oppressed by and isolated from the Christian majority. The outcome has been sporadic civil war.

Islam almost certainly came to South-East Asia through mercantile contacts. Native Chinese Muslims are known to have lived in Canton as early as the ninth century. Marco Polo attested to the existence of a local Muslim sultanate in northern Sumatra in 1292. Surviving gravestones corroborate his testimony. From the fourteenth-century Trengganu stone in northeastern Malaya has come down an edict which was evidently intended to introduce Islamic law in a non-Muslim society. And the gravestones of distinguished Javanese courtiers of the Hindu-Bhuddist Majapahit Kingdom show that Islam had won converts among the aristocracy at least by this time.

Generally speaking the progress of Islam in South-East Asia was marked by four main characteristics:
(i) it was sponsored by the elite, rather than arising out of any deep social movement;
(ii) it was peaceful;
(ii) its expansion was closely associated with major trade routes. The process has been likened to the spreading of an oil stain – slow, irregular and permanent;
(iv) it was intermittent.

Some areas, such as Bali, were never Islamised. In others, such as Java, a syncretist culture emerged. Here, the nominally Muslim majority continued to eat pork and drink alcohol, ignored the *hajj* and the daily prayers and clung to many of their traditional Hindu and Buddhist rituals and beliefs. Even the Santri, the strict Muslims who kept themselves apart as an exclusive minority, practised an Islam which a Middle Eastern Muslim might have found difficult to recognise and accept. A constant struggle for purity is, therefore, a major aspect of South-East Asian Islam.

The opening of the Suez Canal in 1869 and the rapid development of steamship services which accompanied it, greatly diminished the dangers and duration of the journey to Mecca. As the number of pilgrims going to Mecca increased, they brought back with them the influence of Islamic revivalism. By the early years of the present century a reformist Islamic modernism had begun to gain ground in South-East Asia. The re-establishment of political independence and the quickening pace of social and economic change have given groups and movements organised under the banner of Islam a new relevance.

Most Indonesian Muslims are 'abangan', adherents whose faith is largely a matter of allegiance to a cultural tradition. But containing the influence of specifically Muslim political parties has been a continuing preoccupation of successive Indonesian governments since independence. Sukarno banned the largest Muslim party, Masjumi, but took care to proclaim 'Belief in God' as one of the 'Five Principles' of the new State's ideology (Pancasila). In 1977 the Islamic political parties were pushed into a merger which has not stifled their criticisms of the current regime for its alleged corruption and susceptibility to Western 'decadence', Chinese business influence and Christian missionary groups. The government, for its part, fears that Muslim activists are not whole-heartedly committed to Pancasila and that some may harbour secessionist ambitions, a potentially grave threat to a State stretched across a 3,000-mile archipelago. In the short term, however, disagreements focus on the freedom to be given to Muslim *dakwah* (missionary) groups and the balance of secular and religious elements in education.

In Malaysia, Islam is an even more volatile political factor. Muslim dress has become more common. Membership of fundamentalist groups has expanded, especially among the young. On the campus of the University of Malaya liquor, pork, gambling and Western-style dancing have been banned at the insistence of the students. Violent incidents by Muslim extremists, such as the desecration of Hindu temples in August 1978 and an attack on a police station in October 1980 which led to twenty-three deaths, have alarmed the authorities who fear both an explosion between Muslims and non-Muslims and the diversion of popular energies away from the country's ambitious development plans towards more other-worldly preoccupations. Tighter supervision of Muslim lecturers and dakwah movements and especially of their foreign contacts has been one sign of government concern. A more overtly Islamic style of behaviour by government leaders themselves is another.

Further reading

C. Geertz, *Islam Observed: Religious Development in Morocco and Indonesia* (Chicago, 1971).

C.A.O. Van Nieuwenhuijze, 'Indonesia' in J. Schacht and C.E. Bosworth (eds), *The Legacy of Islam* (OUP, 2nd edn, 1974).

Delair Noer, *The Modernist Muslim Movement in Indonesia, 1900–1942* (Singapore: OUP, 1973).

B.N. Pandey, *South and South-East Asia 1945–1979: Problems and Policies* (Macmillan, 1980).

Cambridge History of Islam, vol. 2.

17
Islam
and Art

In his essay on 'Religious Education through Art'[1] Richard Yeomans argues 'that art could provide a more direct and immediate stimulus for the study of religion than textual analysis'. At the most basic level it can be used simply to illustrate the function of buildings and objects with sacred uses or associations; but, Yeomans suggests, far more valuable is its ability to express the 'depth, character and meaning' of a religious tradition. He then considers in some detail how the Alhambra Palace in Granada represents the Qur'anic vision of Paradise and how the Dome of the Rock in Jerusalem, and the mosques designed by Sinan to adorn the Ottoman capital of Istanbul, serve as powerful instruments of religious propaganda.

Titus Burckhardt, in his important and superbly illustrated work *Art of Islam: Language and Meaning*,[2] has argued that

> art appears to have the privilege of being always in conformity with the spirit of Islam, at least in its central manifestations such as sacred architecture . . . provided it is not subject to such deterious foreign influences as lie at the root of Ottoman baroque or to the far more deadly impact of modern technology, which destroys Islamic art by destroying its human base, namely craftsmanship, whose heritage is built on skill and wisdom.

Seyyed Hossein Nasr has observed that the West has neglected Islamic art and suggests that this is because of its symbolism, and because 'its major art forms, such as calligraphy, were considered as "decoration" or "minor arts" and people looked in vain in this tradition for art forms which were central elsewhere'. Richard Yeomans has expressed the hope that 'preoccupation with abstract form in twentieth-century Western art has created the right climate for a fuller investigation of Islamic art'.

But can one talk of 'Islamic art'? The Arabs of the peninsula brought an aesthetic tradition rich in language but impoverished in material terms. Inevitably this affected the subsequent development of the arts in the culture zone that Islam created, modifying the inherited or appropriate skills and motifs of Greeks, Syrians, Persians and others, to create within a couple of centuries a new fusion which can reasonably be characterised as distinctively Islamic which looks like itself and nothing else, and which has preserved that character until modern times.

Richard Ettinghausen emphasises the sources of potential diversity within this cultural tradition – a time span of more than a thousand years, the proliferation of centres of court patronage, the existence of five distinctive ethnic strands (Arab, Iranian, Berber, Turkish and Indian) each with its own aesthetic and technical ideals, the social divisions between courtiers, townsmen, peasants and nomads and the attitudes of different religious groups. And yet, despite clearly discernible regional and chronological differences in such distinctively Islamic phenomena as the minaret or calligraphic scripts, he emphasises that there are such universals as the architectural use of the *eyran* (high vaulted hall) and of flowing water, the ubiquity of carpet production, the willingness to transfer motifs from one medium to another (so that stars and hexagons can be found on plaster, metal, pottery or textiles) and the anonymity of most artists. Ettinghausen identifies the following sources of artistic unity:

(i) Islam itself, which led men, including artists and craftsmen, to see themselves as members of a single *umma* and to share central rituals and beliefs and the use of the Arabic language and script.

(ii) The strength of the artistic legacies of the Mediterranean world – Greek, Syrian, Egyptian and so on – which had long been established in the lands which were to form the core of the Umayyad and 'Abbasid empires.

(iii) The high degree of physical mobility which characterised the Islamic world – involving not only pilgrims, merchants and students, but also nomadic peoples and waves of conquerors, such as the Seljuqs and the Mongols, and, as a result of their activities, refugees and slaves. Long-distance trade, especially in textiles, which are unbreakable and easily transported, also promoted the diffusion of designs which were imitated or adapted elsewhere.

Burckhardt argues that Islamic art is 'essentially contemplative'. The very emptiness of the mosque creates a void within which the soul can expand, just as the endless visual rhythms of elaborately decorated surfaces can match the rhythms of prayer and controlled breathing which may be the prelude to, or climax of, sustained meditation on the divine. The interlacement of repetitive patterns reflects, though it cannot represent, the harmony which underlies the universe and is expressed by the self-reciprocating notion of unity in multiplicity. Burckhardt also stresses that the willingness of Muslim artists to channel their genius into the elaboration or reinterpretation of a few basic forms and motifs does not imply stagnation because this notion is 'highly inapplicable to sacred art, which is either faithful to its principles, and hence active and aware, or forgetful of them, thus entailing decadence and collapse'.

The specific nature of the central beliefs and practices of Islam has given to its artistic tradition certain characteristic qualities and emphases:

(i) The absolute status of the Qur'an as the literal word of God has exalted the significance of the calligrapher and the arts of the book (illumination, binding) in general.

(ii) Muhammad's campaign against idolatry has led to the almost total rejection of three-dimensional or figurative sculpture. The contrast with

Christian, Hindu or Bhuddist iconography could hardly be clearer and, indeed, Grabar has suggested that this convention really dates not from the period of the Prophet's lifetime, but from the period of expansion and conquest when Islam began to define itself culturally by emphasising its distinctiveness against the other religious traditions with which it now had contact.

(iii) The general dislike of figurative representation has extended to other artistic media, such as ceramics, textiles and painting. There is no specific Qur'anic prohibition to support this but there are many relevant *hadith* (for example 'Those who will be most clearly punished on the Day of Judgement are those who murder a prophet, one who has been put to death by a prophet, one who leads men astray without knowledge, and the maker of images and pictures'). Theologically speaking, figural artists were ranked with dealers in stray dogs. Religious art observed this ban strictly; no mosque in the entire Islamic world can be found to contain representatives of the human figure. But secular art, the adornment of palaces and the homes of the wealthy, was often rich in representations of human and animal forms, especially in Persia, India and Turkey. The miniature paintings which adorn the pages of books of poems and fables are the best examples of this, but metalwork, ivories, coins, textiles and ceramics also supply many instances. These representations are, however, stylised rather than naturalistic.

(iv) Limitations on the development of figurative art encouraged development in other directions, notably the elaboration of geometric motifs and the arabesque, and the use of colour as a major element in design, often to produce a most luxuriant impact. This latter may also have been a reaction against the monotony of an arid environment and the dullness of sun-dried mud-brick as a building material.

In discussing the arabesque Burckhardt notes that:

> The shapes of Islamic interlacement are normally built up from one or several figures inscribed in a circle which are then developed according to the principle of the star-shaped polygon, which means that the proportions inhering in the basic figure are re-echoed at each level of development . . . The patterns are those based on dividing a circle by six, eight and five . . . The Muslim artist . . . does not, as a rule, retain the circle which has guided the design and within which the basic pattern has been traced out; this circle is implicit, and felt instead of being seen.

This argument is developed and illustrated at length in Issam El-Said and Ayse Parman, *Geometric Concepts in Islamic Art*.[3]

(v) On the other hand it should be noted that the building of elaborate mausoleums for 'saints' or rulers has no economical justification and indeed runs counter to the belief that all men are equal in death. Yet it has been widely practised throughout the Islamic world, right up until recent times (for example the mausoleums built for Jinnah or Muhammad V of Morocco). Striking examples include that of Tamerlane at Samarkand and, of course, the Taj Mahal.

(vi) The need for water for *wudhu* (ablution), the symbolic importance of water as the source of life, a divine gift, and the daily battle against dust and heat, have made water, both literally and figuratively, a major element in the arts of Islam. Gardens, mosques and palaces, with their fountains, pools and artificial streams show this clearly; but so also do the massive jugs, unglazed so as to cool their contents by evaporation, which can be found throughout the Islamic world. Decorated ewers and basins and the development of the *hammam* (public bath-house) also testify to the importance of water.

(vii) Another environmental factor, the sheer scarcity and, therefore, expense of wood, has meant that the carpenter rather than the cabinet-maker has had a near-monopoly of this material. Doors, shutters, ceilings and wall-panels are made of wood, often elaborately carved and decorated, but furniture is not. Textiles largely took the place of wood, providing cushions, mattresses, carpets, tents and canopies – and employment in the manufacture and distribution of these products. It has been suggested that familiarity with textiles prompted acceptance of flat, infinite patterns in other media as well. Thus carpet designs might be replicated on the walls of mud-brick houses.

The specific qualities of Islamic architecture have been analysed by Grube with the following findings:

(i) There is concentration on the interior of a structure and comparative indifference to its external appearance, which rarely indicates its structure or function. Buildings must, therefore, be experienced from within. The most significant exceptions to this rule, the Dome of the Rock and various free-standing mausoleums, bear witness to the strength of pre-Islamic traditions.

(ii) Specific architectural forms are virtually unrelated to specific functions – the courtyard bounded by four *iwans* (vaulted hemispherical balls) can equally serve as the basic structure of a mosque, a palace, a caravanserai or a private house.

(iii) Structures are seldom conceived as single balanced units and are frequently enlarged, adapted or absorbed into a larger building complex.

(iv) Decoration is focused on the interior and used to convey a sense of spaciousness and weightlessness to what are essentially massive, closed structures.

He concludes that 'Islamic architecture at its best, and at its most "Islamic", is truly a negation of architecture as conceived in Europe . . .'

Anyone seeking a single volume introduction to this field could find no better than the volume in which Grube's brief essay appears, *Architecture of the Islamic World: Its History and Social Meaning*.[4]

Unusually, it tackles the subject thematically, the six distinguished authors covering respectively: (i) Allah and Eternity: Mosques, Madrasas and Tombs; (ii) The Architecture of Power: Palaces, Citadels and Fortifications; (iii) Trade and Travel: Markets and Caravanserais; (iv) Architects, Craftsmen and Builders: Materials and Techniques; (v) The Elements of Decoration: Surface, Pattern and Light; (vi) Vernacular Architecture: The

House and Society. The second half of the book consists of a detailed gazeteer of 250 key monuments, arranged by region including Spain, Africa and the Far East as well as the central Islamic lands.

To make a systematic survey of the major monuments of Islam would be a massive task. But half a dozen or so, even if they could not be taken as 'representative' could form a useful introduction to the field as a whole. Michael Rogers', *The Spread of Islam*[5] gives special consideration, in words and pictures, to fifteenth-century Samarkand, the citadel of Aleppo and the mosque of Sultan Hasan in Cairo. Titus Burckhardt pays similarly detailed attention to The Dome of the Rock, the Umayyad palace at Mshalta, the Great Mosques of Damascus, Kairouan, and Cordoba, the mosques of Ibn Tulun and Sultan Hasan in Cairo, the Shah Mosque at Isfahan and the Taj Mahal.

Sources

1 Richard Yeomans, 'Religious education through art' in Robert Jackson (ed.), *Perspectives on World Religions* (SOAS, 1978).

2 Titus Burckhardt, *Art of Islam: Language and Meaning* (World of Islam Festival Publishing Company, 1976).

3 Issam El-Said and Ayse Parman, *Geometric Concepts in Islamic Art* (World of Islam Festival Publishing Company, 1976).

4 George Michell (ed.), *Architecture of the Islamic World: Its History and Social Meaning* (Thames & Hudson, 1978).

5 Michael Rogers, *The Spread of Islam* (Elsevier: Phaidon, 1976).

Further reading

The literature is extensive and much of it highly specialised. Richard Yeomans' chapter in *Perspectives on World Religions* contains a useful bibliography, to which the following recent outstanding titles might be added:

Joan Allgrave, *The Arts and Practices of Living Religions: Islam* (Ward Lock, 1982).

Oleg Grabar, *The Alhambra* (Allen Lane, 1978).

John D. Hoag, *Islamic Architecture* (Academy Editions, 1977).

Derek Hill and Lucien Golvin, *Islamic Architecture in North Africa* (Faber, 1976).

Claude Humbert, *Islamic Ornamental Design* (Faber, 1980).

B.W. Robinson, E.J. Grube, G.M. Meredith-Owens and R.W. Skelton, *Islamic Painting and the Arts of the Book* (Faber, 1980).

F. Spuhler, *Islamic Carpets and Textiles* (Faber, 1978).

The following titles are relatively inexpensive introductions intended for the general reader:

David James, *Islamic Art: An Introduction* (Hamlyn, 1974).

Carel J. Du Ry, *Art of Islam* (Harry N. Abrams, 1970).

David Talbot Rice, *Islamic Art* (Thames & Hudson, revised edition 1975).

R.A. Jairazbhoy, *An Outline of Islamic Architecture* (J.K. Publishers, 1972).

Edmond Tiffou's, *The Illuminator* (Quartet, 1981) is a fictionalised autobiographical account of an Algerian Frenchman's training in Islamic art.

In pre-Islamic Arabia there was the greatest respect for language but only scorn for writing, and it is perhaps ironic that the civilisation inspired by the revelations given to a self-avowedly illiterate Prophet should come to excel in the art of lettering. That it did so reflects the Muslims' reverence for the Qur'an as the *literal* word of God, worthy in its physical preservation and presentation of the highest aesthetic endeavours. The strength of this reverence is attested by Martin Lings' claim that 'one of the great purposes of Qur'an calligraphy is to provide a visual sacrament. It is a widespread practice in Islam to gaze intently at Qur'anic inscriptions so as to extract a blessing from them . . . so that through the windows of sight the soul may be penetrated by the Divine radiance of the "signs of God" as the verses are called' (*The Qur'anic Art of Calligraphy and Ilumination*).[1]

Titus Burckhardt emphasises that 'calligraphy is . . . the art most widely shared by all Muslims . . . and . . . nothing has typified the aesthetic sense of the Muslim peoples as much as the Arabic script' (op.cit., p.47).

Large claims have been made on behalf of calligraphy and its practitioners. In the fourteenth century Muhammad ibn Mahmud-al-Amuli declared that:

> The art of writing is an honourable one and a soul-accomplishment: as a manual attainment it is always elegant, and enjoys general approval; it is respected in every land; it rises to eminence and wins the confidence of every class . . . Writing is a spiritual geometry wrought by a material instrument . . . Fine utterances in elegant handwriting are a pleasure to the eye, and a joy to the heart and fragrance to the soul.

Burckhardt emphasises the contrasts between Chinese and Arabic calligraphy – the one pictographic, the other phonetic, the one exploiting the potentialities of the brush, the other of the reed pen, each with its own inner symbolism:

> Chinese characters unfold vertically, from the top to the bottom; they imitate the movement of a theogony descending from heaven to earth. As for Arabic script, it proceeds horizontally, on the plane of becoming, but starts from the right, which is the field of action, and moves to the left, which is the region of the heart; it, therefore, describes a progression from the outward to the inward. (Burckhardt op.cit., p.47)

The Arabic script, derived from Nabatean, in its most basic form pre-dates Islam. But at that time many of its letters looked alike and vowels were not indicated, with the result that the meaning of many words could only be inferred from their context.

The first major script of Islamic calligraphy was developed in Kufa, Iraq, and reached its perfection in the second half of the eighth century. Angular Kufic, originally used for writing the Qur'an, was not always very legible, but this mattered less when so many readers knew the entire text by heart anyway. (Another factor making for illegibility, especially in inscriptions, was the fact that it was forbidden – lest the text be corrupted – to quote the Qur'an in abbreviated form; as a result it was sometimes necessary to crowd the lettering or emphasise vertical strokes rather than horizontal ones.) In North Africa a variant of Kufic, Maghribi, survived as a documentary script, but elsewhere it was favoured only for inscriptions and architectural embellishments since it was well-suited to the constraints of such materials as brick, tile, mosaic and plaster.

Ibn Muglah (d.940) a minister under the 'Abbasids, worked out an exactly proportioned cursive script, which, developed by the famed Ibn al-Bawwab (d.1022), became Naskhi, the most widely used form of script, from which other cursive forms such as Thuluth and Nastaliq were subsequently derived. Issam El-Said explains that:

> The thickness of the line drawn by the pen employed was the unit measure for the size of the letters and was referred to as the *nuqtah* (point). The proportion of the thickness to the length of the letter *alif* (the first letter of the Arabic alphabet and written as a vertical straight line) determined the basis of construction of the script. When a circle was drawn with the alif as diameter the shape and the proportional sizes of all the other letters of the alphabet could be derived from this circle . . . (op.cit., p.130)

The art of illumination, intended to complement the beauty of the text, developed later. Its major conventions came to be the use of the tree and the sun (symbols of living, growing things) as motifs and the use of blue and gold (the colours of heaven and the sun, and therefore infinity and light respectively) as colours.

Exquisite examples of the calligraphers' art are to be found not only in fine Mamluk and Mongol Qur'ans but also in the ceramics of Nishapur, the tile-hung mosques of Isfahan and the *kiswa* (cloth covering) of the Ka'ba.

Sources

1　Martin Lings, *The Qur'anic Art of Calligraphy and Illumination* (World of Islam Festival Trust, 1976), p.16.

Further reading

A. Khatibi and M. Sijelmassi, *The Splendour of Islamic Calligraphy* (Thames & Hudson, 1978). Clear text explains historical, technical and aesthetic aspects. Colour and black and white illustrations.

Martin Lings and Yasin Hamid Safadi, *The Qur'an* (World of Islam Festival, 1976). Colour-illustrated catalogue of a British Library Exhibition.

Martin Lings, *The Qur'anic Art of Calligraphy and Illumination* (World of Islam Festival Trust, 1976). Magnificent colour illustrations.

Yasin Hamid Safadi, *Islamic Calligraphy* (Thames & Hudson, 1978). Explains the development of different scripts. 163 black and white illustrations.

Annemarie Schimmel, *Islamic Calligraphy* (E.J. Brill, 1970).

A. Welch, *Calligraphy in the Arts of the Muslim World* (Dawson, 1976).

Naji Zain-al-Din, *The Beauties of Arabic Calligraphy* (Luzac, 1972).

Islam and Science

Seyyed Hossein Nasr insisted that 'Islamic science and technology must not be considered simply a bridge between Greece and the European Renaissance. Rather, they are an independent manner of studying the cosmos based upon the principles of the hierarchic nature of reality, the unity of knowledge and the equilibrium between man and the natural environment.'

The achievements of medieval Muslim scientists were not inconsiderable, particularly in medicine, mathematics and astronomy and in the organisation of collaborative projects of translation and research. But their efforts were, from the modern Western point of view, though not from that of S.H. Nasr, the leading contemporary Muslim writer in this field, constrained by the immense deference they paid to the authority of the ancients – Aristotle, Galen, Ptolemy, Euclid – and by various aspects of the Islamic world view and the hostility of the theologians. Systematic observations of natural phenomena were made and experiments were conducted to verify hypotheses, but these were chiefly directed towards refining or modifying the theories they had inherited rather than advancing new conceptual frameworks or pioneering new techniques of research.

The history of Muslim science can be divided roughly into three broad periods – a phase of reception and absorption, lasting from the early eighth to the late ninth centuries, a phase of florescence, marked by the activities of such remarkable polymaths as Ibn Sina, al-Biruni and al-Rhazi, lasting from about 900 to about 1100, and then a long phase of stagnation, during which little of new value was attempted.

The major aspects of these phases may be sketched as follows:

(i) Under the direct patronage of the 'Abbasid Caliphs an extensive and systematic effort was made at the Bayt al-Hikma (House of Wisdom) in Baghdad, to collect and translate scientific works from Greek, Syriac, Pahlavi and Sanskrit. Prominent in this effort were the Christian translator and scientist Hunayn ibn Ishaq (809–77) and numerous scholars recruited from the famed Persian medical school at Jundishapur, which had attracted refugees from Byzantium and learned men from India.

(ii) During the 'golden age' of Islamic science the Arabic language provided a medium for a truly international exchange of ideas. Scholars travelled widely and corresponded over long distances. The work of three men must suffice to indicate the general level of intellectual activity: Al-Biruni (973– c. 1050), a first-class linguist and a deep student of religious history and literature, wrote standard works on the properties of drugs and minerals, on astronomy and the geography of India; al-Razi (Rhazes) (d.925), an alchemist turned doctor, successfully distinguished between smallpox and measles. His twenty-volume medical encyclopaedia remained a standard reference work in Europe until the nineteenth century; Ibn-Sina (Avicenna) (d.1037), statesman, philosopher and scientist, wrote widely on subjects ranging from music (regarded by Muslims as a branch of mathematics) to meteorology. He is credited with discovering meningitis, the contagious nature of tuberculosis and the way in which epidemics are spread. His *Canon of Medicine* remained a standard reference work for six centuries after his death.

(iii) Although there were still outstanding individuals and institutions after about 1100 they were the exception rather than the rule. The study of geography may be taken to stand for the whole field of science. Virtually summarised in the great atlas prepared for Roger II of Sicily by al-Idrisi, Islamic geography thereafter

> congealed into a mass of received facts, sometimes erroneous and increasingly outdated and spiced with fantasy and conjecture. Islamic scholars of the ninth and tenth century in general knew more about the West than did their descendants of three and four centuries later, and the gap between fact and fancy, real and ideal, was only to widen. (G.M. Wickens, 'The Middle East as world centre of science and medicine')[1]

'Islamic science' is probably, though arguably, a more valuable phrase than 'Arab science'; firstly because its foremost practitioners were Persians more often than Arabs, and quite often Jews (like Saladin's famed physician, Maimonides) or Christians (like Ali ibn Isa, the leading eye-specialist), and secondly because scientific endeavour was bounded by an Islamic world view, which influenced not only its limits but also its priorities. Studies of the natural world and its phenomena, such as plants, and animals, were not motivated solely by a desire to classify and measure and to use the knowledge so gained for practical purposes in such fields as medicine and agriculture. Muslim scholars also sought for symbolic and spiritual significances in the movement of the stars, the colours of gem stones and the behaviour of animals. Thus science in medieval Islam has a large esoteric dimension, alien to and absent from the modern Western view of its proper nature and concerns. S.H. Nasr puts it thus – 'Islamic science is in the most profound sense an art, a sacred art which enables man to contemplate the visible cosmos as an icon revealing the spiritual world beyond it'. He argues, therefore, that alchemy, far from being merely a primitive and deluded proto-chemistry, was a profoundly philosophical enterprise, bridging the gap between the world of technology and the world of the spirit. Astrology is likewise seen as a field of deep and sophisticated reflection on the nature of the universe and man's place.

Whatever view one takes, the significance of the work of Muslim scholars in mathematics, astronomy and medicine is undeniable. In mathematics Islam stood heir to three traditions – Greek, Indian and Babylonian. In addition to the practical needs of merchants, bureaucrats and builders, there was also the stimulus of the Qur'an, with its complex laws of inheritance and the imperative need to determine the hours and direction of prayer. Outstanding among Muslim mathematicians were al-Khwarizmi (d. *c.* 846) and the astronomer Umar Khayyam, who reformed the calendar. Major advances in this field include the perfection of the decimal system and the development of algebra and trigonometry. There was also a persisting interest in mathematical puzzles, such as magic squares and numbers.

Astronomy, based on Ptolemy's Almagest, enjoyed princely patronage. What was probably the world's first time observatory was established at Maragha in Azerbaijan by Hülegü, son of Genghis Khan, in 1259. Here a team of twenty astronomers made regular observations over a period of 20 years and corresponded with other astronomers as far away as Spain and China. Massive observatories can also be seen at Samarkand (fifteenth century) and at Jaipur and Delhi (eighteenth century).

The great strengths of Muslim medicine lay in observation, diagnosis and the use of drugs. This reflected current medical theory postulated upon the basic assumption that health depended upon the harmony of the body's four humours and that the task of the physician was to restore harmony by means of purgatives, soporifics, poisons or by arranging changes in diet and climate.

Surgery was weak because religious doctrines regarding the physical resurrection of the body inhibited research on cadavers. This did not, however, apply to eyes, and as a result ophthalmology was highly developed. It also had the effect of stimulating the development of skilled techniques for coping with fractures and dislocations by external manipulation. The other major achievement of Muslim medicine was the establishment, with permanent, paid staff, of large public teaching hospitals to train and certificate doctors in such cities as Baghdad and Damascus. Nevertheless the opposition of the theologians to 'foreign sciences' increased rather than diminished with the passage of time. Science and philosophy were kept out of the *madrasas*. Crone and Cook do not mince their words on the matter, 'The sciences of the ancients were progressively reduced to a sort of pornography and the elite which had cultivated them to a harrassed and disreputable sub-culture.' (*Hagarism*, p.101)

The fact that the undoubted scientific achievements of medieval Islam never led to the full-blown development of 'modern science', such as occurred in the West, is, however, explained by Seyyed Hossein Nasr, not in terms of intellectual claustrophobia nor of a failure of nerve, but of an inner awareness of its social and ecological implications:

> Islamic civilisation had the means to make complicated machines . . . [But] . . . They did not make practical use of all they knew in this domain, feeling instinctively, the danger of the development of a technology which makes use of metals

and fire, both elements alien to the natural environment, and which, therefore, ultimately results in the loss of the equilibrium *vis-à-vis* nature which is so central to the Islamic perspective and whose destruction is such a danger for modern man.

With regard to the contemporary situation, Ziauddin Sardar has observed that:

> Science in the Muslim world has not made much inroad in spite of grandiose schemes of industrialisation, education programmes that rely on sending students to the West, setting up research institutes modelled on European and American originals, countless aid programmes and massive efforts by well-meaning UN and other consultants. Technology has been transferred on a considerable scale but, on the whole, it has seldom been adapted to the local conditions, and has failed to meet the needs and capabilities of the Muslim countries, led to huge wastage of local potential and resources and tied the importing countries into an overt form of dependency . . . prestigious areas of science, such as nuclear energy, theoretical physics, advanced biology and the like, are given much emphasis and attention at the expense of what may be called bread-and-butter areas of science, such as agriculture, rural development and public transportation.

The same writer concludes that:

> There is a growing awareness throughout the Muslim world that science and technology as practised, researched and taught, are very much a Western enterprise, that their assumptions and axioms are alien to Islam, and their emphasis and priorities have evolved to meet the needs of Western society and culture . . . The task of rediscovering the spirit of Islamic science is a formidable one . . . but at least it is a more real alternative than transplanting a science and technology whose aims and objectives are alien to Muslim cultures and which is taking the Muslim world towards a new, more sophisticated form of colonisation. (*The Guardian*, 3 December 1979)

Sources

1 G.M. Wickens, 'The Middle East as world centre of science and medicine', in R.M. Savory (ed.), *Islamic Civilisation* (CUP, 1976).

Further reading

Seyyed Hossein Nasr, *Islamic Science: An Illustrated Study* (World of Islam Festival Publishing Company, 1976) is wide-ranging, magnificently illustrated and with a distinctly metaphysical orientation. The same author has collected an anthology of original sources, *Science and Civilisation in Islam* (Harvard University Press, 1968).
G. Anawati, 'Science', in the *Cambridge History of Islam*, vol. II, pp.741–79.
Ziauddin Sardar, *Science, Technology and Development in the Muslim World* (Croom Helm, 1977).

A.B. Zahlan, *Science and Science Policy in the Arab World* (Croom Helm, 1979).

Chapter X, 'Science' in J. Schacht and C.E. Bosworth, *The Legacy of Islam* (OUP, 1974), pp.425–505.

Islam in the
Modern World

> The Europeans have now put their hands on every part of the world. The English
> have reached Afghanistan; the French have seized Tunisia. In reality this usurpa-
> tion, aggression and conquest has not come from the French or the English.
> Rather it is science that everywhere manifests its greatness and power.

Thus Jamal al-Din al-Afghani, writing in 1881, neatly summarised the
emerging confrontation between the Islamic world and the apparently
irresistible force of modernism – scientific knowledge harnessed to the
purposes of state power. Since that time the Middle East has borne the
trauma of imperial occupation, the development of the oil industry, unprecedented population growth and the impact of modern means of mass
travel and communication. The railway, the lorry and the transistor radio
have transformed the dimensions of social life and political power. Hence
Gibb's sweeping assertion that 'It is not open to question that all social
changes in the Near East during the past century or so have arisen directly
or indirectly from the impact of Western society and the penetration of
Western techniques and ideas.' To many Muslims these changes have been
bewildering, a threat to a sacred and trusted way of life. But others have
seen the absorption of Western culture as but the prelude to a reassertion of
Arab dignity and a new renaissance of Islamic culture. At least three distinct
reactions can be observed. Firstly, the impulse to return to 'pure Islam',
exemplified by the Muslim Brethren in Egypt from the 1920s to the 1940s
and latterly by Col. Qadaffi in Libya and the Ayatollah Khomeini in Iran.
Secondly, root and branch rejection of the Islamic past. For most Middle
Eastern leaders this would mean political suicide. Only Republican Turkey
(which appealed to a Central Asian myth to legitimise its authority) has
followed this path, and with limited success. Thirdly, Islamic modernism –
the attempt to reach an accommodation between Islam and the Western
techniques and institutions which it must borrow to ensure its own survival.
Rhetoric is liberally employed to maintain the appearance of continuity and
coherence in principles and policies.

The political subjection of the Muslim world has been terminated, but the
task of building nations has scarcely begun. Notions of consent, participation, territorial loyalty are alien to Muslim tradition. Parties and parliaments

are weak and inexperienced and lacking in public support and understanding. The army as the most modern and competent arm of the State becomes, in effect, the State itself, and speaks in the name of the nation which is yet to be. The successor states of the various imperial regimes have, like all modern governments, assumed a wide range of responsibilities in respect of education, welfare and economic development. In effect they are planning the future history of their respective societies and are thus faced with the problem of reconciling traditional Muslim values and attitudes with alien assumptions about the nature of 'normal' political, economic and social relations. Commercial contracts, the inheritance of property, divorce and the content of compulsory education are all matters of intimate daily concern to the lives of millions of ordinary people and each is an aspect of this larger problem of reconciling the old and the new, a problem to which Muslim states have responded in a wide variety of ways.

Seyyed Hossein Nasr has noted that '. . . the vast majority of Muslims remain completely faithful to the teachings of Islam while the small but influential minority which holds power has ceased to belong completely and totally to the tradition because of the influence of the West . . . this cleavage naturally creates a tension within society which characterises much of the Islamic world today'. This tension takes many forms because the traditional teachings of Islam are by no means uniformly interpreted and the directions of desired change are no less diverse, reflecting the conflicting influence of Marxist and capitalist ideas and pressures. All that can be said with certainty is that the tensions are likely to increase in force, range and complexity and that their resolution will affect not only the lives of millions of Muslims but the shape of world politics as well.

Because Islam is a 'complete way of life' its implications for 'modernisation' are all-pervasive. Its rules for inheritance and prohibition of usury affect the transfer and accumulation of capital. Its view of knowledge affects the content of education. Its attitude to the sexual division of labour limits the potential role of women as workers. The diversion of time, resources and educated personnel to religious purposes (prayers, festivals, buildings) and sometimes to the resolution of religious disputes, all have significant implications as do Muslim traditions regarding such literally vital matters as diet or birth-control.

Muslim intellectuals are obliged to confront these issues. The following quotations illustrate two rather differing sets of responses: M. Jamil Hanifi, in *Islam and the Transformation of Culture*,[1] says:

> 'Many vital elements of Islam are likely to persist for centuries to come, but they will need to be related to each other in new ways.'
> 'The difference between the rich and the poor ceases to be a condition and becomes an issue.'
> 'Population is growing more rapidly than production, aspirations more rapidly than accomplishments, opinions more rapidly than consensus.'
> 'Before the modern age it was possible to arm and become more prosperous and more powerful than any neighbour without changing one's mind about anything one's ancestors held dear.'

'The Islamic community of the past was more united in the style of its certainties than in their substance.'

'The secularisation of the masses remains the great unfinished business in the Muslim world.'

Ziauddin Sardar, in *The Future of Muslim Civilisation*,[2] by contrast, while regarding the immediate past as problematic, sees in a reaffirmation of Islamic values not merely 'the straight path' for Muslims but a way forward for mankind as a whole:

'Not only have Muslims failed to live up to Islam, but they have also, to a large extent, failed to understand it.'

'No operational and functional social order of Islam exists in its entirety today or has existed in recent history.'

'He (the Muslim intellectual) knows Islam is supreme but he does not know why. He knows Islam can solve all his individual and collective problems but he does not know how. Islam can certainly solve all problems, but the Muslim intellectuals of today cannot.'

'The majority is uprooted and drifts in the ocean of social change and technological despotism, buffeted by Occidental moral storms, adopting whole-sale alien social habits and outlooks, often sinking into crime and corruption, violence and vice.'

'The Muslim people face two parallel tasks of great magnitude; to operationalise a living civilisation of Islam that was once dynamic and thriving and to make a positive contribution to the predicament of mankind and the stabilisation of Spaceship Earth.'

Sources

1 M. Jamil Hanifi, *Islam and the Transformation of Culture* (Asia Publishing House, 1970).

2 Ziauddin Sardar, *The Future of Muslim Civilisation* (Croom Helm, 1980).

Further reading

J.A. Allan, *Libya: The Experience of Oil* (Croom Helm, 1981).

Morroe Berger, *Islam in Egypt Today* (CUP, 1970). Sociological account of the organisation of popular religion.

Michael Brett (ed.), *Northern Africa: Islam and Modernisation* (Cass, 1973). Collection of scholarly papers.

John I. Clarke and Howard Bowen-Jones, *Change and Development in the Middle East: Essays in Honour of W.B. Fisher* (Methuen, 1981). Useful collection of essays on development, resources, water, oil, nomadism, population growth and urbanisation, plus a dozen case-studies (e.g. agricultural development in Turkey, the industrialisation of Libya).

Alvin J. Cottrell (ed.), *The Persian Gulf States: A General Survey* (John Hopkins, 1980). Compendious and comprehensive.

K. Cragg, *Counsels in Contemporary Islam* (Edinburgh University Press, 1965).

John L. Esposito (ed.), *Islam and Development: Religion and Sociopolitical Change* (Syracuse University Press, 1980). An important collection of essays with case-studies relating to Egypt, Iran, Saudi Arabia, Pakistan, Malaysia, Nigeria and the Arab–Israeli conflict.

H.A.R. Gibb, *Modern Trends in Islam* (Librairie du Liban, 1975). Described by one authority as 'a gem of succinct and lucid analysis'.

Fred Halliday, *Arabia Without Sultans* (Pelican, 1979). Marxist analysis of Gulf politics and development.

Albert Hourani, *Arabic Thought in the Liberal Age* (OUP, 1962). Standard scholarly survey.

Peter Mansfield (ed.), *The Middle East: A Political and Economic Survey* (OUP, 1980). Thematic and survey essays, followed by country by country coverage.

Richard P. Mitchell, *The Society of the Muslim Brothers* (OUP, 1969). Standard scholarly account of major militant movement.

Edna O'Brien, *Arabian Days* (Quartet, 1981). Famous novelist's musings on change in Abu Dhabi.

Rudolph Peters, *Islam and Colonialism: The Doctrine of Jihad in Modern History* (Mouton, 1979).

William R. Polk, *The Arab World* (Harvard University Press, 1980). Political survey emphasising history and international relations.

Maxime Rodinson, *Islam and Capitalism* (Penguin, 1977). Marxist analysis arguing that Islam has not been inimical to capitalism in practice.

Maxime Rodinson, *The Arabs* (Croom Helm, 1981). Elegant interpretative essay.

Maxime Rodinson, *Marxism and the Muslim World* (Zed Publications, 1979).

E.C. Rosenthal, *Islam in the Modern National State* (CUP, 1965).

Anthony Sampson, *The Seven Sisters* (Coronet, 1976). Inside account of the world's major oil companies.

John Waterbury, *Egypt: Burdens of the Past. Options for the Future* (Indiana University Press, 1978).

Rodney Wilson, *The Economies of the Middle East* (Macmillan, 1979). Concise survey.

Ian Young, *The Private Life of Islam* (Allen Lane, 1974). The realities of an Algerian obstetric hospital.

Islamic Revival

There is no hope in returning to a traditional faith after it has once been abandoned, since the essential condition in the holder of a traditional faith is that he should not know that he is a traditionalist. Whenever he knows that, the glass of his traditional faith is broken. That is a breaking that cannot be mended, and a separating that cannot be united by any sewing or putting together, except it be melted in the fire and given another new form. (Al-Ghazzali, *c*.1105)

What is to be revived? For a thousand years after the Prophet's death Islam's history was a history of temporal success. A man from Mars arriving in the seventeenth century might well have thought that the world was on the eve of complete Islamisation. Then the political tide turned against Islam. History started to go wrong. Over the course of subsequent centuries 'revivalists' did what they had often done in the previous thousand years – criticised the current state of society and preached a 'return' to pure Islam, thus offering both an explanation of present ills and a programme for their remedy.

The current 'Islamic revival' has been interpreted as a reiteration of this classic pattern and a reaction against the disruptions of modernisation which reflects both the disenchantment with Western culture of the Westernised elites of the Muslim world and the disenchantment of the masses with those elites.

The term 'Islamic revival' is, however, used in a number of rather different senses:

1   The establishment of Islamic power bases and networks of influence. Muslim states have re-established their political independence and some of them have sought to exercise a greater influence than the mere assertion of their own autonomy. Libya has sought, unsuccessfully, to 'merge' with Algeria, Tunisia and Egypt, to champion the course of Idi Amin, the PLO and the IRA, and to intervene in the troubled politics of neighbouring Chad, perhaps, as some have alleged, as the first step towards the creation of a pan-Saharan Islamic Confederacy. Saudi Arabia has also been active, though less dramatically.

Internationally the Muslim states have begun to organise. Together they account for about a third of the votes in the UN General Assembly. In 1969, in the aftermath of the burning of the Al-Aqsa mosque in Jerusalem, a conference of Muslim foreign ministers was set up. Its 1981 meeting attracted representatives from 42 countries. The *umma* can be said to have adopted a new form of institutional expression.

2   The Islamisation of societies. The idea of applying the *shari'a* across the whole range of social activity seems to have gained increasing acceptance. Iran has witnessed a radical rejection of officially-sponsored westernisation. Pakistan has belatedly embarked upon transforming itself from a state for Muslims into an Islamic state. Saudi Arabia attempts to hold the line against the changes implied by its own development programmes. Even secularised Turkey and Tunisia have experienced unexpectedly strong demands for a reassertion of fundamental Islam.

3   Autonomism. Where Muslims are in a minority, as in much of S.E. Asia, they have been influenced by external developments to demand greater freedom of cultural expression. The implications for such States as India, China and the Soviet Union are problematic.

4   Self-assertion. Muslim minorities in the West have begun to assert themselves more self-confidently and to complain against discrimination in the
mass media and in education. This is particularly true of 'second-generation
immigrants', those not born in their 'country of origin'.

5   Western perceptions. Perhaps the real change has been in the way
Muslims are regarded. Although the general public may remain ignorant of
or hostile to the feelings and aspirations of Muslims, the policy-making elite
has become increasingly sensitive to their reaction. It is, however, one thing
to learn to take Muslims seriously. Learning to take Islam seriously means
going a stage further.

According to Khurshid Ahmad:

> The mechanics of government and society developed in the last 200 years or so
> were steeped in secularism. The last three decades have witnessed the emergence
> of over forty independent Muslim States but the politico-economic systems obtain-
> ing in these countries are based on Western models. This is the contradiction
> which resurgent Islam has tried to challenge. Contemporary Islamic resurgence is
> neither a transient political articulation of militant Islam nor simply an angry
> outburst against Western nations. On the contrary, it heralds the Muslims' positive
> and creative response to the ideological challenge of Western civilisation. For the
> Muslim world it is an attempt to try to reconstruct society by drawing upon its own
> rich but neglected religio-cultural sources. The ultimate objective of this exercise
> is to establish a new and just social order in which the material and the spiritual
> aspects are welded together and in which 'progress' and 'prayer' do not represent
> two watertight compartments . . . ('Resurgence', *The Guardian*, 3 December 1979)

Edward Said has commented that:

> Islam cannot explain everything in Africa and Asia, just as 'Christianity' cannot
> explain Chile or South Africa . . . Under the vast idea called Islam, which the
> faithful look to for spiritual nourishment in their numerous ways, an equally vast,
> rich life passes, as detailed and as complex as any . . . In Iran and elsewhere Islam
> has not simply 'returned', it has always been there, not as an abstraction or a war
> cry but as part of a way people believe, give thanks, have courage and so on. Will it
> not ease our fear to accept the fact that people do the same things inside as well as
> outside Islam, that Muslims live in history and in our common world, not simply in
> the Islamic context? (*Time*, 16 April 1979)

Martin Woollacott, however, emphasises that a real sea-change has taken
place:

> Iran has shown that Islam has once again opened up as a route for political change
> which had seemed only a few years ago to have been closed for ever. Then, Islamic
> political groups were small and isolated and the ulema in most countries had
> grudgingly adjusted to a Western concept of the division between Church and
> State. The prospects for change centred on secular groups, usually of the left.
> Whether the different conditions of other Muslim countries will allow Islam to
> assert itself as fully as it has in Iran is a difficult question. But the mosque, with its
> capacity to appeal to diverse classes and in particular to new urban populations, is
> moving back toward the centre of Muslim politics. ('Coming to Power', *The Guar-
> dian*, 3 December 1979)

Further reading

Mohammed Ayoob, *The Politics of Islamic Reassertion* (Croom Helm, 1981). A wide-ranging, up-to-date survey of recent developments in the Middle East, South-East Asia and the USSR.
A.S. Cudsi and Ali E. Hillal Dessouki (eds), *Islam and Power* (Croom Helm, 1981). See especially A. Kelidar on 'Ayatollah Khomeini's concept of Islamic government' and P.J. Vatikiotis on 'Islamic resurgence: a critical view'.
Altaf Gauhar (ed.), *The Challenge of Islam* (Islamic Council of Europe, 1978). Eighteen papers by leading Muslims on contemporary issues (e.g. women, race, secularism, economic development).
G.H. Jansen, *Militant Islam* (Pan, 1979). Informative and incisive overview.
Martin Kramer, *Political Islam* (The Washington Papers 73: Sage Publications, 1980). Incisive brief survey.
V.S. Naipaul, *Among the Believers: An Islamic Journey* (André Deutsch, 1981). Iran, Pakistan, Malaysia and Indonesia viewed first-hand by a distinguished novelist.

Turkey

Atatürk's root and branch attack upon Islam is well known; its limitations and the continuing resilience of Islam in Turkey are less generally appreciated.

The defeat of the Ottoman Empire in the First World War brought to an end the 600 year history of the most extensive and longest-lived of all the Islamic states. The dynastic principle was replaced by nationalism as the motive force of political obligation as Atatürk, having successfully defended the Anatolian heartland against invasion, set about creating a secular, Turkish republic. This task, in his view, required a rigid separation of the religious and political spheres and the rapid introduction of 'civilisation' – which he equated with Western culture – to remedy Turkey's 'backwardness'. The accomplishment of these objectives necessarily involved an assault on the place of Islam in Turkish life because it was regarded as the major barrier to modernisation and the development of a Turkish sense of identity.

So, in 1924, the Caliphate was abolished. In 1928, Article 2 of the first republican constitution was amended to disestablish Islam as the State religion, and in 1937 the principle of secularism was enshrined in the constitution. Civil servants who continued to make regular attendance at the mosque often did so in fear of their promotion prospects. In 1926 the *Shari'a* was replaced by a new legal code based on the Swiss, German and Italian systems.

Education was regarded as having a key role in the creation of a new Turkish consciousness. It would promote the reformed language and script, teach (rewritten) history and civics, fostering ethnic pride, and familiarise the young with national symbols and rituals.

In 1923 the Ministry of Education took over all religious schools and their endowments and the teaching of religion was forbidden in state schools. In 1929, Arabic and Persian were expunged from the secondary curriculum and in 1933 the faculty of theology at Istanbul University was abolished. (Nevertheless many families continued to arrange Qur'anic instruction in the privacy of their own homes.)

Extensive efforts were also made, through the press and adult literacy campaigns, to popularise the new Latin-style written script. Official attempts were made to purge Turkish of Arabic and Persian words and even the call to prayer was ordered to be made in Turkish.

Great symbolic importance was attached to costume. In 1925 the wearing of the fez was banned and an official campaign launched to popularise European-style head-gear. In the same year it was ordered that only religious officials should be allowed to wear religious garments and insignia. In 1934 religious vestments were forbidden for all faiths except in holy places or during actual ceremonies. Atatürk did not, however, attempt to ban the veil; even he recognised that there were limits.

Popular piety also incurred official displeasure. In 1925 the dervish orders were banned. Pilgrimages to Mecca were not allowed. In 1927 the beating of drums to announce the hours of fasting during Ramadan was forbidden. The clock and the calendar were also changed to the Western pattern.

The religious reaction occurred during the years 1946–50, when the transition to a multi-party system allowed religion to re-emerge as a political and cultural issue. In 1947 pilgrims were once again allowed to go to Mecca. In 1949 a faculty of divinity was established at the university of Ankara and in the same year parents were allowed to opt for courses on Islam for their children in the fourth and fifth grades. In 1950 the tombs of saints were once again opened to the public. In the same year the first free elections were held and the Republican People's Party, which Atatürk had founded, was decisively defeated. A major factor in this defeat was popular dislike of the programme of enforced secularisation. During the years of Democratic Party rule (1950–60) Islam was restored as a compulsory school subject, a programme of mosque-building was sponsored, the call to prayer in Arabic was restored, the Qur'an was allowed to be broadcast over the radio and the rules on religious dress were relaxed. The dervish orders re-emerged, having maintained the training of new recruits throughout the period of their supposed abolition.

Most post-war researchers have testified to the resilience of Islam among the Turkish masses. In village life it is still seen to justify basic social relationships – sex roles, the authority of the father, respect for age, the honour of women and 'kismet' (destiny). The prestige of the *imam* may be less than it was, modern technology may be accepted, but the value system is still very largely, in Lerner's words, 'a "courage culture" in which absence of curiosity is a primary component'. This is particularly true in the eastern provinces, where polygamous marriages are still by no means rare. Cultic practices, incorporating animistic elements (sacred trees) and Christian symbols (the lighting of candles) but which are regarded as authentically Islamic, also still survive.

Urban, educated Turks have been much more completely secularised. A survey of *lycée* pupils (15–18 years) in 1964 found that only 2 per cent said that as parents they would teach religious values to their children. Most ranked a religious career low in prestige and only 7 per cent mentioned religion as their greatest source of personal satisfaction. But 69 per cent agreed some form of religious belief was necessary for a fully mature approach to life, and most upheld traditional attitudes to authority within the family. Even if intellectuals neither accept the doctrines of Islam, nor observe its precepts, they still accept it as the framework of their cultural heritage.

At no level, however, is there much enthusiasm for neo-Islamic movements. Turkey belongs to NATO, trades with Israel and refuses to allow the position of Turkish minorities within the USSR to jeopardise her cool relationship with that country. In part this reflects a realistic appraisal of Turkish national interests, in part a feeling that Turkish Islam is sufficient to itself. Nor, within Turkey, is support for the main religious party, the National Salvation Party, either large or increasing; electoral support runs at less than 10 per cent. But it is significant that even the Republican People's Party admitted in the 1970s that its previous hostility to popular religious sentiment had been a 'misjudgement'. With the exception of the Marxists (who have no parliamentary representation) all parties now accept the legitimacy of popular religious expression. To a very considerable extent this represents a realisation on the part of the educated and urbanised elite that the development of Turkey cannot be accomplished without the positive support of the masses and that this cannot be achieved without respect for Islam.

Further reading

Bernard Lewis, *The Emergence of Modern Turkey* (OUP, 2nd edn, 1968), is the standard account of the modern period. Geoffrey Lewis, *Modern Turkey* (Benn, 1974) is shorter, with the emphasis on more recent times. David Hotham, *The Turks* (John Murray, 1972), is a well-informed journalistic survey. Paul J. Magnarella, *Tradition and Change in a Turkish Town* (Wiley, 1974), is a detailed anthropological case-study in which the technical analysis is interspersed with verbatim comments from local informants. Joe E. Pierce, *Life in a Turkish Village* (Holt, Rinehart and Winston, 1964), is written around the life experiences of a growing boy and includes much first-hand description of local rituals, festivals, folklore and family life.

Pakistan

Pakistan (literally 'the land of the pure') was created as a specifically Islamic state but has still to define its Islamic character. Taking its cultural inspiration from the poet, Sir Muhammad Iqbal, who died in 1938, and its political impetus from the lawyer, Muhammad Ali Jinnah, the Qa'id-i Azam ('great founder') (1876–1949), Pakistan came into being in 1947 as two territories (including Bangladesh, which became independent in 1971) separated by more than 1,000 miles of India. Beset by all the practical difficulties facing a developing country, such as low levels of health, literacy and productivity, this 'moth-eaten' Pakistan (as Jinnah called it) was hampered in tackling them by the fact that the very idea of a separate Muslim state in the sub-continent, and, therefore, the preparation for its establishment, had emerged only at a late phase in the struggle for independence. Although the formation of the Muslim League goes back to 1906 it was not until the 1930s that the concept and name of Pakistan were formulated and not until 1940 that the demand for its existence became the official policy of the Muslim League, now fearful of permanent domination by a Hindu majority should the British bequeath to a single sub-continental state. (As one Muslim put it – 'it was not Iqbal who produced Pakistan, it was the Hindus'.)

Pakistan has been troubled by its inability to establish a stable form of government which would be both uncorrupt and efficient and at the same time acceptable to both the masses and such powerful interests as the army, the large landowners and the Islamic elite. Jinnah's death deprived the new nation of its charismatic leader, though his memory is revered. In 1958 Ayub Khan, backed by the army, took over to root out corruption, but was himself displaced in 1969 by another general, Yahya Khan, who fell as a result of the war which brought independence to Bangladesh. His successor, Zulfikar Ali Bhutto, was undoubtedly a most able politician with wide popular appeal, but, despite his success in binding the nation's wounds, proved unable to satisfy the hopes he had aroused.

Opposition to the rule of the secular and socialist-minded Bhutto took on a strongly Islamic coloration and under the catch-all slogan *Nizam-i Mustafa* (roughly translated as 'we demand the introduction of the system of the Holy Prophet') pressed him to give the state a more specifically Islamic character. (It seems clear that in this the Jama'at-i Islami, the main political party of the Islamic fundamentalists, received both financial and diplomatic support from the Saudi regime.) Accordingly the 1973 constitution decreed that Islam should be the state religion, that the president of the country had to be a Muslim and that all the laws should be in conformity with Islam within seven years.

The preamble to the constitution declares that sovereignty belongs to God alone, that the authority of the people must be exercised 'within the hints prescribed by Him', and that the 'Islamic Republic of Pakistan' is to be a state 'wherein the Muslims shall be enabled to order their lives in the individual and collective spheres in accordance with the teachings and requirements of Islam as set out in the Holy Qur'an and the Sunna'.

Other institutional changes were also made – the Red Cross became the Red Crescent, Arabic was to be taught in state schools and Friday rather than Sunday became the official day of rest. Prohibition was eventually introduced, night clubs closed down and horse-racing banned.

What is remarkable, surely, is that these changes were not made until a quarter of a century after the new 'Islamic' State came into being. During that period the problems of development and the traditional structures and attitudes inherited from the British colonial period appear to have played a far larger part in determining the character of the State than did any concerted effort to develop its specifically Islamic identity, such effort as there was being largely devoted to showing that the legal codes and policies of the new nation did not conflict with the Qur'an. This approach of essentially negative reconciliation was far from implementing the shari'a in full.

Under Bhutto's successor, General Zia ul-Haqq, the Islamisation of the State has proceeded apace with state-sponsored schemes for the *hajj*, the collection of *zakat* and the enforcement of fasting during Ramadan. Popular support for such moves derives, at least in part, from the belief that not only is Islam superior in itself and at one with the character of the people (for example in its views on sexual misconduct) but it also represents a radical and comprehensive break with the muddle, corruption, indecision and social injustice of the last three decades.

Islam as ideology and Islam as life-style can often seem far apart. An exploration of these different aspects in the context of Pakistan can be found in Robert Jackson (ed.), *Perspectives on World Religions*.

The various positions taken by different Islamic ideologues in Pakistan are clearly explained by Peter Hardy in chapter XV, 'Modern trends in Islam in India and Pakistan':

(i) Iqbal 'interpreted Islam as essentially a religion of the action of free human self-expression given moral direction by God but not pre-destined by Him'.

(ii) Ghulam Ahmad Parviz emphasised the Qur'an in opposition to the shari'a of the ulema which he regarded as obscuring its essential truths.

(iii) Professor Fazur Rahman, former Director of the Institute of Islamic Research established in 1960 by Ayub Khan, called for a reinterpretation of shari'a in the light of man's historical struggle to realise the moral order it seeks to express.

(iv) Sayyid Abul A'la Maududi, founder of the Jama'at-i Islami (1941), stood as the most uncompromising fundamentalist. Under General Zia it is his ideas which appear to have triumphed.

The grass-roots level is described by Ralph Russell in chapter XVI, 'Islam in a Pakistan village: Some impressions'. The village is isolated, without electricity, and depends on subsistence farming and the remittances of emigrants. Russell emphasises that:

(i) purdah is not observed and women play an active, although subordinate part in the daily life of the village;

(ii) Muslim identity is simply accepted and it is inconceivable that it should be questioned;

(iii) the mosque is the centre of community life;

(iv) even those who are lax in their religious observances have a genuine respect for those who are not. The fast of Ramadan is generally observed;

(v) the name and views of Maududi are widely known but villagers resent his criticism of *pirs* (spiritual mentors and intercessors), whether living or dead;

(vi) the egalitarianism of Islam is fully reflected in the social relationship between villagers.

Writing more than twenty years ago, Wilfred Cantwell Smith[1] drily observed that 'to "apply Islam" to the concrete affairs of national life quickly proved vastly more difficult than many had foreseen', and noted that the fervour which existed for an Islamic state was 'seemingly accompanied by a vast obscurity as to its nature'. He emphasised, however, that for Pakistanis what was important was that their State existed, not what it had accomplished. Significantly he also identified Maududi as 'much the most systematic thinker of modern Islam' and his movement as 'one of the most significant forces in contemporary Pakistan'. He concluded that 'The Islamic State is the ideal to which Pakistan . . . should aspire. It is the aspiring that has been fundamental; not this or that pattern of the ideal.' By 1980, when Maududi died, the aspiration can be said to have at least acquired a sharper political edge.

Sources

1 Wilfred Cantwell Smith, *Islam in Modern History* (Princeton University Press, 1957).

Further reading

General studies include Ian Stephens, *Pakistan: Old Country, New Nation* (Penguin, 1964), Rafiushan Kureishi, *The New Pakistan* (G. Bell & Sons, 1974), Satish Kumar, *The New Pakistan* (Vikas, 1978) and Hamid Yusuf, *Pakistan in Search of Democracy 1947–77* (Afrasia Publications, 1980). B.L.C. Johnson's well-illustrated *Pakistan* (Heinemann, 1979) focuses on economic development. Donald L. Wilber, *Pakistan: Its People, its Society, its Culture* (HRAF Press, New Haven, 1964) is a comprehensive survey by a team of authors. The historical background is neatly summarised in an article by Ralph Russell, 'Strands of Muslim identity in South Asia' (*South Asian Review*, October 1972). Books written for a school-age readership include Jon A. Teta, *Pakistan in Pictures* (Oak Tree Press, 1972) and Richard Tames, *India and Pakistan in the Twentieth Century* (Batsford, 1981). See also Hafeez

Malik, *Siv Sayyid Ahmad Khan and Muslim Modernisation in India and Pakistan* (Columbia University Press, 1980). Three essays on Maududi and his thought can be found in Khurshid Ahmad and Zafar Ishaq Ansari (eds), *Islamic Perspectives* (Islamic Foundation, 1979). Recent events in Pakistan can be followed in the pages of the overseas weekly edition of *Dawn*, the newspaper founded by Jinnah (from Tanzil (UK) Ltd, 2C Cricklewood Lane, London NW2).

Saudi Arabia

Saudi Arabia in its modern form is a little more than half a century old. Its territory was unified by force by 'Abd al-'Aziz ibn Sa'ud, whose extensive family now rules the country, with the assistance of large numbers of Western-trained technocrats and non-Saudi Arab advisers. The regime derived its ideological *raison d'être* from *Wahhabism*, the doctrine of return to pristine Islam, uncluttered by the cult of saints and with the most rigid adherence to strict Hanbali legal code, preached by Shaik Muhammad ibn 'Abd al-Wahhab in the eighteenth century. Modern administrative and technical skills were provided by Aramco, the US-based oil corporation.

Saudi Arabia is unique among developing states. It was never colonised by the West. It is fabulously wealthy, having the second largest foreign reserves in the world after West Germany. It controls vast reserves of the world's most traded commodity and most flexible source of energy. It also controls the holy places of Islam and organises the hajj. More than a million square miles in area, it is an influential factor in the international politics not only of the Middle East but of Africa and South Asia as well. Committed by its 1975 Development Plan to the expenditure of $142 billion on the modernisation of its economy, it is yet crippled by a chronic shortage of manpower, an inadequate infrastructure, low levels of skills, health and literacy, heavy dependence on foreign expertise and imported technology, a harsh climate, few resources other than oil and severely limited agricultural potential. Not until the 1974 census was the population of the kingdom known and even now the figure remains a subject for dispute, estimates varying from four to seven million.

The very notion of modernisation is problematic. The 1970 Development Plan stated that 'The general objectives of economic and social development policy for Saudi Arabia are to maintain its religious and moral values, and to raise the living standards of its people, while providing for national security and maintaining economic and social stability'. The order in which these objectives are stated is not without significance. The central problem which they pose can be stated quite briefly – can Saudi Arabia proceed along the path of rapid social and economic change while maintaining its Islamic identity?

The strength of the Saudis' adherence to Islam cannot be doubted, even if it does seem to sit lightly upon a few headline-catching princes when they are abroad. But neither should the urgency of their commitment to modernisation be under-estimated. Consider the following statement by the Saudi Minister of Industry in 1977:

> When I was born (1940) my mother died of typhoid because there was no doctor in town. Later I almost lost my eyesight because there was no eye doctor in town . . . I don't believe I saw soap until I was more than ten . . . unless you take into account the yearning of our people for human existence after more than 3,000 years of inhuman existence, you can't understand why we hurry so much. (*Newsweek*, 6 June 1977)

Foreign visitors are in no doubt that the Saudi authorities seek to uphold strict Islamic standards as they understand them. Alcohol is banned and its production, sale and consumption severely punished. Business meetings are interrupted for prayers and business life as a whole disrupted during Ramadan and the month of hajj. In 1980 the ulema secured a ban on the printing of pictures of women in newspapers and on dolls and teddy-bears as un-Islamic representations of God's creatures. The punishment of criminals according to Shar'ia law is carried out in public, usually on Fridays near the mosque, to maximise its deterrent value.

The Saudi authorities insist that the country's only constitution is the Qur'an and its only law the Shari'a. But the exigencies of development have prompted many royal decrees and thus led to the proliferation of a body of administrative law which is neither uniform nor uniformly enforced. The result in often confusion, delay and corruption – to surmount the confusion and delay. Traditional institutions can, however, be adapted to modern needs – thus banks eschew interest but will take 'commission' and a share in the profits of ventures they finance.

The traditional Saudi view is that woman's place is in the home. Women always go veiled in public, are not allowed to drive and may be employed only in all-female institutions such as schools and hospitals. Public buildings do not have lavatories for females since women are not expected to enter them. Schools for girls were introduced in 1964 but are controlled by the religious authorities, not the Ministry of Education. Ninety per cent of women are estimated to be illiterate. In teacher-training and higher medical education women receive instruction from male lecturers via closed circuit television. Because the government is worried about under-population the sale of contraceptives is banned.

Restrictions on the role of women in employment (only 27,000 were estimated to be working in 1975) deprive Saudi Arabia of badly needed labour. Restrictions on the education of women limit understanding of modern knowledge of health and nutrition and thus the fulfilment of the mothering role. It has also led many Saudi men to 'import' educated women from Egypt as wives.

Saudi Arabia's chronic manpower shortage has led to the importation of expatriate labour at all levels. The most important groups are:

(i) Non-Saudi Arabs, notably Egyptians, especially in education, and Palestinians in all sectors. These have been seen as potential sources of ideological

contamination, spreading Nasserist and nationalist ideals. Yemenis form the bulk of the unskilled labour force and number perhaps a million.
(ii) South and East Asians. The Pakistanis are fellow Muslims and some have achieved positions of influence. Like the Indians, they have been prominent in engineering, medicine and trade. Indonesians and Koreans living under military-style discipline have been important in construction.
(iii) Western technical experts, notably Americans (20,000) and British (12,000), living in isolated communities, largely divorced from Saudi society. The increasing number of Japanese should be included in this group.

With the possible exception of the non-Saudi Arabs, the expatriates are less significant as a source of foreign notions than the actual experience of the West itself which has become accessible to Saudis seeking education, entertainment or medical treatment.

Modernisation in Saudi Arabia dates back to the 1920s when telephones and armoured cars were introduced by the king to consolidate his grip on the newly unified kingdom. In the face of resistance from the ulema a few schools were established with a more Western-style curriculum. The oil began to flow in commercial qualities in 1938. But comprehensive, directed development really only began in the 1950s. At first the emphasis was on the creation of physical infrastructure – roads, ports, schools, and so on – until it became clear that extra emphasis had to be given to the creation of a stable, skilled, motivated workforce, loyal to the national community and committed to its further progress. Development had not created this of its own accord, but rather spawned a massive, idle, overpaid and inefficient bureaucracy and increased rather than diminished reliance on foreigners. In 1980 a new emphasis was promised – more technical training, fewer bureaucrats, compulsory primary education for both sexes and conscription for the nation's youth. Enforcement of such policies seemed bound to provoke resistance, both from conservatives opposed to further change and from the newly privileged, resentful of any attempt to limit their freedom.

Saudi Arabia's political structure is itself under strain. The assassination of King Faisal (1975) was a great shock and King Khaled suffers from poor health. The 4,000-strong royal family is divided into factions on foreign policy and development issues. Open allegations of corruption and the abuse of high office are increasingly to be heard. Educated Saudis outside the policy-making elite are demanding greater participation in government. Desertions from the armed forces have weakened a central pillar of the regime. The bloody attack on the Grand Mosque at Mecca in December 1979, almost certainly a bungled *coup d'état*, reveals the existence of organised and determined opposition. A rejuvenated *majlis al-Shura* (consultative assembly) was promised in 1980 but, even if successfully established, would seem inadequate by itself to defuse current tensions.

Further reading

For the early twentieth century see H. St J. Philby, *Arabia of the Wahhabis* (Cass, 1977); D. Howarth, *The Desert King: Ibn Saud* (Quartet, 1980); Sheikh Hafiz Wahba, *Arabian Days* (Arthur Barker, 1964); and Elizabeth Monroe, *Philby of Arabia* (Quartet, 1981).

On recent changes see Fouad Al-Farsy, *Saudi Arabia: A Case Study in Development* (Stacey International, 2nd edn, 1980) for a technocratic analysis; Helen Lackner, *A House Built on Sand: A Political Economy of Saudi Arabia* (Ithaca Press, 1978) for a leftist critique; and Peter Hobday, *Saudi Arabia Today: An Introduction to the Richest Oil Power* (Macmillan, 1978) for an informed journalistic account. Shirley Kay, *Saudi Arabia: Past and Present* (Namara Publications, 1979), is an atmospheric travelogue; while Willard A. Beling (ed.), *King Faisal and the Modernisation of Saudi Arabia* (Croom Helm, 1980), contains case-studies of various aspects of state-formation, development processes, foreign policy and social change (law, mass media and women). Tim Niblock (ed.), *State Society and Economy in Saudi Arabia* (Croom Helm, 1982), follows a broadly similar pattern. For an 'inside view' by a bestselling author see Robert Lacey, *The Kingdom* (Hutchinson, 1981). *The Kingdom of Saudi Arabia* (Stacey International, 4th edn, 1979), is sumptuously illustrated and comprehensive. Eugene Gordon, *Saudi Arabia in Pictures* (Oak Tree Press, 1975), is an illustrated survey written for a school-age readership. Trevor Mostyn (ed.), *Saudi Arabia: A MEED Practical Guide* (Routledge & Kegan Paul, 1981), is a handbook for businessmen. Janet Robinson, *Dubai Arabia* (New Horizon, 1981), is a personal account of expatriate family life.

Iran

Any evaluation of the Iranian revolution must inevitably be tentative and provisional. But of its significance, for Iran, for Islam, for the Third World and for the West, there can be little doubt. Its causes are complex and not all of them can be explained in terms of Islam, but the Islamic dimension is essential both for an understanding of the origins of the revolution and of its subsequent development.

Persia (the name Iran was adopted in 1935) followed the Sunni tradition until the sixteenth century, when the Safavid dynasty came to power and Shah Ismail, who saw himself as a semi-divine figure and descendant of Ali, enforced Twelver Shi'ism as the national religion, with the assistance of Shi'a divines from other countries.

Safavid power collapsed in the early eighteenth century but this did not prevent the emergence of a new doctrine, that in the absence of the twelfth Imam the leadership of the Muslim community should be exercised by a *mujtahid*. From time to time a mujtahid would 'emerge' as the *marja al-taqlid* (source of imitation), to whom the others, and therefore the community as a whole, would look for guidance. Because the mujtahid, by definition, had the authority to exercise *ijtihad* (individual judgement) Shi'a divines were less constrained than Sunni ulema by the heritage of codified law, and thus the ulema in Iran were, at least potentially, able to assert a claim to wider power in Iran than in other parts of Islam.

Shi'a doctrine had a more or less general basic objection to secular government as such on the grounds that, since it was usurping the role of the twelfth imam, it could not be legitimate. On the other hand, some sort of Islamic social order was better than none at all and, therefore, some Shi'a divines were prepared to accept judicial posts but they have, on several occasions, also orchestrated popular resistance to tyranny and alien influence. In 1891–2, when the trade in tobacco was conceded to a British company, the mullahs organised a mass non-smoking campaign and obtained the cancellation of the concession. In 1906–11 the mullahs played a leading part in the constitutional movement which sought to establish a *majlis* (parliament) and limit the power of the monarchy. The 1906 constitution, which empowered a council of five ulema to veto laws incompatible with the Qur'an, was a dead letter in practice, but its restoration was to become a major demand of the anti-Shah opposition. The mullahs were less prominent when Mossadegh's nationalist movement took over the oil industry in 1951–2 but were to take up the theme of economic nationalism as a means of criticising the Shah's involvement with major US corporations. During the liberalisation which followed the launching of the Shah's White Revolution in 1962–3, mullahs protested against his land reforms, autocracy, and ties with the US and Israel. The most direct result was Khomeini's exile.

Pahlavi policy towards Islam had two major strands:
(i) A certain amount of lip-service was paid to Islamic traditions. Pilgrimages were made to major shrines from time to time. A docile court-orientated body of ulema was cultivated. And, more significantly, attempts were made in 1961 and 1970 to influence the succession of the marja al-taqlid.
(ii) At the same time the general trend of Pahlavi policy was to downgrade both Islam and the power of the ulema. In 1933 a number of ulema were massacred in Meshed on the orders of Reza Shah, who also tried to suppress the Ta'ziya play. Systematic efforts were made to promote a nationalist historiography – the institution of monarchy was exalted as authentically Iranian; in 1971 the '2500th anniversary' of the monarchy was celebrated at Persepolis and in 1975 a new calendar, dating from the reign of Cyrus the Great, was established. As state education and Western-style universities developed and Western-based legal codes were introduced, the ulema saw their traditional sources of social influence eroded. Even policies which were not specifically intended as such could have anti-Islamic outcomes. Reza Shah attempted to enforce the abolition of the veil. The 1967 Family Protection Law established a specific procedure to limit polygamy and did so by generally refusing permission for it. (Outside the cities it was simply ignored.)

There can be little doubt that, while various groups kept alive the idea of opposition by passive or active resistance to the regime, the Pahlavi dynasty sowed the seeds of its own downfall:

(i) The break-neck drive for the modernisation of the economy created immense social strains. Firstly, millions of peasants fled to the cities, attracted by the lure of higher wages. On arrival they found themselves the victims of inadequate housing and public services, galloping inflation and insecure employment. In the countryside agricultural productivity declined and the nation, which had once been self-sufficient in foodstuffs, became increasingly dependent on imports. Secondly, the gap between rich and poor expanded. In the northern suburbs of Tehran the beneficiaries of the regime revelled in conspicuous consumption. Elsewhere the poor shivered and starved. Thirdly, traditional economic interests, the bazaari (merchants, craftsmen and money-lenders) were damaged by the extension of the state sector, the penetration of multi-national corporations and modern banks and the anti-inflation policies of the government.

(ii) The political structure itself was riven by the most profound contradictions. The rhetoric of the 'Shah-People Revolution' was exposed as sham by the corruption of members of the royal family, just as the claimed benevolence of the Shah was belied by the brutality of the secret police (SAVAK). Also the armed-services, the major pillar of the regime, were weakened by inter-service rivalries and the Shah's fear of a military coup which led to a 'divide and rule' attitude towards the elite of the officer corps. The resulting mutual distrust goes far to explain the indecisiveness of the military in the final phase of the regime's crisis. In addition the problem of participation was never satisfactorily resolved. The spread of education, increased contact with the West and the growth of a state-employed affluent middle class created demands for political rights which the regime could only control, and ultimately frustrate, by its experiments with sham parliamentarism and the lavish distribution of official sinecures and awards.

Ultimately the Pahlavi regime fell because it acted indecisively in the face of a hostile coalition of the following dissident elements:

(i) Students and intellectuals alienated from the regime's official goals and outraged by direct repression.

(ii) Mullahs, with a long history of anti-government agitation, smarting from the diminution of their social role and erosion of their economic base (for example by state take-overs of *waqf* land).

(iii) Rootless, newly-urbanised peasants with few prospects of sharing in the nation's apparently fabulous wealth.

(iv) Bazaari, conscious of losing out to new economic interests almost beyond their comprehension and certainly beyond their control. Traditionally the bazaari have looked to the mullahs for spiritual leadership and education for their children, and in return they have provided the main source of financial support for the mullahs and their charitable institutions, such as hospitals and orphanages.

(v) Left-wing activists, with forty years of oppositional activity behind them, obviously added a leavening element; but it is doubtful whether they could have created the proto-revolutionary situation as such.

None of these groups had been able to challenge the Shah's regime effectively on their own, but together they were to prove irresistible.

During the final crisis of the Pahlavi regime Islamic aspects were variously revealed:

(i) Islamic tradition provided a set of symbols with broad popular appeal. Firstly, Khomeini specifically identified the Shah with Yazid, the Umayyad Caliph who killed Hussein at the Battle of Karbala in 680, and with Mu'awiya (in Persian Moavieh) who contested Ali's succession to the Caliphate. Secondly, denunciations of Western materialism and social injustice could be couched in the egalitarian and collectivist rhetoric of Islam as a brotherhood of believers. Thirdly, the religious calendar provided numerous occasions for emotional mass processions which could easily be turned to political purposes (for example 4 September 1978 – Eid al-Fitr rallies demand reinstatement of the 1906 Constitution and release of political prisoners). Attempts to ban processions during Muharram (2 to 29 December) met with general defiance – on the 9th Muharram (10 to 11 December) crowds estimated at more than five million demanded an Islamic republic. These demonstrations were later interpreted as a *de facto* referendum in favour of such a step. Fourthly, students and intellectuals, disillusioned with Western liberalism and repelled by Marxism because of its association with the Soviet Union, whose foreign policy had so often run counter to Iranian national interests, were attracted by the radical Shi'ism of writers like Ali Shariati, who portrayed the history of Shi'ism as the history of the oppressed and its traditional martyrs as revolutionary heroes.

Even in its traditional representation Shi'ism, with its millennarian cast, its emotional rituals and its expectation of a righteous messiah to usher in the reign of justice, seems to have been peculiarly appropriate to the circumstances of Iran in the late 1970s.

(ii) The Islamic counter-establishment put an extensive network of communications and mobilisation (180,000 mullahs, 80,000 mosques and shrines and similar numbers of ritual gathering centres) at the service of would-be insurgents. Traditionally used for preaching and the organisation of pilgrimages and religious processions, this network could readily serve the purposes of propaganda and mass mobilisation.

(iii) Armed guerrilla Mujahedin played a direct role in the open insurrection of the final phase.

(iv) Shi'a divines played a prominent part in dividing and demoralising the military (for example by making direct appeals in provincial dialects and languages to conscript troops and junior officers in terms of *jihad* against corruption and fraternity with fellow Muslims – i.e. civilian demonstrators).

The internal logic of Islam alone cannot, however, account for the impetus achieved by the Iranian revolution. The strains of forced modernisation, the agitational efforts of left-wing elements, the uncertainties of American policy, the internal weaknesses of the Pahlavi regime and the alienation of the indigenous intelligentsia all played their part. Islam supplied a structure, slogans and spokesmen. But the specifically religious coloration of the popular movement should not obscure other significant aspects:

(i) The rural masses played almost no part in the general confrontation with the regime. (This is in marked contrast to the Mexican and Russian revolutions.) Indeed a critical role was played by groups from the modern sector – oilfield workers and air-force technicians who, respectively, crippled the economy's key industry and initiated the open disintegration of the armed forces.

(ii) The struggle was essentially an urban one in a nation which had just achieved fifty per cent urbanisation. The major weapons of the insurrectionists were the strike and the mass demonstration; armed assaults on personnel loyal to the Shah remained peripheral until the final phase of the crisis. In both these respects the contrast with the Chinese and Cuban revolutions is significant. A civilian movement defeated a powerfully armed regime whose international allies were powerless to assist it.

The significance of the Islamic dimension of the Iranian revolution will doubtless be the subject of prolonged debate, but two points at least seem worthy of note at the present time. First, a chiliastic and backward-looking ideology, couched in explicitly religious language, has been shown to be entirely relevant to the aspirations of a revolutionary movement in the 1970s. Secondly, the old Leftist charge that religion is the opium of the masses and that the religious classes side with imperialism and feudal landlordism has been decisively refuted.

At the time of writing the Iranian revolution is moving out of its first, essentially negative stage, which concentrated on the destruction of the old order. The general trend of the movement is now towards the creation of institutions which will give effect to the aspiration for an authentically Islamic society. But the attempt to establish a new and effective social and political order is complicated by the need to cope with immediate problems of economic dislocation, sporadic lawlessness, external pressures, threats of regional secession and ethnic dissent and the competing claims to authority of the numerous bodies which were spawned by the process of revolution itself.

A Marxist pamphlet, published in London in May 1978, noted that 'This religious movement wants to establish an "Islamic society" with an "Islamic economy" – a completely Utopian concept . . . by that definition it is unworkable'. Utopia was Sir Thomas More's imagined perfect society, based on true fraternity. The word is derived from the Greek for 'no place'. In which sense is the vision of an Islamic Iran to be realised? We shall see.

Further reading

Iran's Revolutionary Upheaval: An Interpretive Essay by Sepehr Sabih (Alchemy Books, 1979) is clear, concise and informative. Fred Halliday, *Iran: Dictatorship and Development* (Penguin, 2nd edn 1979), provides much detail on the Shah's regime, its policies and their breakdown and the nature of the opposition to his rule. The author's Marxist perspective, however, makes it difficult for him to take full account of the religious factor, whose significance he belatedly acknowledged. Robert Graham, *Iran: The Illusion of Power* (Croom Helm, revised edn 1979), likewise analyses the contradictions of the Shah's drive for modernisation. On the oppositional role of the ulema see Nikki Keddie (ed.), *Scholars, Saints and Sufis: Moslem Religious Institutions in the Middle East since 1500* (University of California Press, 1972). A number of Ali Shariati's lectures have been translated as *On the Sociology of Islam* (Mizan Press, 1979). *Iran Erupts* edited by Ali-Reza Nobari (The Iran–America Documentation Group, 1978) contains a number of key documents, interviews and analyses relating to the crisis of the Pahlavi regime. Michael M.J. Fischer, *Iran: From Religious Dispute to Revolution* (Harvard University Press, 1980), is a full-length academic study based on first-hand knowledge with the emphasis on religious thinking, education and practice and their political implications. See also Marius Barr, *The Unholy War: Oil, Islam and Armageddon* (Henry E. Walter, 1980); the title is indicative of the tone of the contents. *The Hard Awakening* (Triangle Books, 1981) by Hassan B. Dehqani-Tafti, and Paul Hunt, *Inside Iran* (Lion Publishing, 1981) are first-hand accounts by the Anglican Bishop of Iran and his Chaplain. General illustrated accounts for a school-age readership include Jon A. Teta, *Iran in Pictures* (Oak Tree Press, 1973), and Emil Lengyel, *Iran* (Franklin Watts, revised edn 1978).

21

Women in Islam

Contemporary Muslim writing on this subject argues that non-Muslims misunderstand this aspect of Islam more than any other. Aisha Lemu suggests that 'the popular view combines the fantasy of a Hollywood version of the Arabian Nights, with a picture of deprived and repressed victims of a man's world' (*The Challenge of Islam*, ed. Altaf Gauhar).[1] The same author argues that in Islam 'women lead a life balanced between freedom and protection possibly more fitting to their needs than the competitive struggle the more "liberated" women are embarking on in the West'. Malika Citrine asserts that whereas in the West the movement for female emancipation occurred not through the influence of Christianity but when it was on the wane, 'Islam . . . contained at its very inception, in the Holy Qur'an, a charter for women's rights and legal equality such as the world had never seen before. Here indeed is to be found the very origin of the movement for feminine emancipation, centuries before the Western world had even thought of it'. (*The Minaret*, vol.1, no.2.)

An accurate and sympathetic understanding of this topic is not easily obtained, for the following reasons:

(i) The subject matter is both vast and vaguely defined, covering not only the full sweep of time and space embraced by Islam and the very different conditions which apply to nomads, villagers and townspeople, but also such diverse aspects of 'women's role' as legal status, sexual mores, education, the division of labour, folklore and religious observances.

(ii) Evidence is often misleading, biased or scanty. Legal statements, pious exhortations and the reported speech and actions of literary heroines may be far from the realities of everyday life. And, until modern times, statistical evidence of basic demographic trends, enrolments in education and so on, are either non-existent or applicable only to small groups or short periods of time. Even modern statistics must be treated with considerable caution, especially on such matters as property-holdings, illegitimacy or abortion where considerations for honour and shame may colour the picture. Muslims' high valuation of privacy in personal and family matters is also a major barrier to research.

(iii) The viewpoints adopted by writers on this question are frequently polemical in both purpose and tone, whether to justify the 'traditional' position of women in Islam or to advocate 'reform'. The apparently more objective accounts of anthropologists are often no less committed to a firm (often feminist) value-position, though this may be masked by impenetrable jargon.

Most commentators are agreed that Islam improved the position of women in Arabian society in a number of ways:

(i) Female infanticide was suppressed. Girl children had been regarded as an economic burden – their labour was worth less than a man's and would pass to another family in their mature years, while their existence until marriage was a potential source of danger given their vulnerability to dishonour (16: 58–9; 17:31).

(ii) Polygamy was limited. Men could have only four wives and were enjoined to treat them equally.

(iii) Female property rights were guaranteed by law. Women were allowed to retain their own property upon marriage and were given a guaranteed share in the estates of their male relatives (4:7). (English women had to wait until the late nineteenth century before they gained legal rights over their own property.)

(iv) Women were recognised as the spiritual equals of men and equally obliged to observe the five pillars of the faith (though with certain dispensations during menstruation and childbirth) (4:124; 33:35).

(v) The search for knowledge was likewise regarded as incumbent upon male and female alike. It should be noted, however, that a degree of male authority and the right to beat wives is recognised in the Qur'an (4:34).

(vi) Women were to receive only half as much property as men in inheritances. This reflected the non-reciprocal economic responsibility of men for women.

(vii) A woman's testimony in law was to count for only half as much as a man's.

The Prophet repeatedly urged Muslim men to treat their womenfolk with kindness and respect. One of the most widely quoted of his sayings is, 'Paradise is to be found at the feet of your mother', and another is that divorce is the most detestable of all permitted acts. He laid special emphasis on kindness to women in his last sermon.

It has been argued that Muhammad was obliged to compromise with prevailing sentiment and to limit or reform customs which, ideally, he would rather have abolished (for example polygamy). This view of the Prophet as a social engineer is difficult to reconcile with a straightforward belief in the divinity of his mission or with the fact that such evils as drinking and gambling were forbidden outright.

It is important to distinguish between the requirements and injunctions of the Qur'an and Sunna and what has often been the practice of Muslim communities. For instance, the Qur'an urges women to modesty of dress and demeanour but makes no mention of purdah or the veil (24:30–1), while women have often been unable to exercise their rights of inheritance and property, owing to family pressures.

A number of features of the position of women in Muslim societies before the impact of the West were common to many pre-industrial societies and reflect socio-economic pressures as well as religious prescriptions:

(i) Arranged marriages are common in agrarian societies where marriage is an alliance between extended, multi-generational families rather than between two individuals. Because the wealth, status, piety and personality of the proposed partner are of concern to the whole family, practical considerations of domestic harmony lie behind the rhetoric of family pride and honour.

(ii) The widespread Arab preference for first-cousin marriages (especially among the bedouin) can be related to an understandable desire to keep the inheritance of property within the same lineage and thus avoid the fragmentation of herds, lands or water rights so detrimental to agricultural productivity.

Great emphasis is placed in Islam upon the importance of the family unit as the basic building-block of a healthy society. Even Crone and Cook, who generally take a critical view of Islam as a culture, explain its resilience in these terms: 'The Muslim mosque points across the desert to Mecca but the Muslim house contains its *qibla* within itself' (*Hagarism* p.149). Many Muslim writers insist that the position of women in Islam cannot be understood unless this context of concern for the family unit is appreciated. It is also significant that the Qur'an is more explicit on the subjects of marriage, divorce, inheritance and sexual relations than on almost any other aspect of social behaviour and that on this basis a complex and durable corpus of Islamic family law has been erected.

What follows can, therefore, only be regarded as a sketch of some of the major aspects of Muslim views of marriage and related subjects:

(i) Marriage is regarded as the sole proper channel for the expression of sexual energies. Pre-marital and extra-marital relations are strictly forbidden and severely punished. On the other hand, Islam has never, unlike Christianity, venerated celibacy or looked upon sex as sinful in itself.

(ii) Marriages are often better arranged by parents, who know, and are trusted by, their children, and are less likely to be swayed by superficial qualities and more likely to take account of factors of personality and background which will assist the long-term stability of the relationship. Marriages are not, however, valid without the consent of both partners. (In practice familial pressures may be exerted to bring this about.) The prohibited degrees are set out in the Qur'an (4:23–4).

(iii) The form of the ceremony is simple, its essence being a contract and not a sacrament. The presence of a religious official is not necessary.

(iv) The wife has a right to a dowry (*mahr*), which is not a bride-price, paid to her father, but a gift of love, paid to her. This may be used to pay for furniture, utensils, trousseau upon marriage. These remain her property, even after divorce (2:229), when she should receive a second installment of the dowry as compensation (unless the divorce was of her seeking). These arrangements serve as a powerful economic disincentive to divorce.

(v) Husband and wife have mutual rights and obligations (30:21). These are not identical but complementary. The prime responsibility of the wife is to care for her home and family, of the husband to provide for their maintenance. The closeness of the relationship is symbolised in the Qur'anic description that 'They are your garments and you are theirs' (2:187) – the implication of warmth, protection and privacy is clear.

(vi) Divorce should be preceded by extensive efforts at reconciliation (4:35) and followed by a waiting period (*iddat*) of three months before being regarded as final. This is to ensure the acknowledgment of paternal obligations in the case of pregnancy, and to serve as a 'cooling-off' period during which further attempts at reconciliation may be made. Family pressures for reconciliation are not regarded as meddling but as a pious and charitable act. Women's rights, in regard to divorce, are more restricted than those of men (impotence, incurable disease or refusal of maintenance constitute adequate grounds).

(vii) After divorce a man must pay over to his ex-wife any outstanding portion of her dowry and provide her with maintenance for a limited period until she becomes once again the financial responsibility of her male relatives. His financial obligations to his children, however, continue. Custody of children is usually given to the mother (or a female relative) unless she remarries.

(viii) An adopted child in Islamic law has no legal rights (for example, of inheritance) vis-à-vis his adoptive family and is not regarded as being within the prohibited degrees of marriage. On the other hand, a foster-child who has been suckled is regarded as coming within the prohibited degrees.

(ix) Polygamy is permitted in Islam, but has generally been the exception rather than the rule. Small landowners and businessmen still sometimes take a second wife as a mark of status but among the urbanised and educated this is now rare. Circumstances held to justify polygamy include the illness, infertility or sexual incapacity of the wife, or the presence in the community of large numbers of surplus females (for instance after a war). Most Muslim countries now require extensive judicial and bureaucratic proceedings to ensure that a husband can afford to support a second wife. A wife may insert in her marriage contract a requirement that if her husband should wish to take a second wife he must obtain her permission.

Some Muslim reformers have argued that, in the words of Sayyid Amir Ali, 'as absolute justice in matters of feeling is impossible, the Koranic prescription (4:3) amounted in reality to a prohibition' of polygamy. Tunisia has banned polygamy on these grounds.

The social role of women in Muslim countries is being re-defined under the impact of powerful forces for change:

(i) urbanisation – which leads to the abandonment of rural life-styles and exposure to alternative ways of life. The impact is greater in big cities than in small or medium-sized towns, which tend to be more conservative and to attract fewer migrants.

(ii) the spread of mass media – which can present different – especially

Western – attitudes and life-styles, but can also reinforce existing ones.

(iii) the growth of new occupations – economic development requires not only large numbers of secretaries, clerks and telephonists, but also nurses, teachers, pharmacists, and so on.

(iv) the consequent growth of educational opportunities – these not only open up new employment possibilities but also affect attitudes within the family. Research suggests that male opposition to 'women's emancipation' diminishes with the degree of education of the male's mother. Of the 400,000 students in Arab universities a quarter are now women.

(v) emancipationist government policies – which can be promoted not only by granting legal rights but also through the State's control of education, employment and welfare. Article 12 of the constitution of the Ba'ath party states that 'Arab women will enjoy all the rights of citizenship. The party will strive to raise the status of women so that they become worthy of these rights.' Professor W.J. Goode has emphasised that legal and social changes were promoted from the 1950s onwards because:

> Arab leaders have generally recognised the importance of women's contribution to the nation, and even their potentially greater contribution to marital life, if they are permitted to take part in the occupational sphere and obtain the education to prepare them for it . . . these changes have occurred without the impact of a substantial amount of industrialisation . . . as a political and ideological revolution in anticipation of, or perhaps in preparation for, the changes that are beginning in the economic sphere. (*World Revolution and Family Patterns*)[2]

'Modern' political attitudes can, however, co-exist with other, very 'traditional' attitudes. As a 'revolutionary' Algerian postmaster told a young British doctor:

> In Islamic Socialism . . . woman is a mother . . . the keeper of the house, the educator of the children. She's the cornerstone of the family, its vertebral column . . . provided these obligations are fulfilled, she may leave the house to work . . . But that is not the same as 'being allowed out'. A street, believes the Postmaster, is a straight line joining two places of work. It is not a place in its own right, for idling, dallying and striking up dubious relationships. (Ian Young, *The Private Life of Islam*)[3]

The employment of women is opposed by many men, not only on the grounds that it is unIslamic or dishonourable, but because employment is scarce and women are, therefore, unwelcome competitors in the labour market.

E.C. Hodgkin asserts that:

> The fate of a majority of Arab women is still that of poor peasantry everywhere – early marriage to a husband arranged for by the family, followed by child-bearing and household drudgery. Most Muslim women are still subjected to the further handicap of the veil . . . For the most part Arab women are ignorant, superstitious and overworked . . . The battle for emancipation has really only begun. (*The Arabs*)[4]

Generalisation is, however, hazardous. Conditions vary greatly from one

nation to another, and between city, town and village. In Tunisia, Bour-
guiba has sought to promote Western-style female emancipation while its
neighbour, Colonel Gadafi, has used oil revenues to preserve traditional
roles, paying widows to stay home with their families rather than support
them by working. Palestinian women have become symbols of revolutionary
heroism; Algerian women, however, used the veil as a banner of revolutionary resistance to French colonial rule.

Some conception of the variety of women's condition in Muslim countries
can be gained from *Women in the Muslim World*,[5] a collection of 33 essays,
largely by anthropologists, most of which refer to non-elite women in the
Middle East. (Nine of the essays refer to Iran, five to Turkey and four each
to Morocco and Egypt.) The essays cover such topics as legal reform,
folklore, Sufism, illness and women in modern novels as well as case-studies
of the life-styles of women in nomad, village and urban settings. In their
introductory essay the editors make a number of pertinent observations:
Firstly, male–female relations in the Middle East are marked by: (i) basic
emphasis on bridal virginity; (ii) preference for early marriage; (iii) strong
preference for sons – as a source of labour and prestige and a guarantee of
security in old age; (iv) consequent devaluation of wives who are sterile or
produce only daughters; (v) freer roles for women who are not sexually
vulnerable – i.e. children and old women; (vi) the belief that female education is useless; (vii) the assumption that men and women cannot safely be left
alone together.

Secondly, women have always performed a large proportion of the region's work – especially in agriculture and textiles, but also in handicrafts and
domestic service. This work has been underpaid, or more usually unpaid,
and of low status. Factory employment may lead to further exploitation but
also the possibility of remedy through the provision of literacy programmes,
minimum wage legislation and child care facilities.

Thirdly, male dominance long predates Islam. Women have moderated
and manipulated it through their control of sexual access, hospitality, and
house-care, and by means of gossip and ridicule, real and feigned illness and
invocation of the supernatural.

Fourthly, 'What most Middle Eastern women lack when compared with
their wealthier and better educated compatriots or with Western women of
many social classes, is freedom of choice regarding basic life decisions' (for
example education, marriage, work and divorce).

Lastly, the region's very high birth-rate is likely to be a major factor in
forcing a revaluation of women's traditional roles.

Fatima Meruissi, in her study *Beyond the Veil*[6] argues that it is the State
itself, by providing education and opportunities for paid employment
which is doing most to erode traditional male dominance. The author's
main argument, however, is concerned with working out the implications of
her assertion that, unlike the West, Islam does not view women as passive
and inferior: 'On the contrary, the whole system is based on the assumption
that the woman is a powerful and dangerous being. All sexual institutions

(polygamy, repudiation, sexual segregation) can be perceived as a strategy for containing her power'. Her most basic contention is, therefore, that

> the Muslim system is not so much opposed to women as to the heterosexual unit. What is feared is the growth of the involvement between a man and a woman into an all-encompassing love . . . Such an involvement constitutes a direct threat to the man's allegiance to Allah, which should be the unconditional investment of all the man's energies, thoughts and feelings.

Freedom is so much a matter of consciousness and perception that the Western observer must be aware of seeing restrictions where they do not exist. One woman's straightjacket is another woman's suit of armour – protective rather than restrictive. Muslims might well argue that the regime criticised by some Westerners has given generations of women physical and economic security in a harsh environment and has supported rather than inhibited their ability to lead honourable, pious and socially useful lives, performing the tasks assigned to them by God through his Prophet. In the words of Colonel Gadafi:

> You [in the West] force women to work in factories; this is the oppression of women. In Islam we do not sacrifice women for material gain. You have initiated the abortion of pregnant women. You have dispersed the family and broken up society. We have no problems whatsoever. You simply have to apply the Koran for ideal social living.

Whatever changes in women's role and status may occur in Muslim countries in coming years, one thing is certain – that they will be debated and justified in terms of the precepts of the Qur'an and Sunna and the practice of the early Muslim community.

Sources

1 Altaf Gauhar (ed.), *The Challenge of Islam* (Islamic Council of Europe, 1978), p.248.

2 W.J. Goode, *World Revolution and Family Patterns* (Free Press, 1964).

3 Ian Young, *The Private Life of Islam* (Allen Lane, 1973).

4 E.C. Hodgkin, *The Arabs* (OUP, 1966).

5 Lois Beck and Nikki Keddie (eds), *Women in the Muslim World* (Harvard University Press, 1978).

6 Fatima Meruissi, *Beyond the Veil: Male–Female Dynamics in a Modern Muslim Society* (Wiley, 1975).

Further reading

On the pre-modern period see:
R. Levy, *The Social Structure of Islam* (CUP, 1957), chapter 2. Literary evidence can be found in J. Kritzeck (ed.), *Anthology of Islamic Literature* (Pelican, 1964), pp.140–8, 233–7 and 355–61; and in A.J. Arberry, *Aspects of Islamic Civilisation* (Allen & Unwin, 1964), pp.169–90, 316–23 and chapter 9. Short stories by Yusuf Sharouni, Yahya Hakki and Laila Baababaki relating to female themes can be found in Denys Johnson-Davies, *Modern Arabic Short Stories* (Heinemann, 1976).

For a contemporary Muslim view of the role and status of women see the following: K. Ahmad, *Family Life in Islam* (Islamic Foundation, 1974); Jamila Brijbhusban, *Muslim Women: In Purdah and Out of It* (Vikas/Croom Helm, 1980); Abul Al Maududi, *Purdah and the Status of Women in Islam* (Islamic Publications, Lahore, 1973) and B. Aisha Lemu and Fatima Heeren, *Women in Islam* (Islamic Council of Europe, 1976). Naila Minai, *Women in Islam – Tradition and Transition in the Middle East* (John Murray, 1981) offers a concise survey. A brief outline of *Islamic Family Law* by Shaikh Sayyed Darsh can be obtained from the Islamic Cultural Centre.

On contemporary conditions in the Middle East see *Arab Women* (Minority Rights Group, 36 Graven Street, WC2) and E.T. Prothro and L.N. Diab, *Changing Family Patterns in the Arab East* (American University of Beirut, 1974), especially chapters 3, 6 and 7.

Middle-Eastern Muslim Women Speak (University of Texas Press, 1977), edited by E.W. Fernea and B.Q. Berzirgan, is an anthology of interviews, profiles, poems and stories dealing with the everyday lives of ordinary women and such significant figures as Aisha, the wife of the Prophet, Rabi'a, the ninth century mystic, Huda Sh'arawi, the founder of the Egyptian women's movement, and Umm Khulthum, the celebrated singer. Nawal El Saadawi, *The Hidden Face of Eve: Women in the Arab World* (Zed Press, 1980), is a personal account by a celebrated Egyptian feminist, dismissed as Director of Public Health after publication of her book *Woman and Sex*.

22
Muslims in Britain

The nature of the Muslim community

There is no definite figure for the number of Muslims in Britain. Estimates range from half a million to one and a half million. Despite the vagueness surrounding the exact size of the Muslim community a number of its most significant features are beyond serious dispute:

(i) It is an old-established community. Muslims have lived in Britain since the early nineteenth century. The mosque at Woking dates from 1889.

(ii) It is larger than the Jewish community, the second largest non-Christian minority. This has important policy implications where Muslims seek to claim parity of treatment with Jews from public authorities in such matters as burials, or employers' acceptance of religious obligations and festivals.

(iii) It is a permanent community, despite the continuing expectation of many of its members that one day they will return 'home', and, wherever that may be, 'home' is almost certainly changing as much as British society. This necessarily raises the question – in which future society are Muslim parents in Britain bringing up their children to participate? The host society as they perceive it today? The Pakistan that may exist in ten years time? Or a self-conscious minority community which may or may not continue to define itself in religious terms?

(iv) It is, demographically speaking, an increasingly balanced community, in which men no longer greatly outnumber women, and the very young and the old also have a place. This new balance diminishes some of the tensions of previous decades but contains the possibility of new conflicts between the generations.

The Muslim community is also a fragmented community. Indeed, Verity Saifullah Khan has suggested that Muslims may be more accurately defined as a category than a community, a group sharing common characteristics rather than a group participating in a single common structure. In so far as they constitute a community, she argues, they do so as a result of an external act of definition by the host society.

The fragmentation of the Muslim community is the result of the significant cleavages which divide its members. Some of the most important ones are as follows:

National Islam may recognise no frontiers but the fact remains that Muslims hold passports from many different countries and their national status naturally involves differing rights and obligations and, therefore, also differing loyalties and expectations.

Linguistic Muslims in England may speak Malay, Hausa, Turkish, Bengali, Farsi, Arabic or even English as their first language. Even common passport holders from Pakistan may be divided by allegiance to Urdu, Panjabi, Baluch or Pushtu, or by differences of dialect between one region and another.

Education Differences in education imply not only varying degrees of exposure to 'modern' or 'Western' values but also carry major implications for a person's employment prospects in Britain and, therefore, his or her economic and social status. At one end of the educational spectrum one finds the young professional person with a post-graduate qualification from a Western university, at the other end an elderly illiterate who has never attended any kind of school at all. In between one may find the drop-out from a colonial era secondary school, the graduate of a post-independence primary school and the graduate of a non-Western university, frustrated by non-recognition of his qualifications. Differences in educational experience are, of course, likely to be strongly correlated with other key variables such as age, sex, urban residence and socio-economic status.

Sectarian In one sense Islam knows no 'sects' but it would be misleading to deny any significance to the distinction between Sunni and Shi'a. And highly organised minorities within the Muslim community, such as the Isma'ili and the Ahmadiyya, are often among its most active and vociferous spokesmen.

Length of Residence A minority of Muslims are true transients, living in Britain for a few years or less. Most of these are studying or training for some sort of professional career. The majority probably come from the Arab States, Iran, Malaysia and Nigeria. Their temporary residence and relatively small numbers do not, however, diminish their role for, being highly educated and, by their own experience, sensitised to the differences between their Muslim homeland and the non-Muslim society in which they must perforce live, they supply a large number of spokesmen, demonstrators and opinion-formers who catch the attention of the media and often appear to represent the outlook of the Muslim community as a whole. FOSIS, the Federation of Students' Islamic Societies, is only the most visible instrument of their influence.

A much larger proportion of Muslims can more accurately be described as 'transilients', migrants who have no permanent adherence to any single society but who pass between one society and another. 'Classic' nineteenth-century migration involved a once-for-all abandonment of the 'Old World' for the 'New'. Few emigrants from Poland ever left Chicago to revisit 'the old country'. Their migration was an act of total commitment to a new way of life. The jet has changed all that. A Bradford resident can be in the Punjab in less than a day. But the extent of transilience may vary greatly from one family to another. Though most will maintain strong links with 'home', some may make a return visit their highest economic priority while others may return only in response to a family crisis, to seek a marriage partner for a child or to die.

One major implication of this fragmentation is that claims that the Muslim community in Britain shares a common viewpoint on any particular issue should be treated with a certain initial scepticism. Another is that many of the self-styled 'spokesmen' of the Muslim community may be less than representative of those whose views they claim to represent. The largest single category of Muslims in Britain are probably first generation migrants from rural areas in South Asia. They are less often consulted than the *imams*, businessmen and students from the Middle East, East Africa or Malaysia, whose more articulate views receive a wider hearing. Riadh El-Droubie noted in an article in *The Times Educational Supplement* as long ago as 1973 that:

> In Islam we have no religious authority whose opinion is binding on every individual in regard to everyday living . . . with regard to this matter, any Muslim Centre or Mosque could be approached for advice . . . but not the presidents of certain societies or groups of Muslim immigrants who put themselves in authority.

Another outcome of fragmentation is that some Muslim associations are, in fact, almost completely dominated by members from a single region or even a single village or kin-group. Islam is a religion with a strong communitarian impulse and a proliferation of small-scale and short-lived Muslim organisations cannot represent the best way to serve the interests of Muslims, or collectively facilitate their efforts to promote wider understanding among non-Muslims. The efforts of the Islamic Cultural Centre and the Union of Muslim Organisations to promote more effective co-ordination between the efforts and activities of the multifarious bodies already in existence is, therefore, to be welcomed.

The phenomenon of transilience implies that there are strong linkages between Muslims in Britain and elsewhere. These linkages have political and social effects. Problems affecting Muslims in Britain are reported in the press in Pakistan and other Muslim countries and thus become potential issues in Britain's foreign policy. And influences may equally flow from the wider world of Islam back into Britain. The recently established Dar Ul Uloom school in Lancashire was founded with the help of £40,000 from Saudi Arabia.

The notion of transilience challenges a basic assumption that the national community is fixed, stable and closed in its membership. Rather a situation has arisen in which the members of a multi-cultural society must cope with expectations and obligations which, because they transcend national boundaries, legally or territorially, may diverge or even conflict.

In practical terms this can mean the repeated disruption of social relationships, discontinuity of education or employment and loss of language competence.

The prime motive for migration for most South Asian Muslims was probably economic, the promise of higher incomes in Britain than could be earned in Pakistan, India or Bangladesh. Economic improvement achieved in England is frequently translated into social advancement in the community of origin. Badr Dahya has suggested the following order of priorities for the expenditure of remittance money:

(1) Pay off migration debts
(2) Buy more land
(3) Build a Pakka (brick) house
(4) Arrange own/sibling marriage
(5) Establish a business

Linkages are not, however, purely economic. Patricia Jeffery in her studies of Pakistanis in Bristol has emphasised the continuing importance of kinship ties. Members of a common kin-group (*biradari*) exchange gifts, favours, visits and hospitality, and watch over each other's property and errant relatives. The desire to maintain and increase the honour (*izzat*) of the group and the individuals composing it remains a powerful incentive for mutual assistance and solidarity and the threat of ostracism remains a powerful sanction against non-compliance. Jeffery emphasises the authority which heads of families command, the expense and trouble taken to re-unite families and to observe social conventions and maintain traditional life-styles. She also argues that because for many Muslims the 'significant others' whose approval they value are resident in another country, the result is to inhibit the development of ties with the host society and with fellow-Muslims outside the kin-group with which they identify. In other words, 'kinship groupings in Pakistan have satellite groupings in Britain, and the satellites have few ties with one another.'

Another revealing case-study of the migrants' situation is Verity Saifullah Khan's 'The Pakistanis: Mirpuri villagers at home and in Bradford'.[1] The author emphasises the significance of the migrants' individual perception of his situation, and describes the motives for migration, the disillusionment which frequently accompanies both the sojourn in England and the periodic return visits to Pakistan, the re-establishment of kinship ties in Britain for purposes of mutual support and assistance and the tensions which can arise between home and school and between members of different generations.

Muslims and the host community – identity, adaptation and assimilation

The Muslim immigrant faces not one but several dimensions of 'culture shock'. Like the Hindu or the Sikh he may be moving from a rural to an urban environment and may encounter difficulties arising from problems of language, climate, housing, employment and racial prejudice. But he must also learn to cope with other difficulties which arise not simply from the fact that he is an immigrant or an Asian but from the fact that he is a Muslim. Some may arise in the context of work (how to find the time and facilities for prayer when he is working on a production line), some in relation to State and its agencies (can he claim an allowance from the Inland Revenue for a second wife? – no, but family allowances are payable in respect of all children) and some in the general context of social and community life (refusing to join in 'social' drinking).

Ivor Morrish has summarised the tensions which can face the Muslim migrant:

> The Pakistanis find themselves in two worlds – the world of the stable, close-knit extended family, and the world of mobile individualism within the host society. The Pakistani village with its mosque, school and imam; the English town with its partial re-creation of the village kin-group; the English school with its new and strange demands upon individuality; the newly-created mosque and its attempt to re-establish Muslim values, beliefs and customs; the English opportunities for permissiveness, freedom and personal choice; the Muslim demands for submission, obedience and group identity – all these symbolise the polarities of the two worlds. (*The Background of Immigrant Children*)[2]

In resolving conflicts and tensions the individual Muslim is likely to be influenced by the strength of his own personal convictions and habits, reflecting his own upbringing, education and life-experience, and by the influence of the local Muslim community, its degree of organisation, quality of leadership and social coherence. Most Muslims are certainly determined to maintain their identity as Muslims. In the words of Khurshid Ahmad, former Director General of the Islamic Foundation, 'They want to live in Europe as Muslims and not as a culturally uprooted people' (*Impact International*, 28 February 1975). Their motives are partly positive, springing from a fundamental commitment to the truth of Islam and the validity of the way of life it enjoins, and partly negative, deriving from their condemnation of many aspects of contemporary British society.

Muhammad Iqbal, a frequent writer on educational matters, once commented that 'Muslim parents are increasingly aware of the moral degeneration of society through the news media'. If, like many Muslims, you had no close friends in the host community, what sort of picture would you form of its morality from the mass-circulation newspapers? According to Patricia Jeffery, 'British people are associated with the drinking of alcohol, pre-marital sex and illegitimate children, dancing and the neglect of the elderly. Pakistanis compare themselves very favourably with British people when it comes to morality and religion'. If mixing with the British means risking a threat to the *izzat* of one's family, common prudence alone would dictate that it would be safer to hold apart.

Many Muslims are shocked by television with its advertisements for alcohol, its plays about sex, its parades of scantily-clad dancers on 'family variety shows'. The discotheque, a central social institution of the young, can be seen as a prime source of moral danger, combining as it does emotive music and dancing, unaccompanied women and access to alcohol.

Muslims may see British society not as non-religious but as irreligious and, therefore, without any check on its materialism and selfishness. Public acceptance of the phenomenon of the single-parent family can be seen as a shameful admission of failure rather than a praiseworthy instance of enlightenment. Pluralism can look like chaos.

Some of these criticisms are lacking in perspective. Charges of gross materialism ill become those who left a Muslim society for a non-Muslim one for largely economic reasons. A Muslim teacher's charge that 'a majority of immigrant children leave school without qualifications' ignores the fact that so do a majority of non-immigrant ones. Nevertheless, the fact remains that whether their views are based on misinformation, misperception or painful and indisputable personal experience, many Muslims cannot wholeheartedly endorse the social values and life-style of the host community in their entirety.

Many of the practical problems involved in maintaining a Muslim identity in a non-Muslim society are dealt with in a useful publication from the Islamic Foundation – *The Muslim Guide: For Teachers, Employers, Community Workers and Social Administrators in Britain*, by Mustafa Yusuf McDermott and Muhammad Manazir Ahsan (Leicester, 1980). This outlines Muslim beliefs and conduct, practices and attitudes, and focuses particularly on the difficulties likely to be encountered in the contexts of school, work, hospital and prison. Particular emphasis is laid on the need for facilities for prayer, the maintenance of Islamic standards of privacy, hygiene and dietary purity, the proper conduct of rites of passage associated with birth and death, and the adjustment of working hours to enable Muslims to meet their obligations regarding Friday prayers, Ramadan and the Eid festivals.

Given the existence of negative attitudes to the host community and the continuing strength of social and economic linkages with the community of origin, it is not surprising that many Muslims develop a sort of 'insider-outsider' relationship with the host community. Some of the varying dimensions of such a relationship are indicated in the survey of forty-nine male Punjabi factory workers conducted in Slough in 1971 by Levine and Naijar. Ninety per cent of the sample wrote home frequently and sent money back to their relatives; a similar proportion kept close contact with people from their own town or village living in Britain. Active involvement in the life of the Asian community in Britain, whether measured in terms of cinema attendance, newspaper readership or organisational membership, tended to vary greatly, though those with more skilled, better-paying jobs and a greater length of residence in Britain tended to be involved more in the Asian community *and* in the wider host society. (This would imply that the significant dimension is not an either/or choice between involvement in the host society and a sub-culture, but rather a matter of social competence versus withdrawal and alienation.) As far as involvement in British society went some 69 per cent of the sample went to pubs frequently, and 61 per cent belonged to a trade union but only 29 per cent claimed to read British newspapers regularly and only 8 per cent to go to British cinemas. More significant, perhaps, was the widely held view that British society was perceived to be open for the British but unwelcoming to foreigners. Eighty per cent of the sample asserted that substantial discrimination existed and 90 per cent saw themselves as but poorly integrated. Eighty per cent thought the British were not clean, 76 per cent thought they were not warm and 61 per cent thought they were not trustworthy. It is worth noting, however, that a better opinion of the British was clearly correlated with a better job, status and education and longer residence.

J.H. Taylor's interesting study of Asian youths in Newcastle-upon-Tyne, *The Half-Way Generation*,[3] suggests that the Muslim boys in his sample of sixty-seven school-leavers had a much stronger sense of their identity as Muslims than did their Sikh or Hindu counterparts. The Muslims *knew* that they were Muslims, were confident (though not always right) about what this involved in terms of belief and behaviour and were unwilling to surrender their identity as Muslims. The Hindu boys, by contrast, were inclined to reject traditional myths and vegetarianism and were unable to explain such aspects of their culture as Diwali or to acquire satisfactory explanations from their parents. Taylor attributes the difference not to the life-experiences of the youths but to a basic difference between the religious systems. Islam can be made explicit and is a much more 'portable' religion than Hinduism, which requires the supportive structure of village life for its maintenance and realisation.

Inter-generational tensions are explored in *Between Two Cultures: A Study of Relationships between Generations in the Asian Community in Britain* (CRC, 1976). The survey shows a strong attachment to the ideal of a united and prestige-conscious family by young Asians of all religious backgrounds and a continuing commitment to the obligation of younger generations to look after their elders. Muslims, it should be noted, laid particular stress on these. Some other significant findings were:

(i) Muslim *parents* were concerned about the difficulty of finding adequately trained religious teachers.

(ii) A majority of Muslims, both parents and youth, disagreed with the idea of girls wearing Western clothes. Religion was given as the main reason for this.

(iii) Marriage within one's own religious group was endorsed by a large majority of both parents and youth of all religious groups. Most saw it as a way of avoiding inevitable difficulties consequent upon inter-faith marriages. Muslim youths were more strongly in favour of arranged marriages than Hindu or Sikh youths.

(iv) Muslim youths were less inclined to demand more freedom with regard to leisure and social life, and less likely to concede such licence to the next generation. They were more inclined to want to spend their spare time with other Asians.

'Integration' must be distinguished from assimilation. Integration means that members of a group, sharing certain cultural characteristics (languages, dress, rituals, and so on), which enable them to identify themselves and be identified by non-members, are able to function effectively in terms of the dominant values of the larger society. Their lifestyle has both adapted and been accepted, and they are able to secure for themselves adequate access to incomes, amenities and the processes of public decision-making. Assimilation means that the process of integration has proceeded to such a degree that identification is no longer possible. The group is no longer identified as a group by its members or by non-members; it is no longer a group. Sub-culture and host-culture have merged rather than co-existing, the former within the framework of the latter. The French and Dutch Protestant refugees of the sixteenth and seventeenth centuries provide an English example of this process of total assimilation; within a century little remained of their distinctive identity except their surnames. This is not likely to be the case with Muslims, not least because they, like the Jews, are able also to identify with, and call upon the resources of, a wider community of Muslims beyond Britain itself.

In attempting to clarify the notion of assimilation Glazer and Moynihan, in their classic study of American immigration, suggested that assimilation could take place along eight dimensions: (i) acceptance of external patterns of culture and life-style such as dress, food and sport. This could be limited by the ritual significance of some externals; (ii) absence of prejudice towards the newcomer; (iii) absence of discrimination towards the newcomer; (iv) acceptance of prevailing norms regarding basic social values and power relationships; (v) economic representation at all levels of society; (vi) membership of face-to-face groupings, such as clubs and cliques (some minorities are large and concentrated enough to form their own); (vii) inter-marriage (again some groups are large enough to provide each generation with partners from within the group or are able to 'import' partners from elsewhere); (viii) identification with the host society.

The authors point out that Jews in America can be regarded as having been deeply assimilated along the first five dimensions but not along the last three. Perhaps the same will be true of Muslims in Britain. Another complicating possibility is that the continuation of racial prejudice and discrimination could create among British-born Asians a common identity, based on these experiences, in which Muslim, Sikh and Hindu distinctions were at least partly submerged. 'Re-Islamisation' in response to the growing self-confidence and assertiveness of Muslim States abroad is yet another possible strand in the social tapestry which is yet to be woven.

Sources

1 In James L. Watson (ed.), *Between Two Cultures* (Basil Blackwell, Oxford, 1977), chapter 3.

2 Ivor Morrish, *The Background of Immigrant Children* (Allen & Unwin, 1971), p.231.

3 J.H. Taylor, *The Half-Way Generation* (NFER, 1976).

Further reading

M.A. Zaki Badawi, *Islam in Britain* (Ta-Ha Publishers, 1981), is a useful Muslim overview. Patricia Jeffery, *Migrants and Refugees: Muslim and Christian Pakistani Families in Bristol* (CUP, 1976), gives much useful background information, especially on life-styles (housing, diet, leisure, dress and so on). In discussing social change the author not only notes the trend to westernisation but also the counter-current of 'Ashrafisation' (reassertion of Islamic values in daily life). The position of Christians in Pakistan is also described. Another convenient, if somewhat dated, summary of general background information is provided by Ivor Morrish, *The Background of Immigrant Children* (Allen & Unwin, 1971), part 3. A sketch of conditions in the Mirpur district, from which many Pakistanis in Britain have come, is to be found in V.S. Khan's contribution to James L. Watson (ed.), *Between Two Cultures* (Basil Blackwell, 1977). S.M. Darsh, *Muslims in Europe* (Ta-Ha Publishers, 1980) is a very useful concise statement of the cultural priorities of the Muslim community as seen by a former Imam of the London Central Mosque. Mohammed Anwar, *The Myth of Return: Pakistani Migrants in Britain* (Heinemann, 1979), is a study of male textile workers in Rochdale.

23

Islam and Education

> If you are thinking a year ahead, sow seed. If you are thinking ten years ahead,
> plant a tree. If you are thinking one hundred years ahead, educate the people.
> (Kuan-Tzu)

'Seek knowledge, even as far as China' is a favourite Muslim saying, attributed to the prophet Muhammad. Edward Blyden wrote of the Muslim in *Christianity, Islam and the Negro Race* that 'his religion is educational and his education religious'.

Modern Western liberal education differs from traditional Islamic education in many respects. These differences may be represented, if a little simplistically, as follows:

	Islamic	*Western*
Who?	Self-selecting and voluntary	Universal and compulsory
When?	Discontinuously and life-long	Concentrated on youth
What?	Qur'an and Shari'a via Arabic	'Useful knowledge' via vernacular or metropolitan languages
How?	Teacher as mentor and expert. Pupil as imitator and disciple.	Teacher as organiser and validator of knowledge. Pupil as critic or partner in learning
Why?	Spiritual perfection and incorporation into the *umma*	Individual self-advancement through competition

Western-style education has spread through the Islamic world over the course of the last century. Elementary Qur'an schools and *madrasas* for advanced Islamic studies survived governmental neglect to remain as a separate and supplementary system. Jørgen Nielsen has succinctly summarised this process:

> By a combination of imperialist imposition and own choice, the middle and upper classes of the Muslim world abandoned many of their traditional institutions and

adopted European and later American ways. In the process the traditional education system was relegated to the backwaters of society, to the villages and out-of-the-way places. The top of the new educational system became the universities of Europe and North America, and the traditional system was left headless; being irrelevant to new career structures it led nowhere . . . it then became identified with village Qur'an schools, fossilised and infertile in the methods and concepts of two centuries ago. (*British Journal of Religious Education* Autumn 1980, p.37)

Muslim commentators have been divided in their attitude to Western-style education. On the one hand it introduced undeniably useful knowledge, but on the other it seemed to turn out arrogant young men with no respect for tradition or authority of any sort. As the poet Akbar Allahabadi observed: 'Pharaoh would not have earned notoriety for infanticide, had the idea of founding a college crossed his mind. Rulers of the East break the enemy's head, those of the West change his disposition.'

According to Abul Hasan Ali Nadwi, the author of *Western Civilisation: Islam and Muslims*,[2] Western-style education has spread among the young such erroneous views as that religion can be a purely private matter and separated from politics, that Islam can be equated with a church and the *umma* with clergy, that religion is a hindrance to progress, that females should have equality with males in all social spheres, that Islamic family law is obsolete, that usury, drink, gambling and 'sexual waywardness' are to be tolerated and that 'the passionate upholding of the creed of nationalism is to be desired'. He concludes that 'there is only one remedy of the present malaise, however slow and painstaking it may seem. It lies in a total re-orientation of the educational system in the Islamic lands with the object of bringing it in accord with the spiritual needs and aspirations of the Muslims' (op.cit., p.165). This means ridding the system of 'the poison of excessive materialism' and ending 'the denial of the higher moral and spiritual values' in favour of the 'spirit of piety and Godliness and solicitude for the hereafter'. As the first practical steps to the realisation of these aims the author recommends the dismissal of all teachers not committed to the building of Islam and the establishment of hostels to provide a suitable environment for young Muslims studying away from their families. In the long run, he asserts, Islamic countries must eliminate their dependence on Western methods, materials, languages, expertise and institutions. Because many Muslims see education primarily as a process for ensuring cultural continuity and for preparing individuals to perform predetermined social roles, they see great dangers in imitating educational systems which are not based on these assumptions. Western education they see as being at best neutral towards ideals, laying too much stress on individualism and turning out students with no sense of meaning or direction in life and a fragmented view of knowledge.

Khurshid Ahmad has well summarised the situation facing Muslim educators:

Education performs at least two basic functions in any society: it is a vehicle for the preservation, extension and communication of the cultural heritage, traditional values and social and national ideals and morals of a people; and it is a tool for change, innovation and development and a major means through which new knowledge and skills are discovered and trained manpower produced to meet the demands of socio-economic change. These two functions are not always in harmony with one another. How to reconcile them to produce a new and higher level of convergence is the main concern of the modern educationist in the world of Islam. ('Islam: key to the crisis of alienation', *The Times Educational Supplement*, 1 April 1977)

In April 1977 the first World Conference on Muslim Education was held in Mecca to establish a blueprint for the development of a modern Islamic education system at all levels. According to Shaikh Ahmad Salah Jamjoom, chairman of the conference's organising committee:

> The idea of the conference was generated by the realisation that all branches of knowledge in the modern education system that we have borrowed from the West are dominated by secular and hence anti-Islamic concepts. The permanent norm of a God-given code of life which formed at one time in the West the unquestioned source of assumptions for social, cultural and intellectual life has been torn to pieces. We are facing the communist millennium. (Quoted in *The Times Educational Supplement*, 5 September 1980)

Dr Syed Ali Ashraf, secretary of the conference, argues that 'Islam *must* create its own system of modern knowledge or perish. There is no end to knowledge and Muslims must not close the doors to new learning.'

In 1980 the conference of foreign ministers of the Muslim world ratified proposals for a World Centre for Muslim Education to be established in Mecca.

British education faces many Muslims with a dilemma. Verity Saifullah Khan states it bluntly: 'The highest value is placed on education . . . and yet, in its present form, it is the most fundamental threat to all that is valued.'

Muslim parents have a respect for education which is traditional to their culture. Many are illiterate themselves. This causes great practical difficulty in Britain, a bureaucratically administered welfare society. They also see education as the key to occupational and social advancement and perhaps entertain unrealistic ambitions for their offspring. But the expectations they have of schooling do not always accord with what they experience or perceive. They assume that the teacher claims knowledge and authority as the concomitants of his role, and that school work will be structured and sequential, drilled and disciplined, with regular homeworks and standardised tests. Many, used to village schools, are used to the idea of face to face contact with the teacher who is a familiar figure in their own community. The British secondary school with its complex hierarchy of year heads, pastoral teachers, and so on can seem incomprehensible and forbidding.

As Muhammad Iqbal has noted:

> Very few Asian children satisfy parental aspirations . . . to become doctors and engineers and for some this high aspiration, in fact, proves detrimental, yet pushes up the children's own ambitions. Career-counselling among Asian children is underdeveloped. Parental involvement in school affairs . . . is regarded as

highly desirable. This has been minimal by Muslim parents, mainly because of the father's pre-occupation with work and non-participation of the mother who is often illiterate in English and feels uneasy in mixed company. (*The Times Educational Supplement*, 1 April 1977)

One successful method of bridging the gulf between home and school has been the 'Home Tutor Scheme' pioneered by Dr Iqbal in Huddersfield as a practical means whereby female English volunteers could teach Asian mothers in their own homes, thus breaking down language and cultural barriers simultaneously.

Afzal Rahman, chairman of the Muslim Educational Trust, has outlined in dramatic terms what he sees as the moral and cultural dangers in the British school system:

> The philosophy which dominates Western culture in general and Western education in particular, is not only diametrically opposed but also positively hostile to the Islamic philosophy of life. Young Muslims find themselves in a society where their friends and others dance, drink and freely move in mixed gatherings with persons of their choice and have unrestricted relationships both before and after marriage. They are not bound by any moral and religious values or social norms. In view of these un-Islamic forces and unhealthy social and educational surroundings, Muslim youth must be equipped with sound Islamic education and trained to believe in Islamic philosophy and life in Islamic culture. (*The Times Educational Supplement*, 1 April 1977)

Muslim reactions to British education are concisely summarised in Dr S.M. Darsh's pamphlet *Muslims in Europe*.[3] Dr Darsh accepts that Western imperialist regimes felt themselves impelled to introduce their style of education as a necessary adjunct of their 'civilising mission', but notes that this often seemed to benefit non-Muslim minorities at the expense of Muslims and that its value was obscured by the fact that it seemed to have been imposed by foreign conquest. He concedes, however, that:

> People came to realise the value of the new education and found no objection whatsoever on religious grounds to it. They started to discover their spirit anew and to see that the survival of the Muslim world lay in acquiring the type of education upon which modern civilisation is founded . . . the fears of the social structure or religious values being undermined were dispelled. (op.cit., p.35)

But Dr Darsh also asserts that Muslims have become aware that the basic ethic of British education is derived from Christian values and that Muslims face a challenge in preserving their identity. Their response to this challenge is classified by Dr Darsh under four heads:

The establishment of mosque classes
This is 'the most common type' of Muslim educational provision and corresponds in Darsh's view to 'the very old type, common in nearly all Muslim countries prior to the introduction of modern education'. The teaching concentrates on memorisation (rather than understanding) of the Qur'an and an elementary knowledge of the faith, its rituals and early history. In Darsh's words 'the teaching process is direct, tedious and exacting' and 'not

all who take it on are qualified to do so . . . The imam is stern, long-bearded and intolerant of the most trivial breaches of the behavioural code. In contrast with the atmosphere of the infant or junior country school, the disadvantage is great indeed' (op.cit., p.40). (Writing elsewhere, Muhammad Iqbal has concurred: 'Islamic education can be imparted effectively only in county schools as the teaching in the mosque is, by and large, carried out by unqualified teachers and in an inadequate fashion.')

It is noteworthy that second among the aims and objectives of the Birmingham-based Muslim Education Consultative Committee is a pledge, 'To improve the standard of religious instruction in the mosques and bring it up to the standard of mainstream religious instruction in the schools.'

Weekend classes

These are organised where the Muslim community is too small to sustain regular daily mosque classes. Being under the supervision of central Islamic organisations, such classes are more likely to employ more 'progressive' educational materials and methods.

Muslim teachers in maintained schools

The Muslim Educational Trust was established in 1966 to recruit Muslim teachers who would, on a peripatetic basis, meet the religious educational needs of Muslim pupils within the State system. It is claimed that this system served some 3,000 pupils in 59 schools (a fraction of the whole) and that it used well-prepared materials and methods in doing so. But it is conceded that such form of provision made religious education appear to be an additional and competing burden with school work.

Separate provision

Darsh argues that this response, while widely desired, has been retarded by the divisions within the Muslim community:

> There is no . . . well-planned fully documented project. Until this happens, the Muslim children will continue to be the victims of this gross negligence on the part of their elders . . . until such time as the Muslim community becomes financially able to build its own schools and learn from the experience of other minority groups who have been living in this society for hundreds of years, we have to content ourselves with teaching our way of life whenever and wherever we can. This means that Islamic religious education must take place at all levels. Children and adults, fathers, mothers, boys and girls, all are in urgent need of true education. (op.cit., p.45)

For most Muslims in Britain, education means British State education. A recently published book, *The Muslim Guide*, by Mustafa Yusuf McDermott and Muhammad Manazir Ahsan,[4] outlines some of the problems that Muslims are likely to encounter:

Language

The authors assert that trilingual competence must become the norm – a South Asian vernacular for communication with parents, English for school and work, and Arabic for canonical and liturgical purposes. Admitting the possibility of linguistic confusion, they place great confidence in the resilience of the child.

Role conflict

The same confidence is manifested in the face of the anticipated problem of conflicting social expectations from parents and family, teachers and peer group, textbooks and mass media: 'Given moral support from the family, guidance from the mosque and religious tolerance and respect from teachers and community workers, the young Muslim can learn to fulfil the rights and obligations incumbent upon his/her many social roles in a Muslim environment and within British society without the slightest necessity for religious compromise' (op.cit., p.45).

Co-education

The authors assert flatly that co-educational schooling, especially after puberty, 'goes against the teachings of Islam', and express a fear of the possible development of relationships 'leading to sexual permissiveness and the degradation of morals'. They also claim that 'it should be recognised that in Britain there is a well-meaning and silent section even of non-Muslim parents who would surely favour single-sex school education for their children if there was a free choice and provision of such schools' (p.45).

Religious education

Claiming that the 1944 Education Act gives children the right 'to be taught the religious belief and moral code of their parents' and that 'to practise Islam would not be possible without knowledge', the authors argue the need for instruction in Islam to be given in the schools, not only to foster personal religious commitment and family stability among Muslims but also to dispel the misconceptions about Islam which they believe to be current among non-Muslims.

Sex education

'Islam puts great emphasis on modesty and morality which are badly offended by the mode and contents of prevalent sex education.' Islam, it is asserted, 'has its own method of sex education', which does not involve graphics and starts from the standpoint of personal hygiene.

Dress

'Total covering of the body is so basic to Islamic teaching and practice that Muslim parents rightly argue that their daughters should observe these standards from the very beginning.' The authors suggest that differences between parents and school authorities over dress requirements can usually be resolved by the wearing of shalwar (trousers) and hameez (tunic) made from school uniform cloth.

PE and sport

In line with the stance taken on the two preceding issues, the authors express their disapproval of mixed sporting occasions (especially swimming) and the exposure of the body in the context of PE, games or showers.

Fasting

Conceding that some Muslim children will feel weakened during Ramadan, they suggest that it might be reasonable for them to be excused PE, games and swimming. They also express the hope that teachers will express encouragement and approval for Muslim children's efforts in this regard, rather than treating them with condescension or irritation.

The authors conclude their survey with a list of recommendations, which may be summarised thus:

1   That Muslim teachers in schools with a high proportion of Muslim pupils should act as consultants and co-ordinators on all matters affecting their welfare and that they should encourage Muslim parents to attend PTA meetings.

2   That timetable and classroom provision be made for Islamic religious instruction and that a prayer-room and washing facilities should be available.

3   That *imams* and other Muslims be invited into schools to give talks; that Muslims should present Islam in the context of social studies and RE and that arrangements should be made for non-Muslims to visit mosques.

4   That imams and 'Muslim scholars' be invited to serve on school, youth club and other management committees.

5   That Muslim children should be allowed to withdraw from school assemblies and sex education lessons.

6   That a Muslim cook and separate cooking facilities should be made available where possible and that in any case vegetarian dishes should be provided and that no child should be pressed to eat unlawful food or touch pork in cookery classes.

It is interesting to note that no mention is made in this list of the possibility of withdrawal from art or music (especially music and movement) classes or school visits, or of the provision of Islamic books in the school library, although these have been desired by other Muslim educationists in the past.

Many of the adjustments requested in the above list of recommendations could be made without fundamentally disrupting school life but they would require that commitment of manpower, time and resources which signify that acceptance of the ideal of fostering a multi-cultural society is more than a matter of lip-service. The relationship between principle and practice is a problematic one and in this context neatly illustrates the significance of differing perspectives on the role of religion. English law recognises a right of conscience with regard to withdrawal from corporate acts of worship and religious education. This definition might, from a Muslim point of view, seem to rest very much on Christian assumptions about the nature and scope of religious commitment and the observances that it requires. Given that Islam is a total 'way of life' whose prescriptions cover every aspect of social existence, might not a far wider interpretation of rights of conscience be in order?

Teachers also seem frequently to be unaware of the assimilationist assumptions upon which many of their best endeavours are based. Consider, for instance, the following passages from a successful book written by a teacher on the basis of her experiences with Asian immigrant children:

> Our Authority was wise enough to realise that our particular Punjabi Muslims could not be divested of their shalwar overnight, and that teachers would have to be patient and tolerant in the hope that the next generation might be more Western in outlook . . . A particularly devout branch of Islam to which a number of our Pakistani families belonged insisted that its boys should attend Friday

afternoon prayers at the mosque . . . and it was not easy to persuade fanatical fathers to send their sons to school instead, and to convince them that here in England education had a legal priority . . . In Punjabi villages dancing in public was an activity denied to all but prostitutes or fallen women, yet it was a part of normal English school curriculum and somehow prejudice would have to be overcome . . . (R. Scott, *A Wedding Man is Nicer than Cats, Miss*)[5]

The problem is not so much one of trying to assimilate Muslims to a rigid cultural pattern of fixed rules and norms. Perhaps it might be easier for Muslims to formulate a coherent response if this were the case. It is rather that British schooling appears to have so little normative coherence. What liberal educationists might see as 'healthy pluralism' can look to pious Muslims like moral chaos. In fact British schooling does have a normative coherence, but it consists not so much in an overt commitment to the transmission of fixed societal norms as in its explicit encouragement to queston the very things that Muslims wish their children to take for granted and its general assumption that each child is to be encouraged to develop his or her full potential as an individual capable of making free choices of action and commitment over as many areas of life as possible. This does not accord with traditional Muslim values which stress authority in education and put the emphasis on responsibilities rather than on rights. Writing forty years ago about the impact of British colonial education on the youth of India, Maulana Mohammad Ali concluded that 'it tended to breed in the student an arrogant omniscience and to destroy along with age-old blind beliefs in superstition, all respect for tradition and authority . . . what little it substituted was itself based on blind belief and superstitions, albeit "modern" '. The difference in outlook implied by the assumptions on which liberal Western education and traditional Muslim education respectively rest, reflects differing views of the nature of man and therefore the priorities proper to his social and intellectual development. They are neatly paralleled in the observation made by one of the villagers in Ronald Blythe's portrait of a Suffolk village, *Akenfield*, that in the old days one was asked 'Are you saved?' but now it is 'Have you got your 'O' levels?' Is there a central contradiction in the as yet embryonic ideology of multi-culturalism between the recognition on the one hand of the rights of the parent to bring up his child according to his own religious and moral traditions and on the other of the role of the school, acting in a sense as proxy for the State, to prepare the child to take full advantage of its future status as a citizen in a welfare democracy?

A related issue is the question of mother-tongue teaching. In an issue of *Islamic Ideology*, the official newsletter of the Muslim Welfare Association, Iftekhar Ahmad put the following point of view:

Special attention must be given to the teaching of mother tongue so that the children do not feel isolated from their own families. Teaching of the mother tongue should be given the same weight as any other school subject. It should be taught right from nursery schools and qualified Muslim teachers should be employed to do the job . . . In Scandinavian countries all immigrant children are taught their mother tongue and cultural heritage on the same lines as any other school subject. The EEC gives large sums of money to its member countries for the teaching of mother tongues and cultural heritage to the immigrant children.

Strictly speaking mother-tongue teaching is not an Islamic requirement as such because the canonical language of the faith, and the prime subject of study in the mosque schools, is Arabic. But it could be argued that the solidarity of the Muslim family is essential for the realisation of Islam and that this would be gravely jeopardised by a linguistic generation gap. There are, however, a number of practical problems to be faced:

(i) Punjabi, the *de facto* mother tongue of many South Asian Muslims, is generally regarded as an informal language to be used only among the family and friends. Urdu (with which it has much in common) is the prestigious language of high culture, poetry and administration and is used in schools in Pakistan from the start.

(ii) Muslim parents might actually regard the time spent on learning a mother-tongue as wasted and a qualification such as O level Urdu as useless. On the other hand many would no doubt welcome such provision.

(iii) If mother-tongue teaching were to take place in school hours, thus overriding the stigma of being an extra burden, would it be at the expense of another subject and, if so, which? How do the arguments for teaching the mother tongue compare with those for teaching French or Latin or Welsh?

(vi) Given that potential pupils command of both their mother-tongue and English, spoken and written, varies greatly, how could one make available adequate materials, syllabuses and examinations, which reflect the British and not the mother-country context of mother-tongue use?

(v) How can one recruit teachers who are not only competent in the relevant languages but also properly trained teachers skilled in teaching them as foreign languages, which to many British-born Muslims they virtually now are?

Much mother-tongue teaching is nevertheless going ahead. The first national conference on the teaching of Urdu, held at the School of Oriental and African Studies in December 1979, attracted more than 100 participants, as did a similar conference on Punjabi held at Coventry in June 1980.[6]

Some Muslims have concluded that the best answer to their educational dilemmas lies in a system of separate provision which would not only halt the process of what they regard as 'de-education' or, more dramatically, 'cultural genocide', but would actually make it possible to create the educational environment within which a coherent Muslim identity could be fostered and developed. They find Qur'anic justification for this in Sura 24:30, Sura 33:32–33 and Sura 5:48. In 1975 the Union of Muslim Organisations published a paper on 'Islamic Education and Single Sex Schools' and followed this up with the establishment of a National Muslim Educational Council in 1978. In 1979 the Dar-ul-Uloom ('House of Knowledge') school near Manchester began to take in (male, fee-paying) secondary school age pupils for a traditional Islamic education. Two-thirds of the sum needed for buying the school (a disused hospital) was raised by Muslims from Bolton, the rest was donated by the Government of Saudi Arabia. A visiting journalist found conditions 'spartan' and noted that many of the pupils had only a poor command of English, preferring to speak Urdu. She also noted that two boys she spoke to 'like Dar-ul-Uloom. They were quiet and shy and appreciated the calm atmosphere.'[7]

At the time of writing Dar-ul-Uloom remains unique, but a situation in which falling rolls and cuts in public expenditure make surplus buildings and teachers more readily available eases two of the major obstacles to separate provision. It is noteworthy, moreover, that in February 1980 Mark Carlisle, then Secretary of State for Education, spoke at the annual dinner of the Union of Muslim Organisations and gave what *The Times Educational Supplement* reported as 'cautious encouragement' to the idea of separate Muslim schools, although he added the qualification that 'they must also provide a full secular education'. This qualification might raise some further difficulties, especially where girls are concerned.

The motivation for separate provision has been an essentially negative one, arising from dissatisfaction with conditions in the maintained system. But it would seem quite possible that, once established, separate Muslim schools would begin to develop a distinctive character and ethic of their own, and at least in some respects this might run counter to some basic liberal commitments. Consider, for example, the implications of the suggestion in the UMO's 1975 Report on 'Islamic Education and Single Sex Schools' that maintained comprehensives should have single-sex annexes 'to educate Muslim girls specifically in the art of motherhood, childminding and an element of teaching skills for use at home'. A curriculum which legitimised such a sex-related pattern of division of labour would not be likely to find much favour in the eyes of the Equal Opportunities Commission. Muhammad Iqbal concedes that 'it is feared that separate schools for Muslim girls and boys may perpetuate under-achievement', but argues that Muslim parents' religious beliefs 'insist on a happy balance between the education for life here and the hereafter' (*New Equals*, April 1978).

Sources and references

1 Edward Blyden, *Christianity, Islam and the Negro Race* (Edinburgh University Press, 1967).

2 Abul Hasan Ali Nadwi, *Western Civilisation: Islam and Muslims* (Academy of Islamic Research and Publications, Lucknow, 1974).

3 Dr S.M. Darsh, *Muslims in Europe* (Ta-Ha Publishers, 1980).

4 Mustafa Yusuf McDermott and Muhammad Manazir Ahsan, *The Muslim Guide* (Islamic Foundation, 1980).

5 R. Scott, *A Wedding Man is Nicer than Cats, Miss* (David & Charles, 1971).

6 Further details of recent developments can be obtained from the Centre for Information on Language Teaching (20 Carlton House Terrace,

London SW1Y 5AP) and the Linguistic Minorities Project, directed by Dr V.S. Khan (18 Woburn Square, London WC1H 0NS).

7 Joanna Mack, 'The Muslims get a school of their own', *New Society*, 28 June 1979.

Further reading

The papers presented at the 1977 World Conference on Muslim Education are to be published by Hodder & Stoughton in association with King Abdul Aziz University. The first three volumes appeared in 1980 on *Aims and Objectives of Islamic Education, Crisis in Muslim Education* and *Curriculum and Teacher Education*. The further projected volumes will cover 'Philosophy, Literature and Fine Arts', 'Social and Natural Sciences', 'The Islamic Perspective', 'Education and Society in the Muslim World' and 'Muslim Education in the Modern World'.

The foremost writer on Islamic education in Britain has long been A.L. Tibawi, formerly of the University of London's Institute of Education. Many of his essays and reviews on the subject have been collected together and published in *Arabic and Islamic Themes* (Luzac & Co., 1976) and *Islamic Education: Its Traditions and Modernisation into the Arab National Systems* (Luzac, 1972). The legal aspects of Muslim education in Britain are dealt with in a paper by W. Owen Cole (published by the Centre for the Study of Islam and Christian-Muslim Relations, Selly Oak Colleges, Birmingham) in a pamphlet on *Islam in English Law and Administration: A Symposium* (March 1981).

For case studies of the development of education in Muslim countries see G.N. Brown and M.V. Hiskett (eds), *Conflict and Harmony in Education in Tropical Africa* (Allen & Unwin, 1975); Georgie Hyde, *Education in Modern Egypt* (Routledge & Kegan Paul, 1978); and Ishtiaq Hussain Qureshi, *Education in Pakistan: An Inquiry into Objectives and Achievements* (Maaref Ltd, Karachi, 1976).

On mother-tongue teaching see Ralph Russell, *Ethnic Minority Languages and the Schools* (with special reference to Urdu); and Verity Saifullah Khan, *Bilingualism and Linguistic Minorities in Britain* (Runnymede Trust, 62 Chandos Place, London WC2N 4HG).

The Minaret is a quarterly journal devoted to Islam and education in Britain (obtainable from Minaret House, 9 Leslie Park Road, East Croydon CR0 6TN). *Middle East Education*, published six times a year in English and Arabic, covers current developments in the Arab world (from International Trade Publications, Queensway House, 2 Queensway, Redhill, Surrey). From time to time relevant articles appear in *New Community*. See for instance M. Iqbal, 'Education and Islam in Britain — a Muslim view' (vol. V, no. 4, Spring-Summer 1977); and Geoffrey Driver and Roger Ballard, 'Comparing performance in multi-racial schools: South Asian pupils at 16 plus' (vol. VII, no. 2, Summer 1979).

See also: Ivor Morrish, *The Background of Immigrant Children* (Allen & Unwin, 1971), part 3 and especially chapter 14; Ghulam Saqib, *Modernisation of Muslim Education* (Reach Publishing Company, 1977); and J.H. Taylor, *The Half-Way Generation* (NFER, 1976), chapters 14 and 15.

Part Two

Islam in the
Classroom

24

Introduction

Religious education

That the concept of a curriculum does not admit of easy and unambiguous definition the large number of works which have appeared on 'curriculum theory' in recent years adequately testifies. That there are discrepancies between the formal content and objectives of a course of study ('the curriculum as proclaimed'), and the way such content and objectives are understood by teachers ('the curriculum as perceived'), taught in the classroom ('the curriculum as presented'), and imbibed by the learner ('the curriculum as possessed'), must be obvious. The implications of these discrepancies cannot be examined here, but they must be borne in mind.

In comparison with most other countries British teachers enjoy a considerable degree of freedom in determining what they will teach. Religious Education differs, however, from other subjects in being subject to the limitations of an official 'Agreed Syllabus'; but there seems to be less and less reason for regarding this as unduly restrictive.

The preface to Hampshire Education Authority's 'Agreed Syllabus for Religious Education' (1978) reveals the extent to which teacher autonomy is not merely recognised but positively encouraged and diversity of detail in content regarded as desirable.

> At a time of unprecedented increase in knowledge when *local conditions and needs differ widely*, it would be *unrealistic* to *prescribe* the detailed content of the curriculum. However, some *suggestions* as to appropriate content have been added to help the non-specialist teacher and to illustrate the objectives. This mode of presentation is designed to give teachers the opportunity *to exercise their proper responsibility in developing schemes of work*.
>
> Teachers are urged to approach the document without *pre-conceived ideas* about what constitutes Religious Education. The Advisory Panel for Religious Education and their colleagues on the Working Parties have *taken a broad view of the subject*. They see Religious Education as involving the personal *quest* for meaning and the *search* for values as well as the *encounter* with Christianity and other living faiths. In order to take full advantage of the *developmental approach* which has been adopted, the Syllabus must be considered as a whole. (Emphases added)

Change, flexibility and experimentation have become increasingly characteristic of religious education.

The factors which have led to continuing re-appraisal in this field in the post-war period have been concisely summarised in *Stand Points*, a working paper issued by Essex LEA's Standing Advisory Council on Religious Education:

> The Honest-to-God debate, Vatican II, new liturgies, Buddhist monks in London, sizeable Muslim, Hindu and Sikh communities in England, the reaction against religion of a vocal humanist movement, and the cheerful rejection of religion by great numbers of people are but a few of the factors that affect our attitude to religion . . . Changes in our educational system, new insights on learning skills, new approaches to other subjects in the curriculum . . .

The major constraints facing the teacher are: (i) The time-table; (ii) Pupil interest; (iii) Examination syllabuses; (iv) Resources; (v) The teacher's own competence. (i) and (ii) are constraints whose definition and importance rest in large part upon the preferences and perceptions of the individual teacher. (iii) is a constraint which is far more open to challenge than many teachers seem to imagine, though change does take time. Indeed, many of the examining Boards can fairly claim to have played a significant innovatory role, introducing new syallabuses before any large number of teachers seem to have asked for them (see Appendix 7 for details of CSE, O level and A level syllabuses). (iv) might fairly have seemed a constraint a decade ago, but, although there are obvious areas of deficiency, in terms both of content and format, the major difficulties in this area are probably ones of finance. (v) represents the legacy of past patterns of teacher education and, indirectly, a reflection of the previous state of the relevant academic disciplines, their boundaries and priorities. In the view of this writer, teacher competence – and teacher confidence – represent the most significant single source of limitation on the further diffusion of teaching about Islam in English secondary schools.

In his invaluable survey 'Teaching world religions in England and Wales' Brian Gates notes that 'less than forty per cent of the religious education teachers in secondary schools have specialist qualifications and of these only a minority have had world religions courses in colleges or universities.' He goes on to observe that

> the competence and motivation of those who have sought to introduce world religions in their schools is not always above reproach. It is not unknown for a teacher to set about teaching world religions with no more background understanding than that acquired from an introductory school text intended for twelve to fifteen year olds. The risk of superficiality and distortion is enormous anyway – even for the specialist – but, in such instances as this, 'good intentions' are almost bound to be counter-productive.[1]

When teachers do teach about Islam in English schools, how do they go about it, what difficulties do they feel that they face and what strategies do they adopt? The following paragraphs are based on reports from a dozen or so teachers in different parts of the country whose approaches were recommended to the writer by LEA advisers as examples of 'good practice'.

Teachers often manifest considerable self-doubt in approaching Islam: 'Years of Christian theology at university never remotely touched on comparative religion so anything I do now is entirely instinctive and self-taught.' Some teachers may hesitate to deal with Islam because they anticipate reactions of hostility, ridicule or contempt on the part of their pupils to some aspects of Muslim religiosity. The anticipation of such reactions need not, however, lead to retreat on the part of the teacher but rather to a change of direction or emphasis.

Honest difficulties must be honestly faced and dealt with; but they need not be confronted, either by the teacher or the class, all at once. At times it may be best to set an issue aside to 'cool' for a while until, perhaps, a better appreciation of its background and context puts it into a different perspective. At other times it may be more appropriate to consider the implications rather than the origins of differences of conviction and commitment.

The key may well be found in remembering always that the prime aim of religious education is not simply to impart this or that set of facts about this or that religion but to bring the pupil to some understanding of what it means to be religious, whether at the level of an individual, a group or an entire community. Establishing and nurturing this understanding, therefore, leads us constantly to ask ourselves – what is this lesson *really* about? Is it a lesson about pilgrimage or polygamy? – or have my pupils' reactions turned it into a lesson about stereotyping or how to handle one's immediate emotional reactions when faced with a novel or unexpected pattern of belief or behaviour? Have I built up the atmosphere and relationships which would enable me to respond to the assertion 'Saying prayers five times a day is a waste of time' by asking the pupil who makes it to look at his own way of life and become aware of what other people with different standards might consider a waste of time? In other words, has the pupil yet learned to interview himself?

Apart from the teacher's lack of confidence in his or her own knowledge and training there is, of course, also the problem of personal commitment: 'What is always most difficult is trying to see things through the eye of a believer. I have enough problems teaching about Christianity where I am aware that my own personal views might upset the more fundamental believers.'

And, as another teacher admitted, 'it is so easy to fall into the trap of being patronising, gimmicky or superficial'.

More than one teacher put the blame squarely on the over-crowding of the syllabus: 'There are many exciting things going on in religious education but because the amount of "knowledge to get over" has increased so much a process of selection has to take place. This is where the danger of superficiality arises.' 'I stress that we can only learn a little of the complexities of Islam in the time available.'

But Islam does have a positive attraction for some teachers: 'I open the batting with Islam. Firstly, to start off interest and secondly because I am convinced that the crucible of world politics in the 1980s will be the Islamic world.'

The same teacher invites Muslim students from a nearby language school to come in as visiting speakers and encourages individual project work on such subjects as 'Islamic Decorative Art', 'Twentieth Century Mosques' and 'The Qur'an'. Like a number of schools in the same area, he also uses materials borrowed from a local religious education resources centre so that 'for a couple of weeks my room becomes a mosque complete with taped calls to prayer, prayer mats, incense, etcetera'.

A Midlands teacher organises visits to Birmingham Central Mosque and a 'nearby house-mosque', and is 'at present exploring the possibility of some of the pupils going out in pairs to visit Muslim families in order to eat with them and get to know the lived faith "from the inside" '.

A premature introduction to Islam can be counter-productive. A north Yorkshire teacher noted that:

> The more able first-formers seemed interested in the subject because it was new to them and they responded well. Some of the less able seemed lost though . . . simply confused by matters so far outside their normal 'ken'. This was rather tellingly demonstrated by one who wrote, as an exam answer, that Muhammad was an Irish saint. The child in question was not 'trying it on'!

Another teacher from the same area reported that work on Islam (together with 'Hinduism, Shinto, Sikhism and Buddhism, very much on an introductory basis') was done in the third year with pupils of mixed ability – 'mainly pupils with learning difficulties'.

The third year appears to be favoured in many schools, though the reasons for this are not necessarily adequate ones. As one teacher put it, 'If you argue that this is possibly too young, I would agree. It is simply a case of trying to fit a quart into a pint pot.'

The variety of learning activities employed by teachers can be seen in the following account by a Midlands teacher of his approach to Islam with third-year pupils.

1   Islam – an introduction. (General filmstrip shown. Examinations of some key words such as 'Islam', 'Muslim', 'Allah', 'Monotheism' etc.)

2   The distribution of Islam in the world today (map drawn).

3   Islam in Iran today. (The present-day happenings in Iran are looked at, the two-fold division within Islam explained.)

4   The 'five pillars of Islam' – general introduction. (A chart showing the pillars is drawn, the Arabic terms learnt, and so on.)

5   The first pillar of Islam. (Great emphasis is placed on Islamic Art as an avenue of understanding. Its non-representational tradition and the role of calligraphy are discussed. The pupils reproduce the Shahadah in 'Islamic' style.)

6   Prayer – the second pillar of Islam. (Artefacts concerned with prayer are examined: prayer-mat, prayer-beads, prayer-cap, qibla compass: a recording of the muezzin's call to prayer is heard.)

7   The mosque. (Slides of mosques around the world are shown and common features noted. A visit is made to Birmingham Central Mosque.)

8   Almsgiving – the third pillar of Islam.

9   Fasting – the fourth pillar of Islam. (With some groups a proportion of the pupils have chosen to fast in order to see 'what it is like'. This has given rise to some interesting observations and experiences.)

10   The Festival of Id-Ul-Fitr. (A video-taped television programme is viewed. Id cards are examined and then pupils make their 'own' Id card, remembering what was previously said – in 5 – about Islamic art and calligraphy.)

11   The city of Mecca and Ka'ba. (This forms a prelude to work on the hajj. A map is drawn, post-cards and slides looked at and so on.)

12   The hajj – the fifth pillar of Islam. (The complexity of this is a headache but we try to emphasise the significance of the hajj for the hajji rather than the many activities undertaken during the pilgrimage. A taped interview with an English Muslim who has just returned from the hajj is played.)

This is often as far as time allows us to go, though in the past there has sometimes been time to look more closely at (13) Muhammad, (14) the Qur'an, and (15) Islamic contributions to civilisation.

The same teacher emphasises strongly that

> work on Islam concentrates on the present reality of the faith rather than beginning with 'history' (Muhammad, spread of Islam, etc.) and working up to the present day. In my experience, the latter approach can easily lead to aridity and a sapping of life-force from the present manifestation of a religion. Instead we choose to use the 'five pillars' of Islam as the framework for our study and then move out tangentially from this in order to examine other important features (including historical connections).

Media coverage, particularly of recent events in Iran, has not, in the words of one teacher 'always encouraged the pupils to begin with a "sympathetic" attitude to the subject. They seem to have been left with an impression that the Qur'an is full of instructions to chop off limbs for minor criminal offences.' The response of this particular teacher was, therefore, to begin 'by asking them to assemble recent news reports about events in Islamic countries, so that any prejudice or rather superficial understanding might be brought into the open fairly quickly, and attempts might be made to balance what they saw as negative aspects of Islam, by reference to those features of the religion which they more readily see as positive, for example zakat, or the discipline of Muslim prayer'.

These concerns are echoed by another teacher from the same area: 'The recent happenings in Iran give a lot of useful materials but also create a lot of problems, especially since the Western press takes an "anti" standpoint. It is difficult to know oneself what is really going on. What impressions are our children getting?'

A third teacher from the same area had a slightly different approach to the use of press coverage: 'The pupils cut out, from their newspapers, articles about events in Northern Ireland to show that both Islam and Christianity have "followers" who do things which the rest of us might deplore.'

While some teachers 'do Islam' as such, others 'bring it in' from time to time within the framework of a syllabus organised on thematic lines. The syllabuses for public examinations provide examples of both approaches. With regard to public examinations, the evidence suggests a clear trend towards the provision of 'world religions' options encompassing Islam (see Appendix 7). The policies of the Boards show significant variations. Some have no syllabuses which deal with Islam. But provision of syllabuses at CSE level which do cover Islam is increasing. The recently announced decision to merge CSE and GCE examinations into a common examination at 16 plus may well lead to further significant changes.

CSE level syllabuses vary significantly in detail. Work on Islam could account for up to 60 per cent of the final marks of a candidate taking the examination offered by the North Regional Examination Board, whereas such work would account for only one sixth of the marks under the schemes offered by the West Yorkshire and Lindsey Regional Examining Board and the West Midlands Examinations Board. There are also notable differences in the detail with which the coverage of Islam is specified by the various Boards.

Rather fewer options are available at GCE O and A level. And there are similar differences in respect of the depth of detail and breadth of coverage between the schemes offered by the various Boards; contrast, for instance, the syllabuses specified by the Joint Matriculation Board and the Welsh Joint Education Committee.

Whatever the level and breadth of coverage expected, it is noteworthy that the general approach is almost universally a phenomenological one. Study of selected passages from the Qur'an is rarely specified. (The Welsh Joint Education Committee's A level is one example.) The contrast with the detailed references to biblical passages in most O level and some CSE syllabuses is striking.

It is also worthy of remark that some of the Boards specify affective as well as cognitive objectives. Indeed, the North Regional Examinations Board CSE syllabus stresses that:

> The *principal purpose* of this course is to enable the pupil to understand what it means to be a Muslim. More specifically this implies:
> 1 *Possessing an awareness* of the place which the Qur'an and the mosque hold for the Muslim.
> 2 *Appreciating his sense* of the unity of God and the significance of the other pillars of Islam.
> 3 *Understanding his attitude* to the prophet of Islam, Muhammad.
> 4 *Being aware* of the Muslim's sense of belonging to the community of Islam, the umma.
> 5 *Recognising* the contribution of Islamic culture to civilisation.
> 6 Having some knowledge of *what it means* to be a Muslim in Britain today.
> (emphases added)

The West Yorkshire and Lindsey Regional Examining Board likewise emphasises that with regard to its CSE syllabus theme C – Three Major Monotheistic Religions:

> This course of study is to be seen essentially as a quest for knowledge and

understanding through the fullest use of AVA within the classroom and by school visits wherever possible . . . The teaching should not consist of the presentation of a mass of unrelated facts. It should enable the pupils to understand the main themes and principles of the different faiths, and also to acquire some insight into the meaning and influence these have in the lives of those who believe in them . . .

On the other hand, the rubric of the Associated Lancashire Schools Examining Board CSE level regulations states that 'the aim of the syllabus is to present Christian teaching in a vital and relevant manner and to stimulate the application of it to twentieth-century life'.

The implications of the notion that Islam is not just a religion in the narrow, formal sense, but a complete way of life, the framework and manifestation of an entire cultural tradition, do not seem to have had much impact on the secondary school curriculum as a whole.

Other subjects

Islam has been seen as the concern of the religious education specialist. This is scarcely surprising. But that it should not also be the concern of other specialist teachers simply does not follow from that. Teachers of history and social studies (within which category I include humanities, integrated studies, and so on) have ample scope for introducing topics, examples and materials from 'the world of Islam' but there is little evidence to suggest that any significant steps have been taken in this direction.

Social studies teachers have a remarkable degree of freedom to determine their own syllabuses. In practice the same topics tend to recur and many of these, such as 'the family', 'minorities' and 'education' obviously provide opportunities to bring in an Islamic dimension. Nor would such a perspective be excluded from the course of study prescribed for public examinations. The Cambridge A level sociology syllabus, for instance, prescribes the study of socialisation, kinship relations, modernisation and cultural transmission (Paper I), and education, religion and race relations from the sociological point of view (Paper II). The JMB A level sociology syllabus offers a range of optional studies which includes the family, community, education, politics, welfare and work, any of which might admit the inclusion of examples and case-studies from the Islamic world.

Other subject specialists could also make relevant contributions. Art and design and craft courses could include work on Islamic textiles, ceramics, architecture and calligraphy. Indeed, a number of public examination syllabuses give scope for project work which could be devoted exclusively to a study of such a topic. The background to the way of life of Muslim communities could be provided by the teacher of geography, though it must be noted that the Middle East and South-East Asia have been curiously neglected in British schools, and recent trends in geography teaching, which have emphasised skills, concepts and quantitative methods, do not seem to encourage attention to the cultural and human aspects of man's relation to his environment.

Teachers of English – and of French – could examine some of the novels and poetry produced by Muslim writers or at least which relate to Muslim countries and concerns. Teachers of mathematics and science could pause to consider the contribution made to their disciplines by Arab and Persian scholars. Considering that the most recent British winner of the Nobel Prize for Physics was a Pakistani-born Muslim, this might not be inappropriate.

This book is intended to show that there are many ways of approaching Islam. The choice is ultimately the teacher's but in making that choice, and reviewing it once made, he or she should bear in mind some of the pitfalls which can beset his or her path.

Superficiality   Islam is a vast religion which currently embraces perhaps a fifth or more of mankind. Without inducing a sense of intellectual vertigo, teachers should try to ensure that pupils of whatever age do not receive the impression that they have 'done' Islam and that there is no more of significance to be learned. Teachers should, of course, be aware of the same danger in themselves.

Caricature   A desire to catch and retain the interest of pupils can lead to a damaging preoccupation with the more dramatic or apparently bizarre aspects of ritual and belief. These must be set both in their own context and against the background of more everyday practices. If pressure of time prohibits such careful treatment then this sort of approach is probably better avoided. In any case it is only likely to be truly successful in educational terms with the more informed and sophisticated type of pupil.

Condescension   This is a subtler form of caricature. It often takes the form of an apparently non-evaluative account of Muslim attitudes to such questions as pork, gambling, alcohol or the position of women in society followed by a dismissive curtailment of discussion.

Lack of perspective   This can arise from over-emphasis on the biography of the Prophet, as opposed to the content and impact of his message. Access too, and use of, Muslim literature is a good corrective to this tendency, though care must be taken to avoid relying too much on any single 'sectarian' viewpoint. (Proselytising groups are often the most prolific suppliers of free literature.)

Antiquarianism   Islam is a 'here and now' phenomenon as well as a 'then and there' one. Pupils should certainly know something of the early manifestations of Islam but they should also be aware of its historical development and especially of its current vitality and immediacy.

As the editor of *Learning for Living* once put it: 'Is the ordinary fifteen-year-old interested in the existence of God? If not, what makes us believe that he will be interested in Allah?' (January 1974).

A good question – perhaps we can find an answer in another question: 'To what question that the child is asking is what I am teaching an answer?' (For detailed consideration of the relationship between data from world religions and the questions and concerns of pupils, see the chapters on personal development in Robert Jackson (ed.), *Approaching World Religions*.[2] In particular, see Simon Weightman, 'Religious education and realisation'.)

Younger children concern themselves primarily with assimilating data about the physical, and later the social, world in which they find themselves. Most of their questions are couched in terms of 'what?' and later of 'where?', 'when?' and 'how?'. The answers that satisfy them are primarily descriptive and empirical and they relate them to a framework of reality which they accept as defined for them by the adults that they turn to as sources of information and authority.

Adolescents, by contrast, ask very different questions, not 'what?', but 'why?'. The framework of authority itself is questioned. The interrogation of self and others enters a new phase of intensity, focusing on key issues of authority and identity – the persistent 'why should I?' and the more profound 'who am I?' (sometimes appearing in the guise of 'who would I like to be?').

The relatively early onset and widespread sharing of this rebelliousness and existential unease is a peculiar characteristic of contemporary Western civilisation and it may no doubt arise in large part *because* the average fifteen-year-old (or his parents) is not interested in God.

The most seemingly intractable feature of a classroom situation might therefore provide the starting-point for a discussion of the following questions:

Why do so many teenagers think that religious education is boring and irrelevant?

Why are schools obliged to provide it?

Why do a majority of parents oppose its abolition?

What duties do parents and the State have in respect of children's religious upbringing?

At what age should these duties cease?

Are you aware that this situation is, historically speaking, quite new and very odd?

Traditionally, religion has provided absolute and authoritative answers to these very basic questions – 'Why should I?' and 'who am I?'. Even the sceptic who asserts that the absolute and authoritative status of these answers was self-defining cannot deny the massive historical reality of their consequences.

The study of Islam could be particularly rewarding from this point of view. As Frijthof Schuon observes, 'Islam seeks to implant certitude – its unitary faith stands forth as something manifestly clear without in any way renouncing mystery' (*Understanding Islam*, p. 16). Islam gives very clear and forceful answers to the questions 'why should I?' and 'who am I?'. It aims to leave no room for doubt.

A small illustration may be illuminating. At a teachers' conference in Bradford three Muslim boys nervously approached the guest speaker, a learned *imam*, and asked for an authoritative ruling on a matter of urgent personal concern to them – was long hair 'un-Islamic'? The imam replied, of course, that he would have to consult the *hadith*.

Whether or not non-Muslim teenagers could be brought to an understanding of why Muslims regard such a mode of seeking guidance as natural and reasonable, they could surely benefit by discussing the advantages and disadvantages, both for the individual and for society as a whole, of having an explicit and totally comprehensive code of behaviour covering every aspect of life from dress and diet to sex and war. Ethical and psychological uncertainties dissolve as one finds peace (Islam) through the act of submission (Islam) – 'Who am I?' 'You are a Muslim.' 'Why should I do X?' 'Because it is *sunna* for a Muslim to do X.' The discussion could then be developed along the following lines:

(i) How can a code which is both comprehensive and based on revelation manage to provide answers to the questions raised by social and technological change?

(ii) How can such a code co-exist with other codes of behaviour and what difficulties can this create for the believer (for example the problems of a Muslim in a non-Muslim society)?

One may well, of course, meet such responses as: 'Well, I wouldn't do all those things!', 'I think you ought to be able to make up your own mind about things' and so on. To which one must reply, 'But if you had been brought up as Muslim since birth you would feel differently about it, at least until non-Muslim friends began to put doubts in your mind. And then what would you do in such a person's place? And what would be the consequences of your actions?'

Teachers who make no headway with this approach might find it helpful to come to Islam from the opposite direction, so to speak, by examining the ideas and practices of the Sufis. The difference between the Sufi and what, for want of a better word, one can call the 'mainstream' Muslim, can also be expressed in terms of the problems of identity and authority. Once the mainstream Muslim has accepted his identity as a Muslim, his only problem is to inform himself of the modes of behaviour laid down as 'sunna'. But for the Sufi the question of appropriate behaviour in the everyday world of social relations is both less significant and less urgent than the question of his personal relationship to God. Disregarding most of the 'why should I?' issues as trivial, he seeks a deeper, different answer to the other question – 'Who am I?' – and this leads into a whole realm of philosophical questions, revolving around the central question 'How can I know?'

Any teacher who flinches at the thought of presenting such abstract speculations to students preoccupied by the mundane and the material can take comfort from the fact that many Sufis faced the same difficulties. Not a few decided that it was either futile or unwise to try to lift the scales from the eyes of the blind and they were better left to a treadmill of formalistic observances and fundamentalist beliefs. But some of them expressed their concerns lucidly in poetry or gnomically in ambiguous anecdotes and riddles. No doubt many students would be willing to volunteer a consumer's eye-view of this venerable corpus of teaching material.

Sources

1 In W. Owen Cole (ed.), *World Faiths in Education* (Allen & Unwin, 1978).
2 Robert Jackson (ed.), *Approaching World Religions* (John Murray, 1982).

25
The Multi-faith Situation

Reviewing new books on Islam and Sikhism for school-age readers, an Indian scholar observed that:

> In theory, all religions have exclusivist claims . . . In practice, wherever one religious or philosophical system dominates, the others are cramped. Most people in Britain are not conscious of this, for they have been taught not to regard the rationalist/materialist/hedonist consensus of British society as 'religious'. But its rituals don't take much intelligence to decipher, the price it demands for its adherents is terrible, and its consequences on other religions are clearly debilitating. And it is because of the secularist debilitation of organised Christianity that multi-religious education has finally begun to be acceptable. (Prabhu Guptara, 'Brotherhood of Man', *The Times Educational Supplement*, 8 May 1981)

Acceptable to whom? In a paper given to the First World Conference on Muslim Education at Mecca in April 1977, Afzal Rahman, chairman of the Muslim Educational Trust, emphasised the extent to which 'the nature of religious education is undergoing a dramatic change' and cited such examples as:

(i) The Birmingham agreed syllabus, which 'takes the view that the subject should be Religious Education – emphasising both these words'.

(ii) The Free Church Federal Council's acceptance that the syllabus should include 'the ideological stands of those unable to accept or practise the tenets of any religious faith'.

(iii) The Association of Christian Teachers' acknowledgement that there should be 'an examination of other significant world views', including those 'which have no overt religious basis'.

After further references to the pronouncements of the Religious Education Council, the Christian Education Movement and the Schools Council he concludes that:

> There seems to be a general trend among all opinions, including religious as well as secular, towards more liberalism in religious education leading almost to a non-religious or an irreligious type of religious education in schools . . . This type of education is diametrically opposed to the Islamic philosophy of education. There is bound to be a dominant Christian element in multi-faith studies and all other religions, including Islam, will be taught by Christian or other non-Muslim

teachers who will not, for obvious reasons, present the true picture of Islam. Gradually Muslim children will be integrated in Western society. (*The Times Educational Supplement*, 1 April 1977)

By contrast, Muhammad Iqbal, addressing the same conference, reported that: 'At a conference on "Christian-Muslim dialogue in education" [held in Birmingham in July 1974] when the Birmingham RE Syllabus was being discussed, everyone agreed that a major part of the school timetable should be devoted to the study of Christian traditions, Great Britain being a Christian country.' And elsewhere the same writer has declared that: 'British Muslims realise very well the fact that because of the lack of qualified Muslim teachers Islam will have to be taught by non-Muslim RE teachers, especially in a multi-faith situation, and there is bound to be teaching of Christianity as a predominant element in RE' (*The Times Educational Supplement*, 21 April 1978).

Although some Muslims are still dismissive in their attitude towards what Afzal Rahman has referred to as the 'hotch-potch of all religions . . . taught in schools', an increasing number have come to accept and appreciate the distinction between religious instruction and religious education and, indeed, are likely to be among the most outspoken opponents of moves to deprive RE of its special status in the school curriculum.

School assembly remains, however, a potential cause of friction and difficulty. In a pamphlet on *Problems and Rights of Muslim Parents Regarding the Education of their Children*[1] the following advice is given:

> Section 25 of the Education Act gives the right to Muslim parents to withdraw their children both from Morning Assembly and the religious education periods. It is the legal right of every parent to withdraw his child and no Local Education Authority can ever refuse this request by the parent. This matter is not in the hands of the Local Education Authority, and they cannot force any Muslim child to attend Morning Assembly or religious education periods against their parents' wishes.
>
> It may also be pointed out that Muslim parents and their children should not feel guilty or keep any complex in their mind for taking this step because Jewish and Roman Catholic parents also withdraw their children from Morning Assembly and religious education periods. There would not be any stigma or black mark against Muslim children for withdrawing from these periods. The school authorities even do not bother about such minor issues, especially when they are related to religious beliefs of people.

Whether or not withdrawal from assembly is a 'minor issue' is very much a matter of scale. If one or a few children are involved the impact on the school community is very different, both psychologically and administratively, from a situation in which dozens or even hundreds of children might be involved. And where this leads to the involvement of decision-makers other than the persons directly involved (such as imams and local councillors), a satisfactory resolution of the issue can become extremely difficult. Calderdale Local Education Authority provides a case in point. In 1980 a Halifax mosque leader suggested that all Muslim children be withdrawn from prayers at a local primary school. The Chief Education Officer, noting that in four central Halifax schools there was a 'preponderance' of Muslim children and in two they were in the majority, said it was up to parents to withdraw their children if they wished. A proposal that alterations to the agreed syllabus should be discussed by the Advisory Council on religious education was defeated and talks with Muslim leaders were rejected. One Conservative Councillor was reported as having said that 'This is a Christian country and we assume religious assembly in the mornings will be Christian assembly', and another that 'I don't see why religious education should be altered to suit anybody other than the actual system as it now is.' A Labour Councillor was reported as saying that 'As a Christian I saw my opportunity of being an evangelist and preaching the Christian message to the Muslims . . . There is nothing wrong in that.' And while one Conservative Councillor warned against the danger of creating a 'them and us' situation, the Education Committee Chairman noted that other religions had set up their own aided schools and concluded that 'there is no reason why that should not be a further development if that was the strength of feeling in certain areas of the town' (*Halifax Courier*, 18 April 1980).

Rochdale has supplied another example of such difficulties. In the autumn of 1980 'Asian' children at a middle school brought 'letters of a standard type on standard sheets of paper', signed by their parents, requesting their withdrawal from assembly. The headmaster is reported to have tried 'to reach a compromise formula' and to have observed that 'my feeling of assembly is that it is an expression of shared fellowship in which we should attempt to keep the children together. We can still have hymns; and prayers, say, based on the Bible. No offence in that to Muslims.' When a number of local clergymen wrote to Cyril Smith, MP, to express their concern over changes in the content of assembly in the school he referred the matter to the Secretary of State. A member of the local Council for Racial Equality is reported to have said that 'I doubt that the Asian parents are satisfied yet with the changes that have been made' (*The Times Educational Supplement*, 20 February 1981).

At a conference on Muslim and Christian issues in education arranged by the Church of England Board of Education, Dr Zaki Badawi, Director of the Islamic Cultural Centre, is reported to have made the following plea: 'To simply exclude the child from assembly or religious education lessons is punishment. It amounts to saying the child is not a member of the group. Muslims must seek for modification in assembly. Could not it simply put forward a monotheistic view?'

The opportunities of the multi-faith situation need little elaboration – Islam can be presented as a real and living force in the lives of actual people who can (but obviously should not be pressed to) give a personal account of their beliefs and experiences. Difficulties cannot always be avoided but they can normally be minimised by intelligent forethought and careful preparation. Obviously, the specific situation will vary according to the proportion of Muslims in the class and the school, the presence of other non-Christian groups, the age-level of the children, and the nature and extent of the social and religious organisations existing in the wider and Muslim community. Whatever the particular situation facing the teacher he can usefully ask himself the following questions and take the appropriate action:

(i) How will the Muslims in my class interpret and react to my intention to teach about Islam? How will their parents react? Will they see the difference between teaching *about* a religion and evangelising?

(ii) How much do the Muslims in my class already know about their faith and culture? What do they feel about Islam? Are they receiving formal instruction at a mosque? If so, what is its content and how can I best take account of this in my teaching?

(iii) Should I draw explicit comparisons between Islam and Christianity or other faiths? Should I seek to confront the problem of prejudice and misinformation or not? Should I adopt an indirect strategy (for example introducing Islam via its culture or history)? Can the school situation be changed to assist me (for example Qur'anic reading at morning assembly; books on Islam in the library: Islamic artwork in the corridors)?

(iv) What support and assistance can I look for both among my colleagues and outside the school?

(v) How can I know when I have been successful?

Can a non-Muslim teach Islam?

In an article on 'Can a non-Muslim teach Islam?' (*The Minaret*, vol. 1, no. 2, April–June 1977) Edward Hulmes has given two obvious but salutary reminders: 'If the teacher is wise, he will keep in close touch with Muslims, seeking their advice about matters of detail, and checking his material in order to avoid misrepresentation whenever possible.' '. . . If the Muslim community insists that it is wholly improper for non-Muslims even to begin to speak about Islam, and if a fence is erected between them and those who do not share their way of life, then the understanding that is beginning to emerge will itself be damaged.' He concludes that:

> In an obvious sense, the non-Muslim cannot 'teach Islam', but quite apart from the fact that he is not permitted to proselytise on behalf of *any* religion in our county schools, it is naive to assume that he would want to anyway or that in *teaching about* Islam he sees himself involved in anything other than a strictly limited educational exercise. At the present time his role may be narrowly defined, but it is an important one, concerned as it is with knowledge, attitudes and understanding. It is not to be dismissed lightly.

Sources

1 *Problems and Rights of Muslim Parents Regarding the Education of their Children* (Muslim Educational Trust, n.d.).

Further reading

Agreed Syllabus of Religious Education (City of Birmingham Education Committee, 1975).

Living Together: A Teacher's Handbook of Suggestions for Religious Education (City of Birmingham Education Committee, 1975).

W. Owen Cole (ed.), *Religion in the Multi-Faith School* (Yorkshire Committee for Community Relations, 1973).

W. Owen Cole (ed.), *World Faiths in Education* (Allen & Unwin, 1978). See especially the chapter by Riadh El Droubie and the appendix by Brian Gates.

Edward Hulmes, *Commitment and Neutrality in Religious Education* (Geoffrey Chapman, 1979).

M. Iqbal, *Religious Education in a Multi-Religious Society* (Schools Council, Secondary Schools Bulletin, Summer 1971).

Robert Jackson (ed.), *Approaching World Religions* (John Murray, 1982). This book deals in detail with issues relating to practical classroom work, pluralism, commitment, the personal development of pupils and the relationship between religious education, moral education, political education and world studies. Most chapters refer to the multi-faith situation.

Robert Jackson (ed.), *Perspectives on World Religions* (School of Oriental and African Studies, 1978). See especially the editor's introductory chapter. Available from SOAS, Extramural Division, Malet Street, London WC1E 7HP.

W. Weaver, *Religious Education in a Multi-Racial Society* (Community Relations Commission, 1971.

See also the publications of the Standing Conference on Inter-Faith Dialogue in Education (SCIFDE), e.g. J. Prickett (ed.), *Initiation Rites* (Lutterworth, 1978), and *Death* (Lutterworth, 1980).

26

Primary and Middle Schools

The general problem of teaching about world religions in primary schools has been dealt with by Jean Holm in a companion volume in this series (Robert Jackson (ed.), *Approaching World Religions*).[1] She emphasises the importance of the living aspects of faith as they are experienced by children in terms of festivals, life-styles and personal relationships and recommends that in devising schemes of work, teachers should take account of the following needs:

(i) 'Start with the concrete' ('what can be seen, either literally or in pictorial form').

(ii) 'Lots of detail' – 'Juniors love collecting things, including facts'.

(iii) 'A positive attitude towards religions' – 'we should introduce children first to those aspects which they are likely to admire'.

(iv) 'Pupils should be learning about living religions'.

(v) 'Children need access to a variety of resources'.

(vi) 'Children need to undertake practical activities related to the religions they are learning about'.

The following suggestions are intended to supplement rather than replicate the schemes offered by Jean Holm and other experts in this field. Many of the suggestions are aimed at upper junior and middle school pupils. Teachers may find some of the topics and ideas suitable for use with lower secondary pupils.

Festivals

Younger children could make a first study of Islam through its festivals. A short pamphlet on *Muslim Festivals and Ceremonials*[2] might prove very useful to the teacher wishing to take this approach. See also G.E. Von Grünebaum's *Muhammadan Festivals*.[3]

The following framework might be used:

(i) How do we know when to celebrate festivals? (The Islamic Calendar). What year are we in now? What are names of the months of the Islamic Calendar? (Muharram, Safar, Rabi'ul-Awwal, Rabi'ut Akhir, Jamadi al-Awwal, Jamadi al-Akhir, Rajab, Sha'ban, Ramadan, Shawwal, Dhul-Hijja)

The teacher could go on to explain how classical Islamic civilisation contributed to the more accurate measurement of time through advances in astronomy (perhaps focusing on the astronomer-poet Umar Khayyam, or using pictures of astrolabes or the vast buildings and instruments of the Mughal observatory at Jaipur). This work could perhaps be undertaken in co-operation with colleagues teaching mathematics and geography.

(ii) Friday as Yaum ul-Jum'a (the Day of Assembly – as opposed to the idea of a day of rest). The mosque. The *muezzin* and what he calls. The *imam* (how he differs from a priest). Preparing for prayer by ablution. Prayer – the words and ritual movements. Prayer at other times and places.

(iii) Eid-ul-Fitr (festival of fast-breaking) celebrated on 1st Shawwal, following immediately after Ramadan. Why do Muslims fast? What does fasting mean? Who doesn't have to fast? (the very young, the sick, travellers, soldiers). How is Eid-ul-Fitr celebrated? (Congregational prayer, a sermon on the theme of charity, giving of alms and gifts, exchanging visits and telling stories)

(iv) Eid-ul-Adha (the festival of sacrifice) is celebrated on 10th Dhul-Hijja to coincide with the completion of the rites of *hajj*. Each household sacrifices a lamb or sheep and distributes two-thirds of it as alms and gifts. The teacher could link this festival with a description of the hajj or a description of Muslim dietary practices.

ILEA themes for the primary school

In 1975 the Inner London Education Authority published a booklet of teacher's notes entitled *Religious Education in Primary Schools: Suggestions by an ILEA Working Party*. Dr Hyde's Foreword emphasises that 'The suggestions are not intended to replace more traditional work, but rather to show ways of building foundations for religious understanding as distinct from imparting factual knowledge about religion.' The booklet outlines ways in which ten broad themes can be developed through the exploration of everyday experience to bring out implicit religious significances. A teacher using one of the following themes might introduce Islamic examples and perspectives thus:

Shelter

Different types of shelter in different Muslim countries – contrast bedouin tent, Punjabi village house, modern Cairo flat, mud 'skyscrapers' in Sana'a, to show how types of shelter are conditioned by climate and availability of materials. The implicit theme of security could be developed via fortified towns (physical security) to organised compassion (social security) within the Muslim *umma* by means of *zakat* (almsgiving) and *waqf* (property left as a pious bequest). Older children might begin to understand how Islam, which proclaims God and his Creation and man's place within it, can provide for the individual's psychological security.

Alternatively, one could emphasise the difference between a mere house and a home, the difference lying not just in furnishings and decoration or the meeting of basic human needs (sleep, food, warmth, clean clothes), though all of these could be noted and the differences and similarities between Muslim and non-Muslim homes noted, but in the quality of family life and the concern of its members for one another. Two features of Muslim family life are especially worthy of note:

(i) The great importance that Islam has traditionally ascribed to the wife and mother as home-maker (numerous *hadith* can be quoted).

(ii) The strength of the extended family structure: this could be demonstrated visually via family gatherings at times of festival, weddings and so on or by the ways in which immigrant families help each other with the problems of adjusting to life in England (homes, jobs, school, health) and keep in touch with their families in their country of origin. Children might like to learn other language equivalents for 'mother', 'father', 'uncle', 'elder brother' etc.

Communication

How do Muslims greet one another? How can Muslims recognise one another? (for example dress)
The ritual of Muslim prayer as a symbol of man's willing submission to God.
The Arabic language as a link between Muslims of many nations.
Making a frieze of things that all Muslims would recognise (for example Allah in Arabic script, the Ka'ba, a minaret, a prayer carpet, a Qur'an).

Our senses

Sight: colour and geometric shapes in Islamic design (carpets, tiles, and so on); work of medieval Muslim scientists in optics and eye-diseases; what does it mean to have a vision? (Muhammad's visions).
Sound: sounds of prayer and Qur'anic recitation: importance of recited poetry in Arabic and Urdu; role of the story-teller in the Middle East and South Asia (at festivals, fairs and feasts – the One Thousand and One Nights); music and musical instruments in the Islamic world: making simple flutes and drums.
Touch: materials used by craftsmen and the texture they create (soft textiles, sharp swords); the skill of the craftsman's hands (metalwork, pottery, carpets).
Smells: perfumes, how they are made; trade in perfumes.
Taste: foodstuffs, sweets and spices, where they come from and how they are prepared; how we develop preferences.

Sky and space

Descriptions of the heavens in the Qur'an and Muhammad's use of them as evidence of the majesty of God's creation and of rain from the heavens as the source of renewed life.

The work of Muslim astronomers; the instruments they used (for example the observatory at Jaipur); Umar Khayyam and the Muslim Calendar.

Using stars to guide caravans through the desert by night.

Is Heaven an actual place?

Stones

Worship of stones and idols in Muslim Arabia; hence Muslim prohibition of sculpture and artistic representations of living things because they might be worshipped.

The Black Stone and the Ka'ba as the first 'House of God'; symbolic stoning of devils during the rites of hajj.

Stone used as a building material in mosques, forts, bridges.

Precious stones and their symbolism; the craft of the jeweller.

Sharing – a theme for the multicultural school

British teachers are becoming increasingly familiar with such phrases as 'pluralism', 'a multi-racial society', 'mutual respect' and so on. They occur with ever-growing frequency in speeches by politicians and pundits, newspaper editorials and the reports of numberless committees and working-parties. If they are not to remain at the level of airy platitudes or to fossilise into meaningless clichés, they must acquire not merely a general currency but a more precise and comprehensive usage with clear implications for action and practice. What, for instance, do we mean by 'respect' – merely avoiding open disrespect for the beliefs and customs of others? Or making a positive effort to achieve an empathetic understanding of different cultural standards and seeking an active accommodation between those standards and our own? How far, one might ask, can any accommodation be truly *mutual* in a society whose overall framework bears with it 1500 years of Christian values, assumptions, taboos, customs and prejudices? This heritage – whatever one's estimation of the current state of institutionalised Christianity – is still a living heritage and an active component of our daily lives and thoughts and actions. This Christian heritage may be all but invisible to most people in Britain today. Those brought up in a different tradition will have less difficulty in perceiving it.

Teachers are, then, necessarily engaged in the task of working out in detail and practice the values appropriate for a multi-cultural society which seeks to reconcile the maintenance of social harmony with the continuance of cultural diversity. This will not be achieved in a short time or by good intentions alone. Thought, experience and judgement will be required. In helping children to formulate and clarify their own values, teachers will undoubtedly re-examine their own. Needless to say, a great deal will depend on the primary school teacher, whose many responsibilities include guiding the child's first steps into the world of organised social existence.

As a people, the British do not seem to care much for abstractions. Some teachers may therefore be either suspicious or slightly uncomfortable when confronted with the proposition that they should teach 'values'. But values are very commonplace things and can be seen and heard on any school playground at break-time – 'Hey, that isn't *fair*!' 'I don't *trust* her'. And a value which seems both appropriate and potentially fruitful as an explicit integrating concept for the multi-cultural classroom is the simple idea of 'sharing'.

Islam is about sharing, and sharing can be related both to the overtly religious experiences which bind man to God and to the ethical prescriptions which bind man to his fellows. The Five Pillars of the Faith (see Chapter 6) can be presented in the light of this idea of sharing.

1 *The Profession of Faith* must be made in the presence of other believing Muslims. It is whispered in the ear of a new-born baby. These acts represent the sharing of knowledge of God's truth revealed to man.

2 *Prayer* may be individual, but is more often communal and on Fridays at noon is congregational. Muslims share the experience of worship.

3 *Fasting*. The individual feels the pangs of hunger but does so as a member of an entire community which is fasting. The experience enables him to share the sufferings of the poor and hungry. The ending of the fast is marked by a great communal festival (eid-al-Fitr).

4 *Charity*. The giving of alms exemplifies very clearly the Islamic obligation to share one's property with others. Numerous quotations can be found in the Qur'an relating to the duty of care for widows and orphans. The institution of waqf could also be mentioned.

5 *Pilgrimage* is a great spiritual experience in which the individual and collective aspects cannot be separated. By meeting together at Mecca, Muslims can share their sense of belonging to a world-wide community, the *umma*, which embraces all believers. Sharing the hazards and expenses of a long journey also reinforces this experience.

The idea of sharing could be developed by showing how, in the Middle Ages, Muslims shared useful knowledge with the peoples they came in contact with (new crops, irrigation systems, medical and architectural techniques, 'Arabic' numerals and so on) or by arranging a social occasion (perhaps involving parents) in which Muslim and non-Muslim children could share food and listen to stories. It would be important to emphasise that Muslims do not just share experiences, beliefs and goods with each other. Muslims and non-Muslims can both share a belief in God as Creator and Guide, concern for weaker members of the community, a duty to deal justly and kindly with fellow men, and the delight in the beauty of the natural world.

Caravan

Trade, learning and the hajj (pilgrimage to Mecca), three motives for travel, were all made easier by Islam, which honoured the merchant, the scholar and the pilgrim, prescribed that charity and hospitality be shown toward them and supplied, in Arabic, an international language for travellers. The idea of a camel-caravan of travellers, moving from the fringes of the Islamic world towards one of its great centres (Cairo, Damascus, Baghdad or Mecca itself) and picking up new travellers along the route, could provide a serviceable framework – both comprehensive and flexible – for role-playing or imaginative writing.

Every member of a class (even the largest class) can research and build up for himself an identity as an individual traveller, with a name and character, distinctive dress and preferences in food and leisure, a motive for travel, goods to trade, a background of city and family ties and a story to tell (for example about hospitality to travellers!) at one of the caravan's many stopping-places (which can also be described). It is worth making the point that caravans usually travelled by night (it was cooler) and therefore had to navigate by the stars. This could lead into a discussion of Islamic achievements of astronomy and related fields (geography, astrology, mathematics). The journey can be set in a particular century and along a specific route, affording the opportunity for accurate historical reconstruction through careful deduction from the evidence available (i.e. What could the travellers not have seen? Was a town that is in ruins now in ruins then?). It would probably be helpful to relate role-playing and writing to a large-scale map showing the caravan's chosen route. Drawings of a caravanserai (a building specially designed as a resting-place for caravans) and other buildings seen along the route could be added to make a wall-display. A 'snakes and ladders' or 'ludo' type of board game, illustrating the hazards and rewards of caravan travel, could also be devised. (Instead of throwing dice, contestants could ask each other questions from a prepared pack to enable them to move forward.) 'Caravans' should serve to illustrate the enormous size of the Islamic world and the social attitudes and institutions which made trade and travel possible over vast tracts of inhospitable terrain. E.W. Bovill, *Caravans of the Old Sahara*,[4] would be relevant further reading for this project. Descriptions of caravans can be found in the works of Sir Richard Burton, Edward Lane and Ibu Battuta. An anonymous account appears in Hakluyt, *Principal Navigations*.[5]

Stamps

Postage stamps can be used both to illustrate the vast extent of the Muslim world (perhaps by relating a display of stamps to a world map) and to show the sort of things that Muslims value and are proud of. Famous mosques are a favourite motif. Egypt has issued stamps showing the al-Azhar, Jordan the Dome of the Rock in Jerusalem, Saudi Arabia the Prophet's mosque in Medina and so on. Stories from the 'Arabian Nights' figure in a recent series issued by the United Arab Emirates. Any major catalogue will provide dozens of examples, stretching over a century and from more than fifty countries. The very use of Arabic script on the stamps of non-Arab but Muslim countries such as Iran and Pakistan can be pointed out as an illustration of the unifying power of language and writing.

Shadow theatre

When the Sultan Saladin asked al-Qadi al Fadil if he had liked the show, he answered 'I witnessed a great lesson. I saw some rich people come and go and when the curtain dropped there was only one person who moved them' (quoted in Littman, *Arab Shadow Shows*).

The shadow theatre has been known in the Islamic world since at least the twelfth century and has traditionally been enjoyed in palace and market-place alike. Many teachers of younger children may find that it could be turned to advantage in the classroom. A shadow-theatre production offers scope for a wide range of activities, capable of involving pupils of widely differing aptitudes, interests and levels of ability, for example:

(i)   researching details of costume and architecture;
(ii) drawing and cutting out the shadow-puppets and scenery;
(iii) assembling and working the puppets;
(iv) writing the narration and dialogue;
(v)   performing the narration and dialogue;
(vi) stage-managing (erecting the sheet-screen and light source: organising performers);
(vii) performing background music and sound effects.

In terms of classroom management it may be better to avoid involving the whole class on a single project, especially if this means multiplying characters and scenes, as over-ambitious productions can generate conflicts and may never be completed. It would, therefore, probably be better to divide into groups of five or six, each group aiming to present a five to ten minute play with three or four characters. Groups could take different subjects or, if they were all given the same basic story-line or plot (for example 'write a play about hospitality') offer different versions which would then form the basis for discussion.

Puppets should be made twelve to eighteen inches high, of thick card (tissue-paper and paper doilies could be used to effect) using paper-fasteners to articulate limbs, head and so on, which are moved by means of thin rods (e.g. old knitting-needles). As many Middle Eastern characters will wear long flowing garments the design of body outlines is simplified, but there is a correspondingly greater need to delineate characters by their headgear and accoutrements (for example shepherd's staff, grand vizier's wand of office, soldier's scimitar). Simple scenery (domed mosques, minarets, palm trees, city walls and gates) can also be useful. Animals (camels, donkeys, sheep) should also be in evidence (but *not* pigs). Animals are often main characters in fables.

Many themes suggest themselves for dramatisation. One could use actual historical events associated with the spread of Islam, 'The Thousand and One Nights', the Crusades, the history of the great Muslim dynasties and empires (see Chapter 31) or the folk-tales which have themselves been the basis of shadow-theatre from Istanbul to Cairo. The Islamic equivalent to Aesop's fables are the fables of Bidpai, derived from India. Turkey has given us Nasruddin Hoca, a comic character whose adventures and comments are often very perceptive. For a variant of these stories see Idries Shah's collection of stories *The Exploits of the Incomparable Mulla Hasrudin*.[6] It should be noted that some Muslims might find the representation of *sacred* subjects in this form objectionable.

Numbers and shapes

The practice of Islam has always demanded a knowledge of mathematics to solve such practical problems as working out shares of property according to Islamic laws of inheritance (quadratic equations were useful for this) and calculating the times and direction of prayer. Muslim scholars did, however, come to take a great interest in mathematics for its own sake, making algebra into a systematic field of study and inventing trigonometry. They also passed on to the West the use of 'Arabic' (really Indian) numerals, including the concept of zero, which enormously simplified the tasks of multiplication and division. (Our word 'cipher' comes from the Arabic 'sifr', an empty space, which stood for zero.)

The first great mathematician was al-Khwarizmi (d.846) (the English word 'algorithm' is a distortion of his name) but Umar Khayyam (d.1123) the Persian courtier and poet, who devised a new calendar, is probably better known in the West.

Muslim mathematicians also excelled in geometry and, because Muslims were forbidden to represent living creatures in their art, complex geometric patterns became a leading feature of Islamic architecture and decoration. Variations on the star motif were especially favoured.

Muslim mathematicians were fascinated by 'magic squares' in which the numbers, whether added up downwards, across or diagonally, always came to the same sum. Here is a simple one in which the numbers 1 – 9 are used but not repeated:

8	1	6
3	5	7
4	9	2

This one uses the numbers 1 – 16 without repetition:

16	2	3	13
5	11	10	8
9	7	6	12
4	14	15	1

In this famous square from India not only do all the numbers add up to 34 but so do all adjacent 2 × 2 squares:

15	10	3	6
4	5	16	9
14	11	2	7
1	8	13	12

Further suggestions for 'Multi-ethnic mathematics' can be found in the article by Ray Hemmings in *Multi-racial Education* (Summer 1980). On geometrical patterns see *The Islamic Colouring Book*,[7] J. Bourgoin, *Arabic Geometrical Pattern and Design*,[8] and Keith Albarn, Jenny Miall Smith, Stanford Steele and Dinah Walker, *The Language of Pattern*.[9]

The call of the minaret: A discursive introduction to Islam

Given the practical impossibility of providing a completely comprehensive survey of Islam it might well be argued that the busy teacher should regard the situation as one in which he or she can feel free to follow his or her own interests and those of the class, as they become apparent, rather than attempt to 'cover the ground'. A discursive approach can not only be fun, it can also illustrate the way in which so many facets of Islamic culture link on to one another more clearly than a rigidly structured study might do.

The example given below may seem at first glance rather teacher-centred. In practice it should give plenty of scope for pupil activity. Its emphasis is as much visual as verbal and it could, hopefully, be modified to meet the needs of younger or less academic children.

The minaret

(i) Draw an example of a 'typical' minaret on the blackboard (such as the 'pencil' type developed by Ottoman architects).

(ii) Explain what it is for.

(iii) Ask the class to collect other examples and make their own sketches. One could be taken from every country in which Islam is practised.

(iv) Reporting back. This should include locating the examples on a large sketch-map and noting differences and similarities in style and structure (some are free-standing, some integral; some mosques have only one minaret, others have many; some minarets are round, others square, spiral or octagonal; materials, proportions and decoration also differ from period to period and country to country).

(v) This approach should enable the teacher to emphasise the following major points: the great geographic spread of Islam; the variety of different traditions which have been incorporated in Islamic art (one could use the analogy of an Islamic 'house' with rooms furnished in Arab, Persian, Indian and other styles; and note that after a while the furniture began to get rather mixed up); the way in which these distant regions and diverse traditions are held together by Islamic rituals (prayer and hajj) and customs (relating to food, marriage and so on) – Islam, in other words, exhibits both unity and diversity at the same time; the time-span covered by the spread of the faith (for example by contrasting the eighth-century mosque at Qayrwan with the twentieth-century National Mosque at Kuala Lumpur).

The call to prayer

(i) Play a recording of the dawn call to prayer in Arabic. Write up the words in English and discuss the main beliefs that it expresses (God's greatness and oneness; Muhammad's role as bringer of God's message to Man; the value of prayer).

(ii) Emphasise that throughout the Islamic world the summons to prayer is made in Arabic, regardless of the local language of the country. It may help to refer back to the sketch-map to reinforce this point.

(iii) Discuss the use of Arabic as both the devotional language of Islam and the language of the Qur'an. Are the central features of the faith better understood by ordinary people when it is in their own everyday language? Does understanding lead to more or less piety? Does the use of a special devotional language enhance the power of a ritual or not? Does a religion which uses such language tend to come under the control of the privileged few with access to education? Remember to emphasise that the vast majority of Muslims do not speak Arabic as their native language (but rather Urdu, Hausa, Farsi, and so on) and that Arabic, unlike Sanskrit, Pali, Latin and other devotional languages, is still a living tongue.

The act of prayer

> We cannot express our being in any way more directly than in speech . . . Islam therefore makes it central in its rites which revolve most of all around prayer. (S.H. Nasr)

(i) Show slides of the ritual gestures for the act of prayer. (The class could attempt to learn the cycle right through.)

(ii) Discuss the place of prayer in Islam. Indicate the significance of ritual ablution, precise gestures and words and the timing of daily and other prayers. Compare with Christian, Jewish and other practices.

(iii) Develop understanding of the Islamic conception of God and his relation to man by using Sura 1 ('the Opening') (used in all daily prayers) which could be compared with the Lord's Prayer.

(iv) Locate Mecca on the map and explain why, for Muslims it determines the *qibla* (direction of prayer)

(a) site of the Ka'ba

(b) object of the hajj

(c) birthplace of the Prophet and the scene of his early preaching and eventual triumph.

(v) Repeat the theme of unity and diversity of a world-wide faith by reference to qibla and hajj.

Servants of the Faith

(i) Describe the roles of the muezzin and the imam.

(ii) Compare the role of the imam with that of the Christian priest.

The mosque

(i) Explain that the Arabic word 'masjid' means 'a place of prostration' and that Muslims may pray anywhere. Attendance at the mosque for the noon prayer on Friday is customary for all adult male Muslims.

(ii) Draw a ground-plan and front and side elevations of a mosque, indicating the main architectural features and their significance (court-yard, prayer-hall, dome, minaret, mihrab, minbar).

(iii) Discuss how the mosque is used as a school, meeting place, etc.

(iv) Returning to the original examples of minarets selected above, assign each pupil the task of researching the mosque of which it forms a part, using the following outline:

(a) Draw a ground plan and general view.

(b) Who built it? When? What was happening in the Islamic world at that time?

(c) Does the mosque have any special architectural features (in layout, structure, materials or decoration)? If so, make sketches of them and find similar examples in other mosques.

(d) How has the mosque changed since it was first built?

(e)   Have any famous events happened at or near the mosque? Have any famous people visited it? If so, write a short account of them.

(v) The resulting sketches and written accounts could then be mounted as an exhibition using the original map of the Islamic world as a centre-piece.

Possible variations and developments

(i) Using selected mosques as the starting point for a general exploration of their historical background:

(a)   Cordoba – the conquest – Muslim culture and its influence on Europe – Toledo and Granada – the reconquest and the Cid – the Muslim legacy in Spain.

(b)   Ibu Tulun, Cairo – conquest of North Africa – emergence of Cairo as the cultural and commercial centre of Islam – Al Azhar University – the Mamluks.

(c)   Sulemaniye, Istanbul – rivalry of Byzantium and Islam – emergence of the Ottomans and the fall of Constantinople – the reconstruction of the city – Sulaiman – Sinan.

(ii) Various aspects of Islamic culture could, as has been suggested, be explored as they arise in discussion. Thus the Arabic language could lead on to calligraphy as an art-form. The problem of determining the qibla raises the topic of astronomy.

Meeting a Muslim

Give each child a picture (preferably facial close-up, but showing some clothing) of a Muslim boy, girl, man or woman. It is not necessary for each child to have a separate picture; it would add a further dimension to the exercise to let two or more children write about the same picture and compare their views of the person, and for the class to discuss similarities or differences in their views. The selection of pictures could contain the following: a soldier, a veiled woman, a middle-class woman dressed in European style, an office worker, an engineer/technician, a politician, an oil sheikh, an imam, a teacher. Each child should:

(i) give the person a name;

(ii) make up details of the person's family background (number in family, ages etcetera);

(iii) say what sort of education the person has had/is having;

(iv) describe what sort of home the person lives in;

(v) say what the person likes to do in his spare time;

(vi) say what the most important event/person/influence in his life has been;

(vii) say what the person thinks is important, what he wants most, what he fears most, how he feels his life is changing.

Growing up as a Muslim

Children may be interested to learn something of the customs associated with growing up as a Muslim. These include:

(i) Recitation of the *shahadah* into a baby's ear at birth, shaving the head of the new baby and, if he is male, circumcising him.

(ii) Naming – names are often those of prophets (Daoud – David, Suleiman – Solomon), female relatives of the Prophet (Fatima, Aisha) or qualities of God (al-Hakim – the Wise).

(iii) Learning to say 'Bismillah', to pray, to fast and to read the Qur'an.

(iv) Going to mosque school and Friday prayers.

(v) Muslim habits of personal cleanliness – use of water for toilet purposes and ritual ablution: use of the right hand for eating and the left for washing.

(vi) Greetings.

(vii) Clothes and food.

A visiting speaker might be the most appropriate source of information on many of these matters. It is important to remember that he or she may not always be able to say *why* a particular custom is followed; but most of us are only dimly aware of the origin and full meaning of many of our cultural traditions.

A whole school project on Islam

Infants and First Years

Stories from the early life of Muhammad. His birth and childhood in the desert. His upbringing in Mecca. His marriage to Khadijah. The story of Zayd.

Life in the desert – nomads, camels and other desert creatures.

Second and Third Years

The Five Pillars of Islam, as they are experienced. Belief in One God (calligraphy of Allah or the Shahadah), Prayer, Charity, Fasting and Pilgrimage (role-play, interview or visiting speaker).

Life in an Arab or Pakistani village. Homes, food, clothes and pastimes.

Fourth Year

The mosque (visit and/or model-making).

Muslim countries – frieze, map or wall display incorporating postcards, pictures (travel brochures are a good source), stamps (many show mosques), coins and flags (many have Islamic motifs).

Patterns in mathematics and design.

Music and musical instruments. Examples of inter-faith work (including

Islam) in primary schools can be found in the pamphlet *Religious Education in Primary Schools in a Multicultural Society* published by ILEA, and in *Religious Education and the Multicultural Society* (Christian Education Movement Primary Resource, vol. 5, no. 3, Summer 1978).

A Muslim view of primary education

Muslims emphasise religious instruction rather than religious education. It will be of interest to teachers to know what Muslims regard as desirable objectives for children of this age-group.

In 1976 the Union of Muslim Organisations published a 28-page pamphlet *Guidelines and Syllabus on Islamic Education*. This was prepared by an Education Committee of Muslim scholars under the Chairmanship of Professor Syed Ali Ashraf of King Abdul Aziz University. The Committee did not apparently number any serving teachers among its members. Objectives for the infant (five to six years) and junior (seven to eleven years) levels were summarised as follows:

Infants

'They should learn by heart the Arabic version of the Kalima and through the question-answer method know that they are Muslims, their religion is Islam, their prophet is Muhammad.'

Juniors

'By the time a child reaches the age of seven, he or she should know how to perform wadu (*wudu*) and have some basic knowledge about prayers, fasting and hajj. By the time he or she is eleven . . . he or she should know all the forms of prayer . . . and learn by heart Sura Fatiha and the last ten chapters of the Holy Qur'an . . . They should also know what is Halal and Haram in food, what is permitted and prohibited in dress and social functions and conduct . . . they ought to get a broad idea about the place of Islam in the family of religions. The other ideas which they should imbibe by the time they reach the eleventh year are: The idea of life after death, the idea of the Last Day of Judgement, the idea that Allah the Almighty controls our Fate, but he has given Man freedom to choose between right and wrong.'

Sources

1 Robert Jackson (ed.), *Approaching World Religions* (John Murray, 1982).

2 *Muslim Festivals and Ceremonials* (Minaret House).

3 G.E. Von Grünebaum, *Muhammadan Festivals* (Curzon Press, 1976).

4 E.W. Bovill, *Caravans of the Old Sahara* (OUP, 2nd edn, 1968).

5 Hakluyt, *Principal Navigations* (Everyman edn, vol. 31), p.176 onwards.

6 Idries Shah, *The Exploits of the Incomparable Mulla Hasrudin* (Pan Picador, 1973).

7 *The Islamic Colouring Book* (Wildwood House, n.d.).

8 J. Bourgoin, *Arabic Geometrical Pattern and Design* (Dover, 1973).

9 Keith Albarn, Jenny Miall Smith, Stanford Steele and Dinah Walker, *The Language of Pattern* (Thames & Hudson, 1974).

Resources for primary and middle schools

The situation has improved dramatically in recent years and it may reasonably be expected that the range and standard of materials available will continue to increase. The following selection cannot therefore claim to be comprehensive.

Materials written or produced by Muslims:

The Islamic Foundation, Leicester:
The Children's Book of Islam, Part One, 40 pp. (1975), Part Two, 72 pp. (1975). Revised and expanded versions of the First and Second Primers of Islam published by the Muslim Educational Trust. Basically catechetical exposition of Islamic beliefs and vocabulary, including some guidance on the pronunciation of Arabic words. Aimed at Muslim children aged eight to eleven. Illustrated with photographs and diagrams and accompanied by question and answer workbooks.

Mustafa Yusuf McDermott, *Muslim Nursery Rhymes* (1981). Fifteen English nursery rhymes (Little Boy Blue, Humpty Dumpty etcetera) with new words (such as 'Fatima! Fatima! Where Have You Been!' or 'Where Are You Going To, Oma Abdullah') 'to inculcate an awareness of Islamic values'. Colour illustrations and notes to explain the significance of the rhymes.

M.S. Kayani, *Assalamu Alaikum* (1981). 'A book about the traditional greetings used by Muslims.' Aimed at five to eight year olds. Ten colour illustrations.

M.S. Kayani, *Love all Creatures* (1981). 'Eight stories from the life and teachings of the Prophet . . . showing what he taught and practised about mercy, compassion and kindness to all creatures.' Aimed at eight to eleven years. Eight colour illustrations.

M.S. Kayani, *A Great Friend of Children* (1981). 'Eight stories from the life of the Prophet . . . depicting the love and kindness that he showed towards little children.' Aimed at eight to eleven years. Eight colour illustrations.

Ahmad von Denffer, *Islam for Children* (1981). Seventy pages of stories on the prophets, the same on Islamic beliefs and customs and a section on crafts, puzzles and games. Aimed at six to twelve years. Black and white illustrations.

Muhammad Rashid Feroze, *Abu Bakr: The First Caliph* (1976). Biography of one of Muhammad's closest companions.

MWH. London Publishers:

Jamal-un-Nisa Siddiqui, *Islamic Quiz Book* (1979). Six 20-question quizzes (with answers) on general knowledge about Islam.

The First Man on Earth (1979). Muslim account of creation, Adam and Hawwa (Eve). Colour illustrations.

Dawn of Islam (1976). Illustrated account of Muhammad's preachings.

Muhammad Ibrahim El-Geyoushi, *Primary Islamic Teachings for Children* (n.d.). Two part exposition of beliefs, precepts and rituals (illustrated). Aimed at eight to ten years.

Islamic Information Services:

Heroes of Islam (1978). Brief illustrated biographies of the warriors Khalid ibn al Walid, Salah al Din (Saladin) and the physician-scholars Al Razi (Rhazes) and Ibn Sina (Avicenna) and the traveller Ibn Battuta.

M. Iqbal, *The Guiding Crescent* (Dar-Al-Ihsan, 1973). A collection of short stories for reading aloud. 'They have been chosen not merely for their historical interest but for their portrayal of the essential Islamic characteristics of kindness, truthfulness, forgiveness, honesty, piety, humility . . .' Seven of the stories deal with Muhammad, the other twenty-seven mostly with Caliphs and princes, (Umar, Abu Bakr, Saladin, Aurangzeb) but also with sufis, children and poor people. Most paint a clear 'moral' but some may need interpreting to non-Muslims. Difficult words and important names are explained. Obtainable from the author (The Polytechnic, Queensgate, Huddersfield).

Olive Toto, *Children's Book on Islam* and *Last Prophet of God Muhammad* (1973). Discursive and at times whimsical text but packed with appealing detail for the younger child. Good examples of calligraphy and large selection of black and white photographs from all parts of the Muslim world. Obtainable from the author (10 Tremadoc Road, London SW4).

Muhammad Iqbal, *The Way of the Muslim* (Hulton Educational Publications, 1973). Simple text covering the life of the Prophet (in some detail), the spread of Islam and the beliefs, ideals and practices of Muslims. Black and white drawings. Useful index.

Syed Ali Ashraf, *The Prophets* (Hodder & Stoughton/Union of Muslim Organisations, 1980). Simple stories for reading aloud. Illustrated.

Celia S. Ghajjar, *Stories of the Prophets* ('Concerned Muslims', 2 Verwood Road, North Harrow, Middlesex). Nine short booklets with simple text and brightly coloured illustrations intended to introduce five to eight-year-olds to Adam, Noah, Abraham etc.

Materials written or produced by non-Muslims:

Carol Barker, *A Prince of Islam* (Macdonald and Jane's, 1976). Story of a boy in ninth-century Baghdad. Striking but historically muddled illustrations, some of which might seem improper to Muslims.

Tony Barton, *The Storyteller of Marrakesh* (Evans Bros Ltd, 1980). Traditional tales retold.

M. Blakeley, *Nahda's Family* (A. & C. Black, 1977). Daily life of a Pakistani family in the north of England seen through the eyes of a twelve-year-old girl. Simple text and colour photographs.

D.F. Brennan, *Calendar of Religious Festivals* (Commission for Racial Equality and the Shap Working Party on World Religions in Education). Invaluable annual publication available from the Shap Working Party, 7 Alderbrook Road, Solihull, West Midlands.

Bernard Brett, *Mohammed* (Collins, 1972). Biography set against Arabian background. Includes pictures of the Prophet and therefore not to be used with Muslims.

Anne Farncombe, *Our Muslim Friends* (Denholm House Press, 1977). Describes the journey of Nasima and Tariq from India to England. Outlines basic beliefs and rituals. Includes recipes for Biriani and Chapatis and a list of thirty 'words to remember'. Index. Artist's illustrations.

G.E. von Grünebaum, *Muhammadan Festivals* (Curzon Press, 1976). Scholarly account of prayer, hajj, Ramadan and the 10th of Muharram.

H.M. Nahmad, *The Peasant and the Donkey* (OUP, 1967). Arabic, Turkish, Persian and other traditional stories.

Michael Pollard, *My World* (Macdonald Educational, 1979). Colour-illustrated accounts of the life styles of seven children, including Christopher of Britain and Dipti of Bangladesh. Shows children's games and clothes and includes a folk story.

Amina Shah, *Arabian Fairy Tales* (Frederick Muller, 1969). This series also includes Indonesian, Persian and Turkish fairy tales.

Joan Solomon, *Shabnam's Day Out* (Hamish Hamilton, 1980). London outing of a Muslim family. Simple text and colour photographs. Includes pictures of a mosque class.

Joan Solomon, *Gifts and Almonds* (Hamish Hamilton, 1980). Eid celebrations, illustrated with colour photographs.

27

Lower
Secondary Level

Teachers may find that some of the topics listed in Chapter 26 can be adapted for use at the lower secondary level.

The Pillars of the Faith

This is a familiar framework for a discussion of the central features of Islam, usable with Muslim and non-Muslim pupils alike. As it corresponds to the treatment of the faith given in many books, assignments for individual and group work are easily made.

1 The Creed. Pupils could make their own copies of one of the many elaborate calligraphic versions of the *shahada*, or at least of the name 'Allah'.

2 Prayer. Pupils could examine the two main kinds of prayer in Islam considering the importance both of formal prayer, performed by Muslims five times a day, and less formal prayer – *du'a* (supplication) – which may be said anywhere and at any time.

3 Zakat. This lends itself to discussion and research about how oil-rich countries are giving foreign aid to poor ones.

4 Fasting. This could lead into work on food and festivals.

5 Pilgrimage. This offers exciting possibilities and would make an excellent focus or 'finale'. A number of good films are available and brief personal accounts of the *hajj* could be used to make interesting comparisons of the physical and spiritual circumstances of the hajj in the past and now. A study of the hajj could be used to bring out the following points:

(a) the pre-Islamic tradition of pilgrimage in Arabia.

(b) the central importance (quite literally) of Mecca and the Ka'ba for the Muslim world (relate this to the *qibla* of the local mosque).

(c) the world-wide extent of the Muslim faith (draw a world map showing main routes linking major Muslim communities with Mecca).

(d) the significance of each of the rites of the hajj.

(e) the egalitarianism of Islam (films and slides should show pilgrims of all races wearing the same simple robes and performing the same simple rituals).

(f) other pilgrimages in Islam – such as those associated with the Shi'a in Iran and Iraq.

A project on the hajj using imaginative writing and/or drama should enable the pupil to grasp its emotional and spiritual significance for the believer. The following outline might be used: the personal situation of the believer – his home, occupation and family responsibilities (is he free to undertake the hajj?); his decision to undertake the hajj; preparatory arrangements; the journey; the rites; return home and welcome; effect of the hajj on the pilgrim.

Rites of passage

This is an approach that would lend itself to:

(i) Comparative treatment (taking in Christianity, Judaism and a non-monotheistic religion to reinforce similarities and contrasts).

(ii) A social studies context (connecting with family life, leisure and customs, festivals, and so on). Essentially the objective is to explore the religious significance of social acts:

Birth. Circumcision of male children. Why? (not a Qur'anic injunction but universally observed by Muslims). What are Muslim parents' attitudes to boys and girls respectively? How are they brought up? How does this differ from the upbringing of children of other religions? When are they considered fully adult? (See Qur'an Suras 17:20–25)[1]

Marriage. Marriage is not a sacrament in Islam but a contract (give details of dowry, women's rights in Islamic law). The marriage ceremony (the film *A Mosque in the Park* contains an extended sequence dealing with preparations for a Muslim marriage, as well as the actual ceremony). The Muslim view of the family. Polygamy and divorce in theory and practice.

Death. Muslim burial rites. What do Muslims believe about the after-life? (Develop ideas of Judgement, ethical responsibility, revelation, etc.) See also 'Muslim Burials: A Policy Paper' (CRC).

Worksheets for a lower secondary level course

Arabia before Muhammad

(1) What sort of country is Arabia? Where is it? How big is it? What is the weather like? What would you see if you were to fly over it?

(2) Draw a map of Arabia and the surrounding countries. Mark in Medina, Mecca, Damascus, Baghdad, Jiddah, Riyadh.

(3) Why was Mecca an important city?

(4) Describe the life of:

(a) a bedouin; (b) a merchant from Mecca at the time of Muhammad.

(5) What did the Arabs believe in before Muhammad began to preach to them? What other religions might they have known about? Why was the Ka'ba important? Draw a picture of it.

The life of Muhammad

(1) What sort of childhood did Muhammad have?
(2) Why did people come to call Muhammad 'Al-Amin' (the trustworthy)?
(3) Describe in your own words what happened when the angel Gabriel came to Muhammad. Explain what Muhammad did afterwards.
(4) Why were Muhammad and his followers persecuted?
(5) When and why did Muhammad and his followers leave Mecca? Why is this event important for Muslims today? Imagine that you travelled with him and tell the story of your adventure.
(6) Explain how things changed for the Muslims while they were at Medina.
(7) What did Muhammad do when he came back to Mecca?
(8) What can you tell about Muhammad to show that he was a great leader?

The teachings conveyed by Muhammad

(1) What did Muhammad teach men about God?
(2) What did Muhammad tell people they ought to do? What did he tell them they ought not to do?
(3) What are the Five Pillars of the Faith? Explain why each one is important.
(4) What is the Shahada? Make your own copy of the Shahada as it is written in Arabic.
(5) Imagine you have been on the pilgrimage to Mecca. Write an account of your journey and what you saw and did there.
(6) Why is the Qur'an so important to Muslims?

The expansion of Islam

(1) Draw a map to show which countries had been conquered by the Muslims a hundred years after Muhammad's death. Can you explain how Islam spread so far and so quickly?
(2) Imagine you were a merchant who had travelled with a caravan from Cordoba to Baghdad four centuries after Muhammad's death. Describe some of the things you would have seen and the places you would have passed through.
(3) Find out about the city of Baghdad and the Caliph Haroun al-Rashid. Why are they famous?
(4) What important events happened in: (a) 711, (b) 732, (c) 750, (d) 910, (e) 1258, (f) 1492, (g) 1526? Write an account of one of these events. Draw a map and mark in the places where they happened.
(5) Make a list of the important inventions and discoveries made by Muslims. Explain why any one of these was important.
(6) Explain what is meant by: (a) Caliph, (b) Jihad.
(7) Find out how Jews and Christians were treated by the Muslims.

The Muslim way of life

(1) Describe the most important Muslim customs concerning dress and diet.

(2) What are the most important Muslim festivals? Describe how any one of them is celebrated.

(3) Why is the mosque important to Muslims? Draw pictures of a mosque (inside and outside, top and side). Mark in the *mihrab, minbar* and minaret. In what ways is a mosque different from a church? Make a list of some of the world's most famous mosques. Draw a map and mark them in on it.

(4) Explain how Muslims feel about: (i) marriage and the family; (ii) education and bringing up children. What sort of things do they think are most important? What sort of things do they disapprove of?

(5) Draw a map of the world and mark in all the countries where there are many Muslims. Which are the largest Muslim countries in population? Describe what you might see on a visit to one of these.

(6) What do you think everybody could learn from the Muslim way of life?

Further work

(1) Explain the main things that Muslims and Christians both believe in. Find out what Muslims believe about Jesus and the Bible.

(2) Explain what problems a Muslim family must face when coming to live in a non-Muslim country.

(3) Explain the difference between Sunnite and Shi'ite.

(4) Find out about the Sufis. What did they believe in and what did they do?

(5) What is done by (a) an *imam*; (b) a *muezzin*?

The use of imaginative writing

The writing of formal essays may be an appropriate exercise for the more academic pupil who responds to the challenge of an invitation to 'Explain', 'Discuss' or 'Comment': but many children of average and below average ability are likely to regard formal essays as boring, irrelevant and tainted by association with 'exams', failure and frustration (which is not to say that some of the most lively pupils of above average ability may not also feel the same way). This need not, however, preclude the use of continuous prose writing exercises. At its best, imaginative writing can engage both the emotion and intellect of the pupil, helping him or her to develop the capacity for insight and empathy, exercising his or her ability to express judgements, suggest moods and construct coherent arguments and narratives. It should also encourage the use of works of reference and a critical attitude towards the use of evidence. Some suggestions for a possible exercise are given below.

Although imaginative writing is an exercise in the use of language it is invariably helpful to keep pictorial material to hand to stimulate the imagination and also to serve as another source of information.

Autobiography of an early follower of Muhammad

This exercise invites the pupil to try to 'get close to' the personality and career of the Prophet and to try to understand the motivations and convictions of a believer. A possible outline might be:

(i) previous religious outlook of the believer – what did he/she respect/fear?
(ii) reputation and activities of Muhammad – what sort of man did he seem to be?
(iii) the decision to become a convert – when and why?
(iv) the effect of the new faith on the believer's life, family and outlook;
(v) the part played by the new believer in trying to advance the faith. This outline might be written up in the style of a 'confession' or a diary, or a letter to a friend or relative whom the convert wishes to win over. The resulting efforts could then be compared for similarities of style, emphasis, and so on.

Islam quiz for lower secondary level

Are the following true or false?

(i)   Muslims are not allowed to eat pork.
(ii)   Muslims are allowed to have more than one wife.
(iii)   Muslims are supposed to pray five times a day.
(iv)   Muslims cannot be divorced.
(v)   Muslims believe Jesus was a Prophet of God.

Explain the meaning of the following words:

(i)	Allah	(vi)	hajj
(ii)	salat	(vii)	bismillah
(iii)	minbar	(viii)	muezzin
(iv)	imam	(ix)	hijra
(v)	Ramadan	(x)	halal

Where would you expect to find the following?

(i)   a minaret
(ii)   a Muslim at noon on Friday
(iii)   a bedouin
(iv)   Muhammad's tomb
(v)   a mihrab

Where are the following?

(i)   the Dome of the Rock
(ii)   the Taj Mahal
(iii)   the Alhambra
(iv)   Fatepur Sikri
(v)   the Ka'ba

Sources

1 See M. Iqbal, 'The religious upbringing and education of a Muslim child' in W.O. Cole (ed.), *Religion in the Multi-Faith School* (YCCR, 1973).

Books for lower secondary level

Robert Boyce, *The Story of Islam* (Religious Education Press, 1972). Covers 'The country where Islam began', 'The life of Muhammad', 'Islam spreads to other countries', 'The beliefs of Islam' and 'Islam comes to the present time'. Black and white illustrations.

Riadh El-Droubie, *Islam* (Ward Lock, 1970). This Muslim author conveys a great deal of information about beliefs and life-style in a very small space. Black and white illustrations.

I.G. Edmonds, *Islam* (Franklin Watts, 1977). Covers Muslim beliefs and duties, the career of the Prophet and a sketch of Islamic history. Black and white photographs.

Muhammad and Maryam Iqbal, *Understanding Your Muslim Neighbour* (Lutterworth Educational, 1976). Introduces Islam and Muslim life-styles through the experiences of Muhammad Bashir and his sister Shamim in moving from Pakistan to England. Black and white photographs.

Shirley Kay, *The Arab World* (OUP, 1970). Well-written illustrated information book especially useful on desert life and Islamic history.

Schools Council Religious Education in Secondary Schools Project, *The Muslim Way of Life* (Hart-Davis Educational Ltd, 1977). Simple text, many black and white illustrations and suggestions for work. Dialogues between 'Rawab-Ullah' and 'Peter Taylor', pupils at the same Sheffield school, cover migration, life-styles and the mosque. A second edition was published in 1981; unfortunately it contains pictures of the Prophet.

Many schemes of work for lower secondary level are organised on thematic lines by means of examples taken from different world religions (for example sacred buildings and objects, founders of religions, rites of passage, pilgrimage and so on). The following books would be useful in this connection. All contain an element of Islam.

G. Cleverley and B. Philips, *Northbourne Tales of Belief and Understanding* (McGraw-Hill, 1975). Specially written stories 'concerned with the beliefs and life-styles of immigrant communities which have settled into Britain and in particular their children. They are intended to appeal to children in the fourteen to fifteen age group, particularly those in non-academic streams . . . their main role is to attract attention and arouse interest in the subject . . .' Each story is accompanied by comprehension questions and topics for discussion. Muslims are particularly mentioned in the following stories: 'Fireworks' (festivals, calendars, monotheism), 'Two Children' (birth, baptism, naming), 'Ishmael Stays at School' (fasting, dress rules, group membership and loyalties), 'The Photograph' (marriage, attitudes to women, inter-faith relationships), 'The Cripple' (charity, attitudes to misfortune, attitudes to social change).

P.J. Hunt, *Temples and Other Places of Worship* (Franklin Watts, 1974). Very brief. Illustrated with photographs.

E.G. Parrinder, *A Book of World Religions* (Hulton Educational Publications Ltd, 1965). Text organised around the themes of Men at Prayer, Founders, Holy Books and their Teaching, and Growth and Present State of Religions. Illustrated.

A.E. Perry, *How People Worship* (Denholm House Press, 1974).

D.G. Butler, *Life Among Muslims* (*Friends and Neighbours* series, Edward Arnold, 1980). Eight short plays about Pakistani Muslim life (at home, Qur'an, mosque, Ramadan, growing up, wedding, death). Ideas for follow-up work are given, and a word list is included.

John Rankin, *Looking at Symbols* (Lutterworth Educational, 1979). A pack of illustrated work cards.

Raymond Trudgian, *Who is my Neighbour?* (Denholm House Press, 1975). Considers world religions' answers to 'ultimate questions'.

28

The Fourth
and Fifth Years

A number of Boards now offer CSE and O level syllabuses incorporating Islam (see Appendix 7). The following schemes are offered for those wishing to follow a non-examination course or to devise their own syllabus. An example of a Mode 3 O level syllabus is given in Chapter 30 and an account of the development of a Mode 3 O level syllabus which includes an Islamic component is given by Eric Pain, 'Developing a World Religions Course' in Robert Jackson (ed.), *Approaching World Religions*.

Islam in action

Michael Pye, *Comparative Religion: An Introduction through Source Materials*[1] categorises religious phenomena in terms of Religious Action, Religious Groups, Religious Concepts and Religious States of Mind. His framework of 'Religious Action' offers a possible structure for a study of Islam:

(i) *Special places, times and objects*
Places – Mecca, Medina, mosques, tombs
Times – Fridays, Ramadan, Dhul-Hijja
Objects – Qur'an
(The fact that there are so few 'special objects' associated with Islam underlines its non-material emphasis and anti-idolatrous origins.)
(ii) *The use of the body*
Prayer rituals, dervishes, fasting
(iii) *Separation and ritual cleansing*
Ablutions, diet, ghettoes, endogamy
(iv) *Sacrifice, offering and worship*
Eid-al-Adha, Zakat
(v) *Rehearsal of significant past or myth*
Hajj (e.g. the running which commemorates Hagar's search for water), Tenth of Muharram
(vi) *Meditation and prayer*
Ramadan
(vii) *Seeking specific benefits*
e.g. rain, victory, wealth, health, exorcism

Examples from Muslim history
(viii) *Occasional rites*
Rites of passage, rites associated with work, hunting, building, the harvest
(ix) *Ethics and society*
Highly specific rules are enjoined regarding sexual relations, gambling, alcohol, and so on. These could be compared with the Ten Commandments or Buddhist conceptions of 'right action'.
(x) *Propagation*
Proselytisation by sufis and merchants, Ahmadiyya

Six dimensions of Islam

This outline is based on the six dimensional approach to religious phenomena (doctrinal, mythological, ethical, ritual, experiential, social/institutional) devised by Professor Ninian Smart.[2] It assumes that the dimensions need not be examined according to any one set order but that their inter-relationship should be emphasised, as should the fact that the significance of any particular dimension varies according to the religious tradition in question.

The starting point chosen is Smart's *mythic* dimension. He defines a myth as 'a story of significance somehow depicting . . . the relation between the transcendent and the human and worldly realm', and instances Christ's Passion as the central myth of Christianity.[3] For Islam the central myth is the revelation of God's message to Muhammad; in a sense it is the Qur'an itself. From the fact of the Qur'an one might next proceed to the central *doctrines* of its teaching and in particular, its conception of God and of the relation of man to God. This leads logically to the third, *ethical* dimension, which deals with the relations of man to man. These are the three dimensions dealing with *belief*.

The three dimensions of *practice* can be approached from the starting point of *ritual*, which plays a prominent part in Islam. The rites of prayer, fasting and the hajj produce a deep *experiential* effect in visibly affirming the solidarity of believers in their submission. The power of Islamic ritual to internalise fundamental values is so significant that the *institutional* dimension of the faith has played a less prominent part in its development than it has, say, in Christianity.

In terms of activities and resources this strategy might be implemented as follows:

1 The revelation of the Qur'an (Myth)

Read (or distribute copies for reading) the account of Muhammad's revelation on Mount Hira as described in the *Biography of the Messenger of God* of Ibn Ishaq (d. *circa* 768).[4] The following points could then be made in the course of analysing this passage:
(i) The detailed description of the circumstances of the Prophet's revela-

tion emphasises his human status (contrast with Christ). Teachers may wish at this stage to sketch in the background of Muhammad's early life. The popular tendency to surround him with a miraculous aura could be illustrated by using the previous section of Ibn Ishaq (pp.16–19, op.cit.).

(ii) The passage emphasises the succession of prophets that have been sent by God.

(iii) The passage emphasises that Muhammad observed the ritual aspects of pre-Islamic religion. Teachers could point out that prayer, charity and the rites of the Ka'ba were integrated into Islam.

(iv) In describing the revelation the translator uses the word 'Read'; an editorial footnote advises 'Recite' as a better translation. Teachers could clarify the Islamic conception of revelation as dictation, refer to the tradition of Muhammad's illiteracy and, by contrasting the five lines of Sura 96 quoted with other versions, illustrate the problems of translation and thus bring out the importance of all Muslims learning to use the Qur'an in Arabic. This could be developed into a discussion of the problems facing the illiterate and their attempts to find solutions through emphasis on ritual or recourse to mystics (dead or living) and other intermediaries.

(v) The role of Waraqa, Muhammad's uncle, could be used to develop the idea of the relationship between Islam and other religions (reiterating points made under (i) and (ii) above. Other possible avenues for exploration are *poetry* (its status in pre-Islamic Arabia: the poetic nature of the Qur'an) and *meditation and possession* ('speaking in tongues'): the subsequent life of the Prophet. As an (optional) assignment ask students to write an account of the above passage from the point of view of Khadija or Waraqa.

2 The message of the Qur'an (Doctrine)

Using Sura 96 as a basis, the following basic points could be expounded:
(i) God is the Creator (first 2 lines)
(ii) God is Beneficent (line 3)
(iii) God has sent man a message to lighten his ignorance
(iv) Man needs God (lines 6–7)
(v) Man faces God at death (line 8)
(vi) These things cannot be evaded (lines 9–14)
(vii) A time of reckoning will come (lines 15–19)
(viii) Man must submit to the message of God's revelation (lines 20–21)
Detailed analysis could be followed by a summary of the overall impression of the passage, reflecting characteristic emphases of the Islamic faith: the oneness of God (Tawhid); the inevitability of judgement; the need for submission (Islam).

3 The teaching of the Qur'an (Ethics)

The main precepts of Islamic ethical teaching could either be gleaned through the Qur'an or illustrated by *hadith*. Pupils should be encouraged to review the material thus assembled in the light of three questions:

– What does it tell us about the state of pre-Islamic Arabia? (Develop the idea of Muhammad as a moral reformer.)
– How far are Islamic teachings on ethical matters shared by other major religions?
– Has the relevance of these precepts changed since the time of Muhammad's revelation? Discuss the problems of modernisation (e.g. usury and economic development) and of Muslims living in a non-Muslim society (e.g. pork, alcohol, gambling and monogamy as normal features of the British way of life).
The teacher could outline the development of the *shari'a*.
Optional Assignment: devise a Christian/Muslim dialogue on Charity or Honesty or the Family or War.

4 The practice of Islam (Ritual)

The ritual of daily prayer could be presented by the use of slides plus records. But this should be *preceded* by an exposition of *why* Muslims pray (which could lead into a general discussion of the nature and forms of prayer and other forms of worship).

The practice of fasting could then be discussed – perhaps from the point of view of an Islamic modernist. The *experiential* impact of prayer and fasting leads naturally to the next section.
Optional assignment: argue the case for or against a change in Islamic observances. (Teachers should look for use of Qur'anic citations or historical precedents to justify or refute recommended changes.)

5 The experience of Islam (Experiential)

This might best be approached through an examination of the hajj, using personal accounts or, better still, a film. The equality and brotherhood of all believers can be brought out through the hajj.

Alternatively, one could treat the hajj as an aspect of ritual (under section 4) and focus instead on Sufism as a mode of elevating the individual's direct consciousness of God. Poetry could be used as a starting-point and the section could be developed through biographical accounts of Sufi saints and scholars or descriptions of some of the dervish orders. Care must be taken to avoid descriptive exoticism, but the approach could lead into a useful discussion of the cult and folklore aspects of popular Islam, thus undermining any previous impression that Islam was totally homogenous and monolithic.

Optional assignment essay: 'Islam is a religion of doing rather than of thinking.' Do you agree?

6 The organisation of Islam (Social/Institutional)

A visit to a mosque could be organised at this stage. Failing this, or the opportunity to discuss the role of the mosque with an imam or a Muslim, students could appreciate its importance through visual presentations of its architecture and decor. The imam could be contrasted with a Christian priest thus giving the opportunity to reiterate through examination of social and symbolic roles significant differences of doctrine and ritual. Other aspects which could be explored under this heading are: (i) *waqf*, (ii) missionary activity, (iii) the Muslim family as the basis of the Islamic social order.

Concluding optional assignment: which aspects of Islam do you think you ought to know more about?

The course outlined above not only tries to take account of Smart's six dimensions but also offers scope for a variety of pupil activities and different avenues of development. It also emphasises the centrality of the Qur'an and affords opportunities for exploring the links between Islam and other religions.

Islam: An outline syllabus

This outline is intended to provide a focus for discussion for teachers aiming to produce their own CSE or O level syllabus.

A   Compulsory units

1   Muhammad and the Qur'an: the Arabian setting – social conditions, religious practices and influences; career and character of the Prophet – Muhammad as moral reformer, statesman and model for Muslims; the Qur'an – its structure and contents – problem of translation – its place in Islamic art and daily life.
2   Pillars of the Faith: the treatment to involve an account of meaning as well as description; *shahada* – Tawhid and the Muslim conception of God and man; *Salat* – the value of ritual; *Zakat* – other ethical obligations; *Saum* – other paths to spiritual development; *Hajj* – equality of believers, the umma.
3   Islam as a world religion: what is a world religion? Sketch of Islam's expansion and distribution of Muslims today; case-studies of Saudi Arabia, Pakistan, Turkey, Indonesia, Tunisia, Nigeria, Iran and Libya; how many of these should be studied?

B   Choice units

4   Women and the family in Islam: (i) position of women before Muhammad – his teachings on women; (ii) traditional role of women in Muslim society – their rights in law and practice – divorce and inheritance; (iii) family life – authority in the family – growing up as a Muslim; (iv) forces for change – education, work and nationalism.
5   Muslims in Britain: (i) origins and distribution of the Muslim community; (ii) problems of adjustment to British society (NB distinguish between

problems *qua* immigrant and *qua* Muslim); (iii) divisions and conflicts within the Muslim community and Muslim families – strengths of Muslim community life; (iv) parallels with changes taking place in modernising Muslim countries.

6   Islam and Christianity: (i) shared beliefs and ethical values; (ii) main points of doctrinal disagreement; (iii) Christians under Muslim rule and vice versa – what is toleration? what is respect? (iv) parallels in their adjustment to the modern world.

Points for discussion

Is the extent and balance of the syllabus acceptable? Should anything be cut? Has anything of major importance been omitted?

What does the syllabus imply in terms of the following?

(i)   Resources: are existing materials adequate? for which sections would teacher-produced materials be necessary (e.g. units 3 and 5)?

(ii) Teaching style and strategy: are any specially valuable approaches precluded? is there scope for the development of skills and attitudes, and if so, which?

(iii) Teacher preparation – how could this be accomplished most effectively?

What would be the main obstacles to the effective implementation of such a syllabus? How could they be overcome?

What form(s) of assessment should be employed? (i) multiple choice; (ii) stimulus material; (iii) documents; (iv) essay questions; (v) project.

Sources

1   Michael Pye, *Comparative Religion: An Introduction Through Source Materials* (David & Charles, 1972).

2   Ninian Smart, *Secular Education and the Logic of Religion* (Faber, 1968).

3   See N. Smart, 'What is religion?' in N. Smart and D. Horder (eds), *New Movements in Religious Education* (Temple Smith, 1975), p.15.

4   Reprinted in W.H. McNeill and M.R. Waldman, *The Islamic World* (Oxford, 1973), pp.19–22.

Books for CSE and O level

Jane Bradshaw, *Eight Major Religions in Britain* (Edward Arnold, 1979). Gives a concise outline with the emphasis on the contemporary British situation. Black and white illustrations. Suggestions for work.

W. Owen Cole, *Five Religions in the Twentieth Century* (Hulton Educational

Publications, 1981). 'Designed for O level multi-faith syllabuses such as the AEB.' The religions (Hinduism, Judaism, Christianity, Islam and Sikhism) are considered under the following headings – Messengers of God, The Scriptures, Worship, Pilgrimages, Festivals, The Coming Together of Religions. Numerous black and white photographs and diagrams. Questions, bibliography and index.

Riadh El-Droubie and Edward Hulmes, *Islam* (Longman, 1980). Well-illustrated survey by a Muslim and a Catholic, covering the life of the Prophet, the Qur'an, prayer, hajj, Muslims in Britain and 'Fasts and festivals'. Specially useful features include a comprehensive list of activities (with Qur'anic references) and a detailed index.

Jan Thompson, *The Islamic Faith* (Edward Arnold, 1981). Ingeniously structured text weaves an exposition of Islam around a narrative of the life of the Prophet. Includes many aspects (such as sub-divisions in Islam) omitted in briefer accounts. Black and white photographs. Suggestions for work.

29

The Sixth Form

The following outlines are offered as suggestions for general studies work. A level syllabuses can be found in Appendix 7.

Introducing Islam

The following framework attempts to set out a series of loosely defined topics in a roughly chronological sequence.

1 The Prophet

Discussion – What was the religious and ethical state of Arabian society before Islam? What evidence do we have as a basis for understanding this period? Why was Muhammad persecuted for his teachings? What had Muhammad achieved by the time of his death? How do Muslim attitudes to Muhammad compare with Christian attitudes to Jesus? Why is Muhammad regarded by Muslims as 'the seal of the Prophets'?
Research – Hadith, their origins, validation and significance.

2 Qur'an, doctrine and ritual

Discussion – Why is it incorrect to refer to Muhammad as the author of the Qur'an? What are the consequences of the view that the Qur'an cannot be translated? What part does the Qur'an play in the life of a Muslim? Explain the spiritual and social significance of each of the 'Five Pillars of the Faith'? How far was Muhammad's teaching compatible with the traditional customs and beliefs of the Arabs of his time?
Research – The hajj or Muslim views on free will versus predestination.

3 The expansion of Islam

Discussion – How can one account for the rapid expansion of Islam in the century after the Prophet's death? What were the main characteristics of Muslim rule under the Umayyads? What changes did the Abbasids bring about? Why did the Muslim empire begin to fragment politically from the ninth century onwards? What links held the Muslim world together after the fall of Baghdad? When and where did Islam enjoy its 'golden age'? Research – The career of a Muslim statesman (e.g. Umar, Muawiyah, Nizam-ul-mulk).

4   Science and philosophy

Discussion – What were the main centres of intellectual activity in traditional Islam? What did Muslim thought owe to Greece, India, Persia and China? What problems did Muslims have in reconciling reason with revelation? When and why did the vigour of Muslim intellectual life begin to waver? Research – The life and work of Ibn Sina (Avicenna) or Ibn Rushd (Averroes).

5   Art and architecture

Discussion – What are the distinctive characteristics of Islamic art? In what ways have Western art and architecture been influenced by Islam? Why was architecture the 'queen of the arts' in Islam? Research – The work of Sinan *or* calligraphy as an art.

6   Shari'a

Discussion – Why is law so important in Islam? In what ways do the four great schools of law differ from one another? Research – The relationship between the shari'a and the legal code of any Muslim country today.

7   Sects and Sufis

Discussion – What divides the Sunni from the Shi'a? How has Sufism affected the development of Islam? Research – The life and works of Rumi or al-Ghazali *or* the Isma'ili.

8   Muslim empires

Discussion – What were the distinctive features of Ottoman rule? How do they compare with those of the Mughals and Safavids? In what senses were these empires 'Islamic'? Research – The career and achievements of Akbar or Shah Abbas or Suleyman II *or* the building of Istanbul or Fathpur Sikri or Isfahan.

9   Islam and the modern world

Discussion – What difficulties face Islamic traditionalists in the twentieth century? Is nationalism compatible with Islam? In what ways do the experiences of Muslim immigrants in Britain illustrate the problems of reconciling Islam to the conditions of an industrialised society? How is the dynamism of Islam in modern Africa to be explained? Is Islam a bulwark against communism? How have Muslims fared under communist rule?

Research – The career and writings of Sir Sayyid Ahmad Khan or Muhhamad Abduh or Jamil al-din Al Afghani or Sir Muhammad Iqbal.

10   *Review*

Discussion – What claim does Islam have to be considered as a 'world religion'? What ethical values are shared by Muslims and Christians? Which of the following predictions do you most tend to agree with: 'Islam faces extinction because it cannot meet the challenge of the modern world.' 'Islam will continue to expand its influence and enlarge its contribution to the moral progress of mankind.'?

The challenge of change

What is loosely referred to as 'the challenge of modernisation' must be faced on a number of inter-related levels. It might simplify matters to present the problem in terms of five 'Cs' – *Change* in the *Community's Creed, Code* and *Cult*.

Community – usually defined in terms of the nation-state – how have new definitions of community and citizenship (especially nationalist ones) been reconciled with traditional Islamic ones?

Cult – how far have ritual observances been modified or abandoned?

Code – how far have social behaviour and ethics changed (for example regarding the position of women)? How have these been justified in terms of the Qur'an?

Creed – how far has the interpretation of Qur'an and hadith changed (for example with regard to *jihad* or modern science)?

Change – what is the pace and scope of change? What factors advance or retard it? Useful contrasts could be made between Saudi Arabia and Turkey (both relatively new States, dating in their present form from the 1920s, but both also encompassing old societies) or between Tunisia and Libya (neighbouring States with very different ideas about what constitutes 'Islamic socialism'). Egypt, Algeria and Pakistan also provide well-documented examples. Indonesia and Malaysia could be examined to see how religious change is complicated by other factors in societies which are not only multi-faith but also multi-ethnic. In any case-study, however, it is important to examine divergences *within* as well as *between* nations and also to investigate the extent to which legislative prescription has been translated into actual changes in behaviour and attitudes. Nor is it reasonable to assume that change occurs in one direction only. Improvements in communications have considerably increased the numbers of pilgrims undertaking the hajj.

Imagine

Imagine you are the Minister of Information of . . . (choose a specific, real country with a population which is wholly or mostly Muslim). Draw up an itinerary for a group of visitors, taking into account the following criteria:
(i) their nationality (British, Russian, American, mixed),
(ii) their occupations (politicians, teachers, journalists, scientists),
(iii) time available (3 days, 10 days, 30 days).
Which visits/sights/events/activities would you consider absolutely essential for an understanding of your country? Why? Is there anything you would rather they did not see?

Imagine that a wealthy Muslim philanthropist has established a charitable foundation in Britain with the object of promoting a better understanding of Islam (rather than of winning converts). Draw up a programme of activities for such a foundation.

Imagine you are a Pakistani newcomer to Britain. Write a letter home to your relatives describing your first impressions and experiences. Remember to mention the reactions of other members of your family.

Imagine you are the headmaster of a large comprehensive school. You have been advised that the number of Muslim pupils in your school will increase considerably over the next few years. Draw up a report for the school governors outlining the steps you propose to take.

The world of Islam

This project involves drafting the scenario for an hour-long television programme on 'The World of Islam'. It would probably be most suitable coming at the end of a course, when pupils have acquired a good grasp of basic factual material and have sufficient familiarity with sources of reference to enable them to look up specific points and enlarge their knowledge as necessary.

At first sight this exercise may seem rather strange, even bizarre, but as most students will have watched many hours of television they should soon be able to analyse a programme into its component parts once they have started thinking about it.

The following questions might usefully be borne in mind:

Objectives

Does the programme have any special objectives, other than to inform and entertain? How, and how far, can informing and entertaining be reconciled with each other? Are there any particular impressions one would wish to avoid giving unintentionally (for example reinforcing stereotypes through superficial treatment of complex issues)?

Audience

Is the programme intended for any specific audience (e.g. regional, school)?
Is it intended to reach any specific section of a general audience (defined in
terms of age, sex, class, attitudes)? What level of pre-knowledge and what
sort of attitudes can be assumed to exist among potential viewers?

Having considered these questions (but not necessarily having finalised
the answers) one should then go on to the following:
Which particular aspects of 'The World of Islam' should be dealt with?
Should the treatment be generalised or use specific examples? Think of a
title for the programme.

Islam and development

The movement for 'development education' has gathered momentum in
recent years. Almost all of the world's fifty odd Muslim States are developing countries and their distinctive traditions have profound implications for
the process of development.

Development and basic needs

What are basic needs? Does Islam imply a commitment to their provision?
In what ways and how far are basic needs being met through the development programmes of Muslim States? Do these programmes give sufficient
priority to basic needs?

Development and liberation

Does 'militant Islam' represent a rejection of oppression? Does the Iranian
Revolution represent a 'liberation theology' in action?

Religious values and development

Does Islam imply any particular form of, or priorities for, development?

Social justice

What is the Islamic view of social justice? What does Islam imply in terms of
equality and inequality? What is the Islamic notion of 'human rights'?

Interdependence

In what ways is the world we are conscious of living in interdependent with
the world of developing Muslim States?

The good society

One might compare, for instance, the Shah's view of 'the good society', and
the Ayatollah's, with that of the current Saudi regime and with that of, say, a
World Bank development consultant.

Further topics for research and discussion

'Ritual helps to remove the frontiers between the sacred and the profane and establishes a route by which man gains access from the latter to the former.' Comment, with reference to Islam.

Why does Islam have no priestly class? Why is this important?

'There are no major sects in Islam, only different schools of thought.' Comment.

'It is a cause of much wonder that those who urge celibacy should at the same time hesitate to allow family planning' (Fatwa of the Grand Mufti of Jordan, 1964). Comment.

'To veil the body is not to deny it but to withdraw it like gold, into the domain of things concealed from the eyes of the crowd.' Comment.

'Islam is focused to one point in its geography, its history, its liturgy and its architecture' (Cragg). Why is this important?

'God is essentially inscrutable and the realisation of this is what, in a real sense, submission is about' (Cragg). Comment.

'Religion both encourages and discourages hostile action against non-believers.' In what ways does Islam conform to this paradox?

'I do not see how it is possible . . . for any revival of true religion to continue long. For religion must necessarily produce both industry and frugality, and these cannot but produce riches. But as riches increase so will pride, anger and love of the world in all its branches.' Does the history of Islam confirm this view of John Wesley's?

'Islam never interfered with the dogmas of any moral faith, never persecuted, never established an Inquisition. It never invented the rack or the stake for stifling difference of opinion or strangling the human conscience . . .' (Syed Ameer Ali). How far can this claim be justified?

What is it that Muslims have admired about the West? What have been their main criticisms of it?

What historical contacts have there been between Britain and the Islamic world?

In what ways do you think each of the following can make a special contribution towards improving relations between Muslims and non-Muslims in a multicultural community: (i) Christian clergy, (ii) local government employees, (iii) policemen, (iv) imams, (v) teachers, (vi) local newspaper reporters, (vii) local businessmen. Are there any other key groups or individuals?

Assemble a file of press clippings relating to the Muslim community, using both local and national newspapers. What overall impression is given of Muslims and their faith? Can you find evidence of hostility, trivialisation or ignorance? Are Muslims presented as a problem to the community or as a community with problems?

Explain how the following headlines might come to appear in a local newspaper. What action would you advise in each situation? 'Muslim leader demands single sex schools', 'Councillor condemns "unhygienic" burials', 'Muslim workers fired for festival absence'.

Further reading

In 1978 Franklin Watts published a series of books which give basic information accompanied by black and white photographs: Gilda Berger, *Kuwait and the Rim of Arabia*; George S. Fichter, *Iraq*; Henry Gifford, *Syria*; Don Lawson, *Morocco, Algeria, Tunisia and Libya*; Emil Lengyel, *Modern Egypt*; Gerald Newman, *Lebanon*; Frederick Lane Poole, *Jordan*. See also W.B. Fisher, *The Oil States* (Batsford, 1980) and Richard Tames, *The Arab World Today* (Kaye & Ward, 1980). Both of these are written for upper secondary level.

30

Some Examples of Secondary Level RE Syllabuses

(See Appendix 7 for CSE, O and A level syllabuses)

Selective Girls School, South London

There is a detailed syllabus for the eleven to sixteen age-range. Three 'general aims' are specified: 'an appreciation of the religious quest as a universal phenomenon'; 'knowledge of, and sensitivity to, the dominant religious and philosophical systems of this country, with the greatest emphasis on the Judaeo-Christian tradition but also with attention to the "belief, behaviour and belonging" of Muslims, Hindus, Sikhs, Buddhists and Humanists'; 'a personal search for meaning'.

The first term of the first year is concerned with 'the nature of religion'. Examples from the Islamic tradition might be involved here. The rest of the first two years is devoted to Bible Studies. World religions 'provide the content for years three to five. Three objectives are reiterated: 'to impart knowledge about beliefs and practices'; 'to encourage attitudes of openness and tolerance'; 'to promote a spirit of free enquiry'.

The first term of the fourth year is devoted entirely to 'Muslims', the syllabus being organised as follows:

1 What is Islam? (NB Muslim conception of God.)
2 Life of Muhammad – his revelation and the establishment of a Muslim society.
3 The Five Pillars.
4 The Qur'an – its composition and structure, and discussion of certain selected passages.
5 The form and function of the mosque.
6 The characteristics of Muslim art.
7 The position of women in Islam.
8 The Muslim community in Britain.
9 Project (group work): one of the following topics: (i) A modern Islamic state, e.g. Iran, Pakistan, Egypt; (ii) Everyday customs in a particular Islamic society; (iii) A particular aspect of the history of Islam, e.g. Crusades, Muslim Spain, Ottoman Empire, Mogul Empire; (iv) A depth study of any other aspect of the course.

Mixed Comprehensive School, Essex

The school has its own Mode 3 O and A levels approved by London University for an experimental period of seven years.

Work in the lower school (years one to three) is organised thematically:

Year 1 – The language of wisdom and religion; Religious Founders and Leaders (including Muhammad); A place of worship (project).

Year 2 – Sacred writings (including Qur'an); Choices and decisions.

Year 3 – Rites of passage; Myself and the world about me

Non-examination religious education work in the upper school (years four to six) is largely implicit in its approach, occurring in the context of a 'Design for Living' course and courses on the background to current affairs and general studies.

The school's Mode 3 O level is organised as follows:

Section 1 – *Making a judgement* (personal responsibility including home, money, leisure, community).

Section 2 – *Religious belief*: (i) The place of founders, scriptures and traditions; (ii) Prayer, worship and spiritual discipline; (iii) Religion in the modern world; (iv) The use of music *or* art in religion.

Each section is assessed by a project and an examination (two hours) each of which carries 25 per cent of the total marks. Examples of projects include: 'Have I the right to do what I like?' 'Do women get fair opportunities?' 'People and religion in our neighbourhood' 'Religious poetry' 'The architecture, symbolism and furnishings of a particular place of worship'.

The school's Mode 3 A level is organised as follows:

Section 1 – *Man and religion*: Part A   The candidate's own belief, or one with which they are familiar, an exposition and defence of a point of view and its implications for behaviour. Part B   One other system of belief. Both parts are assessed by a project, each carrying 25 per cent of the final marks.

Section 2 – Part A   A study of one of the following themes in religious thought: (i) Science and religion; (ii) Ideological persecution; (iii) Literary sources of belief – their use and misuse; (iv) Religious leaders and prophets; (v) Religious education and the development of sensitivity. Part B   Philosophy of religion: (i) Religious language – myth, symbol and analogy; (ii) God and the world – creation, determinism and providence, miracles, evil and suffering; (iii) God and man – the existence of God, the nature of religious experience, man and his destiny, religion and morality. Both parts are assessed by an examination, each carrying 25 per cent of the final marks.

(NB Since this scheme was established three other local schools have adopted it.)

London Boys' School with a largely non-academic intake

Islam appears in the Religious Studies syllabus of this school at the following points:

Year 1 Term 1. *Founders of religions – Muhammad*. His childhood and early life. His marriage to Khadija. He is called to be a prophet; the Qur'an is revealed. He meets with opposition and leaves Mecca but later returns in triumph. (Some references might also be made in Term 3 – *Signs and symbols* – which also includes myths, names and parables.)

Year 2 Term 2. *Ways of living – the Muslim way of life*. (i) Home life – The distinction between sacred and secular made in the West is not made in Islam. All of life should be lived in submission to the will of God. (ii) Relationships within the family. Duty to obey and eventually care for parents. (iii) Food and drink – The consumption of pork and alcohol is forbidden. Animal life is taken only in the name of God, so Muslims only eat meat killed by Muslim butchers. (iv) Daily and weekly devotions – Daily declaration of faith. On Fridays prayer at the mosque; children are taught the Qur'an at the mosque. Reference may be made to the Five Pillars which are dealt with more fully in the third year.

Term 3. *Basic questions/sacred writings*. Basic questions about man – Who am I? Why am I here? Where am I going? Basic questions about the world – How did it happen? Why did it happen? To consider the answers suggested in the sacred writings/holy books of various religions.

Year 3 Term 1. *Religion and life* – 'rites of passage' and 'codes for living' both involve consideration of Islam.

Term 2. *How men worship* – covers religious buildings, holy days, 'middle men' (such as the *imam*) and festivals.

Term 3. *Men need hope* – this includes a unit on the significance of Jerusalem for Jews, Muslims and Christians. With reference to Muslims the following main points are made: (i) things they share with Jews and Christians (e.g. Old Testament prophets); (ii) things peculiar to Islam (e.g. Dome of the Rock); (iii) occupation for a long period; (iv) Crusades were holy wars for Muslims.

Years 4 and 5. The syllabus is organised on the theme of *Human Rights*. Islam is specifically mentioned in connection with 'Freedom of Worship' and could well be referred to under such headings as 'Justice', 'Crime and Punishment', 'Education', 'The Family', 'Marriage, Children's Rights, Women's Rights' and 'Peace and International Order' (includes religious attitudes to violence, war and peace in the world's religions).

Further reading

See Eric Pain, 'Developing a world religions course' and Marilyn Thomas, 'Religious education in a multi-ethnic comprehensive school', both in Robert Jackson (ed.), *Approaching World Religions* (John Murray, 1982) for examples of how Islam fits into the overall RE syllabuses of fourth- and fifth-year examination pupils (both CSE and O level Mode 3) and first- to third-year pupils respectively.

The Muslim brush has painted such large tracts of time and space during the last fourteen hundred years that the historical panorama which did not feature them could be nothing but a wild and grotesque distortion of reality. (James L. Henderson, 'The importance of Islam')[1]

Merely to mention Cordoba and Isfahan, Saladin and Sulaiman the Magnificent, the Taj Mahal and the Thousand and One Nights, is to indicate the richness of Islam's splendid heritage. And it could certainly be argued that an awareness of the history of Islam is essential for an understanding of such contemporary matters as the political rhetoric of Arab nationalism, the constitutional law of Pakistan, ethnic rivalries in Nigeria, armed insurrection in the Philippines, the legal status of Jerusalem and the cultural and linguistic policies of the Soviet regime. By examining the past through Muslim eyes we can also reveal new perspectives (for example the Mughal and Ottoman empires at their height, rather than in decline) and discover a new significance in familiar events, (by understanding the Crusades in terms of culture-contact as well as political conflict). Nevertheless it must be admitted that Islam scarcely figures in history as it is taught in British secondary schools. What follows is a brief indication of some ways in which the current treatment of topics related to Islamic history could be enlarged or treated in a more balanced manner, followed by a sketch of a possible area for RE–History co-operation at the lower secondary level.

A level

Nineteenth-century British and European history is one of the most popular options. Two topics which are often dealt with are the Ottoman Empire and the Mahdist conquest of the Sudan. Both tend to be treated rather dismissively, the Ottoman Empire simply being labelled 'the sick man of Europe' and the Mahdi and his followers being dismissed as madmen. That the Ottoman Empire was a sophisticated bureaucratic State, which made strenuous efforts at internal reform and only collapsed after losing a world war, is scarcely noted. That the Mahdi was both a skilful leader and that his movement was only one of a number resisting the advance of European imperialism, from the Atlas mountains to the Caucasus, is likewise ignored. There are, however, a number of accessible scholarly accounts which could go far to correct these distortions, such as Bernard Lewis, *The Origins of Modern Turkey*.[2]

Students working on the 'early modern' period will encounter Muslims in the guise of 'the terrible Turk' who was, in the sixteenth and seventeenth centuries, in the pet cliché of the examiners, a 'threat to the peace of Europe'. (Europe in that period showed itself, of course, to be quite capable of destroying its peace by means of internal religious divisions without external assistance – *vide* the Fronde, the Thirty Years War and the activities of the Inquisition.) That European visitors to the new imperial capital of Istanbul were awed by its splendours is less likely to be noted; that Luther warned the German princes that Turkish rule seemed so benevolent compared with their own that their peasants would gladly change masters if they knew of this, is likewise scarcely likely to be known. This period also embraces the self-styled 'Age of Discovery', which offers an opportunity to consider relations between Europeans and the Mughal empire in India and the Safavid empire in Persia, when they were on a par militarily and technologically. Useful sources are the *Letters* of Ogier Ghiselin de Busbecq,[3] a Habsburg diplomat at the Ottoman Court, Halil Inalcik's masterly survey *The Ottoman Empire*[4] and Norman Itzkowitz *Ottoman Empire and Islamic Tradition*.[5] Bamber Gascoigne's *The Great Mughals*[6] is superbly illustrated. J.J. Saunders, *The Muslim World on the Eve of Europe's Expansion*[7] is a very useful collection of documentary extracts. See also M.A. Cook, *A History of the Ottoman Empire to 1730*[8] and P.M. Holt, *The Mahdist State in the Sudan*.[9]

Medievalists, and indeed any historian with an interest in historiography, should be aware of the career and works of Ibn Khaldun (1332–1406). He was deeply involved in the turbulent politics of North Africa but his enduring significance lies in 'The Muqaddimah', an introductory essay which precedes the main text of his universal *History* (Kitab al-Ibar). Ibn Khaldun has been hailed by Toynbee as the true father of modern historical writing. Others have seen him as a founding father of sociology.[10]

M.A. Enan, *Ibn Khaldun: His Life and Work*,[11] sketches the historian's adventurous career and then considers his contributions to sociology and political science, the relation of his thought to that of Machiavelli and how modern commentators have regarded his work. See also Aziz Al-Azmeh, *Ibn Khaldun in Modern Scholarship*.[12]

O Level

A number of GCE Boards now offer papers in twentieth-century world history. The 'Arab-Israeli dispute' is quite a popular topic and is also the subject of one of the four modern world studies of the Schools Council's History 13 to 16 project; but the Islamic dimension of this conflict is often ignored. Atatürk's attempts to limit the influence of Islam in Turkey provides the other main topic relating to the Middle East. These efforts are invariably presented from an uncritically Eurocentric viewpoint as long-overdue 'reforms' and their limited impact is often overlooked. Little is taught about the recent history of such obviously important countries as Iran and Saudi Arabia. An especially useful resource is therefore Richard Lawless' recently published *The Middle East in the Twentieth Century*,[13] an illustrated account written for this age group. Also useful for teachers are Walter Laqueur, *The Israel-Arab Reader*,[14] Martin Gilbert, *The Arab-Israeli Conflict: Its History in Maps*[15] and T.G. Fraser, *The Middle East 1914–1979*.[16]

Lower secondary level

Teachers of history, generally speaking, have a fairly free hand in terms of syllabus construction for the eleven to fourteen age group (NB about half of all British children give up history after the age of fourteen). The following topic outline is aimed at this level:

The expansion of Islam

Before the Prophet Muhammad, the Arabs were a pagan tribal people inhabiting a vast, barren peninsula, despised by the great empires which bordered their territories. A century after his death they were the rulers of a sprawling empire of their own, which stretched from the Pyrenees to the borders of India. Their language had taken a decisive step towards world status. They had created whole new cities and a new style of architecture. Their laws would give distinctive shape to the lives, commerce and customs of an entirely new civilisation for a thousand years to come, without chal-lenge. As W.H. McNeill has put it:

> Never before or since has a prophet won such success so quickly; nor has the work of a single man so rapidly and radically transformed the course of world history. Through his inspired utterances, his personal example and the organisational framework he established for Islam, Muhammad laid the basics for a distinctive new style of life, which within the space of two centuries attracted the allegiance of a major fraction of the human race. (*The Rise of the West*)[17]

How did this come about? What have been the lasting results of these momentous changes? The following points might be considered:

1   The conquest

Was it planned or did it 'just happen'? Why was it so rapid? Why did the degree of resistance vary greatly in different areas? What problems were created by the speed and scale of the conquest? (for example the need to control many different ethnic groups and to adapt their customs, laws and tax-systems). What were the aims of the conquerors? How important was the 'purely' religious factor? McNeill observes that:

> . . . daily prayers must have had much the same psychological effect upon an army on campaign as does modern close-order drill. Precise gestures and recitation of

prayers inculcated sentiments of solidarity within the ranks and habits of obedience to the commander, who, in the early days, was also prayer leader. Such
exercises no doubt did much to overcome the chronic weakness of any nomad
confederacy – insubordination resulting from tribal and personal rivalries. (*The
Rise of the West*, p.428)

The enduring impact of Islam can be illustrated clearly by contrasting a
map of the Islamic world a century after the Prophet's death with a map of
the Islamic world today. This would illustrate two important points – that,
with the notable exceptions of Spain, Sicily and the Balkans, Islam has never
been dislodged from an area in which it has established itself, and that Islam
continued to spread as a creed (for example Africa and S.E. Asia) for
centuries after it had ceased to expand militarily. Pupils may get a more
accurate impression of the scale and process of Muslim expansion if they
work in groups, each looking at one particular area in one particular phase.
Imaginative writing and/or role-playing could be related to the experience
of, for instance, Bedouin warriors in the first wave of conquest, encounter-
ing great cities for the first time, or Christians in such cities, perhaps fearing
the worst at the hands of their new masters. A dramatic scene could be
improvised around the negotiations which might have taken place between
the leaders of a Muslim army and the representatives of a conquered city.
This could be used to bring out the fears of the latter and the policy of the
former. (Three examples of treaties are to be found in P.K. Hitti, *Islam and
the West*.)[18]

2 The culture

Perhaps the most important question is – why was the conquest so permanent? Empires built on rapid conquest may prove ephemeral (for example
the Mongols). They endure when conquerors have a positive world view to
impose and live by, in this case Islam, with its Qur'anically inspired law codes
expressed in Arabic. In the long run the lasting victories are won in the
battle of ideas.

The Arab empire was Arab, as it were, all round but not all through. Islam
supplied the framework of law, Arabic the language of the elite, and Arabs the
leading office-holders. But the sheer size of the conquered territories and their
populations necessitated the incorporation of non-Arabs into the system. The
Arabs ... needed Persian and Greek officials to collect their taxes, keep their
records, maintain public works ... The Arabs were likewise grateful to take
advantage of the advanced technical skills of their subjects in such fields as
medicine and architecture in which they themselves had little expertise. What
emerged was a synthesis, something truly new, an Islamic culture compounded of
Arab values, Greek technique and Persian style. (Richard Tames, *The Arab World
Today*)[19]

It might perhaps be difficult to explain to lower secondary pupils just
what it was about the Islamic empire that made it Islamic; but the material
significance of its achievements in terms of buildings, trade, technology and
the introduction of new products and crops to Europe can more easily be
grasped. The word-list reproduced on page 236 can serve to remind us that

there was a time when Europe played the role of 'developing world' to Islam's 'developed world', borrowing its vocabulary as it imported the fruits (literally as well as metaphorically) of its more advanced civilisation. One way in which the cultural achievements of medieval Islam might be presented is through the personality and career of the child prodigy and polymath Avicenna (Ibn Sina) whose writings were well known in the West and referred to by Chaucer.

3   The crusades

The crusades fall into a more proper perspective when seen in the general context of cultural contact between Islam and Christendom. Militarily they were never more than a side-show, compared with, say, the impact of the Mongols. But their effects on European culture range from changes in techniques of castle-building to styles and themes of lyric poetry. Nor should concentration on the Levant lead one to ignore the brilliance of the encounter of Christian and Muslim in Sicily and Spain.

4   An overview

The Islamic world cannot be summarised but it could be surveyed. This was the achievement of that tireless traveller, Ibn Battuta, who is estimated to have covered some 75,000 miles between 1325 and 1353, visiting not only the central Arab lands but also Spain, West Africa, India and China. His observations on every subject from coconuts to the Black Death were recorded in a lengthy account of his travels. Extracts from his African travels appear in Said Hamdun and Noel King, *Ibn Battuta in Black Africa*.[20] The full version of the 'Travels', edited by H.A.R. Gibb, is published by the Hakluyt Society.

Sources

1 James L. Henderson, 'The importance of Islam', *World Studies Bulletin* no. 29, December 1973.

1 Bernard Lewis, *The Origins of Modern Turkey* (OUP, 2nd edn, 1968).

3 Ogier Ghiselin de Busbecq, *Letters* (OUP, 1967).

4 Halil Inalcik, *The Ottoman Empire* (Weidenfeld & Nicolson, 1973).

5 Norman Itzkowitz, *Ottoman Empire and Islamic Tradition* (Alfred A. Knopf, 1972).

6 Bamber Gascoigne, *The Great Mughals* (Cape, 1971).

7 J.J. Saunders (ed.), *The Muslim World on the Eve of Europe's Expansion* (Prentice-Hall, 1966).

8 M.A. Cook (ed.), *A History of the Ottoman Empire to 1730* (CUP, 1980).

9 P.M. Holt, *The Mahdist State in the Sudan* (OUP, 2nd edn, 1970).

10 Ibn Khaldun, *The Muqaddimah: An Introduction to History* (Routledge & Kegan Paul, paperback edn, 1978).

11 M.A. Enan, *Ibn Khaldun: His Life and Work* (Kitab Bhavan, New Delhi, 1979).

12 Aziz Al-Azmeh, *Ibn Khaldun in Modern Scholarship* (Third World Centre, 1981).

13 Richard Lawless, *The Middle East in the Twentieth Century* (Batsford, 1980).

14 Walter Laqueur (ed.), *The Israel-Arab Reader* (Bantam Books, 3rd edn, 1976).

15 Martin Gilbert, *The Arab-Israeli Conflict: Its History in Maps* (Weidenfeld & Nicolson, 3rd edn, 1979).

16 T.G. Fraser, *The Middle East 1914–1979* (Edward Arnold, 1980).

17 W.H. McNeill, *The Rise of the West* (University of Chicago Press, 1963), p.421.

18 P.K. Hitti (ed.), *Islam and the West* (Van Nostrand Reinhold, 1962), reading no. 6.

19 Richard Tames, *The Arab World Today* (Kaye & Ward, 1980), pp.23–4.

20 Said Hamdun and Noel King, *Ibn Battuta in Black Africa* (Rex Collings, 1975).

Resources on 'The Expansion of Islam'

For pupils

Viola Bailey and Ella Wise, *Mohammed: His Times and Influence* (Chambers, 1976). Illustrated. Many questions and exercises. Special sections on Baghdad and Cordoba.

Carol Barker, *A Prince of Islam* (Macdonald & Jane's, 1976). Fictionalised account of a Baghdad boyhood. Superb illustrations but historically inconsistent.

Trevor Cairns, *Barbarians, Christians and Muslims* (CUP, 1971). Contains brief ten-page account of Islam.

P.W. Crittenden, *Islam in the Middle Ages* (covers the conquest); *The Achievements of Islam* (covers the culture) (Macmillan, 1971). Illustrated. Some questions.

John Duckworth, *Muhammad and the Arab Empire* (Harrap, 1974). Illustrated. Many extracts from contemporary sources.

Gerald Hawting, *The Moors* (Sampson Low, 1978). Colour-illustrated survey of Moorish Spain and North Africa. Sections on government, warfare, daily life, sports and the arts. Links past and present at many points.

Trevor John, *East and West at the Time of the Crusades* (Ginn, 1972). Mostly on Europe but with chapters on Byzantium, the Arab Empire, Arab civilisation and 'How Byzantium, Islam and the West saw each other'.

Antony Kamm, *The Story of Islam* (Dinosaur Publications, 1976). Brief, inexpensive and well illustrated. Especially useful on cultural aspects, including science and music.

Brenda Ralph Lewis, *Islam* (Wayland Publishers Ltd, 1978). Some useful illustrations, but also many nineteenth-century engravings over-emphasising 'romantic' and exotic aspects. Text must be used with care.

Brenda Ralph Lewis, *The How and Why Wonder Book of the Crusades* (Transworld, 1975). Question and answer narrative history. Inexpensive.

H.A.O. McWilliams, *Muhammad and the World of Islam* (Longman, 1979). Illustrated account in the 'Then and There' series. Accompanying slide set available.

Anton Powell, *The Rise of Islam* (Longman, 1979). Colour-illustrated survey with the emphasis on culture, including sections on court life, women, slaves, trade, technology, Spain and Baghdad.

David Sweetman, *The How and Why Wonder Book of The Arab World* (Transworld, 1979). Inexpensive, question and answer narrative history. Useful sections on the crusades, the 'Arabian Nights' and cultural exchange between Islam and Christendom.

Richard Tames, *The World of Islam* (Jackdaw No. 143, 1976). Useful visual material on mosques, cities, arts, science and leading personalities.

Boswell Taylor, *The World of Islam* (Hodder & Stoughton, 1976). Inexpensive, visual source book; mostly line drawings based on contemporary sources.

Duncan Townson, *Muslim Spain* (CUP, 1973). Illustrated case-study, setting Spain in the context of Muslim expansion.

Kathrine Sorley Walker, *Saladin: Sultan of the Holy Sword* (Dennis Dobson, 1971). Full-length biography for school-age readers; based on contemporary sources.

Malcolm Yapp, *Ibn Sina* (Harrap, 1974). Illustrated brief biography of leading Muslim intellectual (Avicenna); with documentary extracts.

There are also many historical novels for younger readers, set against the background of the crusades – for example Alfred Duggan, *Knight in Armour* (Penguin), Ronald Welch, *Knight Crusader* (OUP).

For teachers

Aziz Ahmad, *A History of Islamic Sicily* (Edinburgh University Press, 1975). Concise scholarly account.

A.S. Atiyah, *Crusade, Commerce and Culture* (OUP, 1962). Scholarly essays on culture contact.

Edward Atiyah, *The Arabs* (Librairie du Liban, Beirut, 1968). The first two chapters give a concise account of 'The rise and fall of the Arab Empire' and 'The place of the Arabs in history'.

Michael Brett and Werner Forman, *The Moors: Islam in the West* (Orbis Publishing, 1980). Beautifully illustrated account with the emphasis on social organisation, cultural achievements and the intellectual outlook of the age.

Norman Daniel, *The Arabs and Medieval Europe* (Longman, 2nd edn, 1979). Scholarly survey of the interaction of Christendom and Islam; especially useful on Spain, the crusades, Sicily, scientific and theological exchanges and mutual perceptions.

D.M. Dunlop, *Arab Civilisation to AD 1500* (Longman, 1978). Scholarly survey.

Sir Hamilton Gibb, *The Life of Saladin* (Oxford, 1973). Brief scholarly biography based on the works of two historians closely associated with him.

John Bagot Glubb, *A Short History of the Arab Peoples* (Quartet, 1978), *The Great Arab Conquests* (Quartet, 1980). Detailed popular narrative histories.

G.E. Von Grünebaum, *Medieval Islam: A Study in Cultural Orientation* (University of Chicago Press, 2nd edn, 1953). Scholarly essays on institutions and culture, including one on 'Christendom and Islam' and another on 'Creative borrowing: Greece in the Arabian Nights'.

G.E. Von Grünebaum, *Classical Islam: A History 600–1258* (Allen & Unwin, 1970). Scholarly survey with the emphasis on the political. Useful detailed chronology and bibliography.

P.M. Holt, Ann K.S. Lambton and Bernard Lewis (eds), *The Cambridge History of Islam* (CUP, 2 vols, 1970). Standard scholarly work of reference. vol. I covers Islamic expansion. vol. II, Part VIII deals with 'Islamic society and civilisation', including a chapter on 'The transmission of learning and literary influences to Western Europe'.

Philip K. Hitti, *History of the Arabs* (Macmillan, 10th edn 1970). Exhaustive survey including nine chapters on 'The Arabs in Europe'.

Philip K. Hitti, *Makers of Arab History* (Macmillan, 1968). Useful brief biographies of Umar, Muawiyah, Al-Mamun, Saladin, Ibn Sina, Ibn Khaldun and others.

Reuben Levy, *The Social Structure of Islam* (CUP, 1971). Introduced by a fifty-page sketch of Islamic expansion, this study focuses on social organisation and institutions.

Archibald Lewis, *The Islamic World and the West 622–1492 AD* (John Wiley & Sons, 1970). Edited extracts from documentary sources and scholarly essays on commercial, literary, and scientific contacts, including the crusades.

Bernard Lewis, *The Arabs in History* (Hutchinson, 5th edn 1970). Standard brief scholarly survey.

Bernard Lewis (ed.), *Islam from the Prophet Muhammad to the Capture of Constantinople* (Harper & Row, 2 vols, 1974). Selected extracts from contemporary sources. Vol. I deals with war and politics, Vol. II with religion and society.

Peter Mansfield, *The Arabs* (Penguin, revised edition 1978). Popular history. See especially chapters 2 and 3, 'The great Arab explosion' and 'The long decline'.

William H. McNeill and Marilyn Robinson Waldman, *The Islamic World* (OUP, 1973). Very useful collection of extracts from contemporary sources, including Usamah and Ibn Battuta.

Jan Read, *The Moors in Spain and Portugal* (Faber, 1974). Detailed popular narrative history.

Michael Rogers, *The Spread of Islam* (Elsevier Phaidon, 1976). Superbly illustrated historical survey through architecture and archaeology: useful glossary.

R.M. Savory (ed.), *Introduction to Islamic Civilisation* (CUP, 1976). Eighteen essays including 'The Middle East as world centre of science and medicine', 'What the West borrowed from the Middle East' and 'Christendom vs. Islam: Fourteen centuries of interaction and co-existence'.

R.W. Southern, *Western Views of Islam in the Middle Ages* (Harvard University Press, 1962). Concise scholarly narrative.

W.M. Watt, *The Influence of Islam on Medieval Europe* (Edinburgh University Press, 1972). Concise scholarly synthesis.

The Genius of Arab Civilisation: Source of Renaissance (Phaidon, 1976). Scholarly essays on cultural, commercial and technological linkages with the West. Outstanding illustrations. See also: Richard Tames, 'Studying Islamic culture' (*The New Era*, vol. 56, no. 7, September/October 1975) and 'Islam in history' (*Teaching History*, no. 17, February 1977).

32
Social Studies

Whatever social studies may or may not be taken to embrace, social relationships should surely form their central focus. Social relationships imply some elementary understanding of what it means to be a person in a particular society, what this means in terms of rights and responsibilities, and how the concept of being an individual relates to the idea of being a member of a family and a community.

One could take a 'cultural universals' approach – examining a particular society in terms of those features which are held to be common to all societies, such as:

(i) social stratification – differentiation between individuals and families on the grounds of wealth, power and status (and piety?);

(ii) kinship – the significance of blood and marital linkages, both actual and fictive;

(iii) conflict management – by means of law, feuding, gossip;

(iv) social mobility and equilibrium – by marriage, education, inheritance, etcetera;

(v) socialisation – patterns of child-rearing and 'rites of passage' (birth, initiation into the community, marriage and parenthood, death).

Alternatively, one could take an 'idealist' approach; given that Islam is a religion which implies a total view of man and society, one could consider what an ideal Islamic society might be like and how far any existing society measures up to this ideal. Apart from the Qur'an and *hadith*, proverbs and folk-heroes might be useful indicators of social values in this regard. Could one, perhaps, arrive at a definition of 'the good man' in Islamic terms?

Because Islam is, as so many writers have stressed, a 'complete way of life', it should be of especial importance and interest to the teacher of social studies, whose concern is the whole range of structures, relationships and processes sustained by 'man in society'.

All of the world's great religious traditions deal with man's relationship with the 'ultimate', with the question of his origin and purpose and with the problems of death, suffering and evil; but between, and within, these various traditions can be found widely varying emphases regarding the significance of the here and now and of man's relationship to his fellows, ranging from an ideal of total withdrawal to that of positive striving through active involvement in public life. In Christianity one can find strong traditions of monasticism on the one hand and of evangelism on the other, both manifesting themselves in individualistic and collective forms. Islam has likewise given birth, through Sufism, to individual mystics and to brotherhoods of devotees but its main concern has been to emphasise the value and importance of a life lived not just in conformity with the divine ordinance, but within the social order. Worldly success is not decried but the obligations of family life must take precedence over it. The Qur'an has many apocalyptic passages describing Heaven and Hell and the Day of Judgement; it also contains very detailed prescriptions and guidelines for men's dealings with one another.

Why should Islam display this social emphasis? One explanation might be that it appeared in the midst of a social crisis and prospered just because it offered a basis and framework for a new social and moral order, capable of reintegrating a society which had shown itself incapable of reconciling the tribal mores of the desert with the novel conditions of urban life in rapidly expanding Mecca. Islam offered an attractive and workable alternative to a social order based on force and cunning rather than a coherent pattern of mutual rights and obligations. Muhammad's preaching singled out the social evils of his day – the arrogance of the rich, the neglect of what we would now call the socially disadvantaged – but he went beyond analysis and indictment into the realm of prescription and practice (hence the buttressing of the rights of women and orphans, and obligation to pay the poor-due (*zakat*) and so on). During the Medinan period successive revelations dealt with such mundane matters as marriage, property rights, crime and the ethics of trade and war.

After the Prophet's death, and while the boundaries of Muslim influence were expanding rapidly to embrace millions of subjects scattered over a vast area and divided by religious beliefs and ethnic ties, the framework of the Islamic social order was elaborated by the ulema, the learned judges who were the architects of the great edifice of holy law (*shari'a*) which represented the Muslim ideal. The rituals of the faith themselves express and reinforce its social character – the *shahada* is a *public* profession of belief, prayers may be said in any public place, fasting is likewise a communal activity, alms are given as a social obligation and the *hajj* acts as a visible affirmation of the universal brotherhood of all believers.

Islam is both a fact and an aspiration. Historically speaking an Islamic community has existed here on earth since the lifetime of the Prophet, but constant self-development is a condition of its continuing existence. Islam must, so to speak, constantly strive to become more Islamic. As Van Nieuwenhuijze has put it

> Islam is a state of mind and a continuous act. It is the implementation of a pre-established given norm. This norm is at once this-worldly and other-worldly. It is an eternal part of the divine order of existence. Yet at the same time, an account of revelation, it is decisively part and parcel of the transient order of being. (*Sociology of the Middle East*)[1]

What then are the salient features of this normative social order which the earth-bound Muslim community aspires to realise? The diagram attempts to represent some of its major characteristics, albeit crudely.

	ALLAH		D
	PROPHETS		A
	QUR'AN		R
ULEMA		KHALIFA	A
			L
	SHARI'A		
	ADULT		H
	MALE MUSLIMS		A
			R
DHIMMI	WOMEN	SLAVES	B

1 Allah, the Creator, the Omniscient, the Omnipresent presides over the reality He has established and whose boundaries in space and time He determines.

2 Allah has revealed Himself to man through His prophets (culminating in Muhammad). Man as a conscious agent and the summit of creation is free to follow the divine ordinance and thus to create the ideal Islamic community on earth.

3 The Qur'an stands as the final and complete revelation of God's purpose. It contains the principles upon which the Islamic social order must be based.

4 The *ulema* are the guardians, interpreters and through the devices of *ijtihad* (expert independent opinion) *qiyas* (analogy) and *ijma* (consensus) also the elaborators of the Shari'a.

5 The *Khalifa* (Caliph) is Muhammad's successor as temporal head of the Muslim community and ultimately responsible for maintaining conditions or order within which men may pursue righteousness. In practice his power may be deputed to an able politico-military commander (sultan) or devolved to local leaders (*amirs*). Ideally, the Khalifa should model himself on the first four Caliphs (the Rashidin or 'rightly-guided').

6 The Shari'a sets out a complete framework for social existence. Every act is classified in one of five categories – forbidden, discouraged, neutral, permitted, obligatory. Four Schools of Law (*madhab*) offer varying interpretations on points of detail.

7 Adult male Muslims constitute the active core of the community. They are all equal to one another in rights and obligations. Other social categories (such as women, children, slaves, and *dhimmi* – protected Christians and Jews) are essentially dependent upon them.

8 Outside Islam lies the *dar al-harb* (House of War).

Traditionally three ways of life have co-existed in the Middle East, those of the nomad, the peasant and the townsman. Each has its own distinctive character but each also depends upon the others for its continuance.

Detailed examination of each in turn can often lead us to ignore the vital links between them. The extent and manner of their inter-relationship becomes all the more significant when we come to consider the rapid and fundamental changes which have overtaken each of them in the present century.

In the twentieth century the entertainment industry has nourished the stereotyped image of the desert nomad as the type of the Arab which generations of travel writers have firmly established in the mind of the average Westerner. Stirred by the romantic picture of the hawk-eyed, aquiline prince of the wastelands, many Westerners still find it difficult to associate the term 'Arab' with such figures as the white-collar office-worker, or the hard-working peasant, though these far outnumber the nomads and are playing a far more significant part in creating the new societies in which the nomad is more and more likely to be cast in the role of victim than of master.

Nevertheless, a study of the nomad and his way of life is of value for at least three major reasons:

(i) It enables us to appreciate some of the most distinctive features of Arab culture (such as the importance of 'face') which may have originated in the desert but which became generalised to townsmen and villagers alike.

(ii) It enables us to gain new insights into the history and literature of the Arab peoples, in which the nomad and his values figure so largely.

(iii) It provides unusually clear and well-documented exemplification of some of the most fundamental social patterns and processes and it thus can be of great value in any programme designed to give some elementary insight into the workings and structure of human groups. It is also worth noting Lenski's observation that:

> Herding societies are extremely interesting from the religious stand-point. No other societal type so closely resembles Judaism and Christianity in its conception of God. In forty of the fifty herding groups for which the Ethnographic Atlas has data, there is a belief in a Supreme Deity who created the world and remains actively concerned with its affairs, especially with man's moral conduct. This combination of beliefs is rare in other societies . . . (G. Lenski, *Human Societies*)[2]

Historically speaking, the village and its inhabitants have played an essentially passive role in the development of Middle Eastern society. The culture of the village is less distinctive than that of the city or the nomad camp because it stands at the mid-point of the sociological spectrum of which they are the two extremes. The villager has, moreover, been looked down upon both by the townsman and by the nomad, his passive relationship towards both symbolised by the exaction of taxes and rents by the one, tribute and plunder by the other. Deprived of its surplus products by these payments, the village has been forced towards subsistence levels of existence. A tempting and vulnerable target for attack, the village cannot afford the defences and armed guards of the city or resort to flight like the nomads. An essentially isolated (both physically and psychologically) community, it cannot summon or expect help from the outside world when under attack.

Given these circumstances the tenaciousness and stability of the village community is all the more remarkable. And it must be stressed, moreover, that the vast majority of the population of the Middle East are villagers and that this has invariably been the case. Without the peasants and the surplus foodstuffs they produce, city life, with its concentrations of non-agricultural specialists (priests, craftsmen, clerks), and nomadic life, with its heavy dependence on stock-raising, would both have been impossible. From the nomads the villagers have acquired their meat, milk products and stock for breeding and transport; from the city they have received luxuries such as tea, coffee, tobacco and fine cloth and such specialist services as can be provided by the religious and the literate. In return they have supplied crops, men, and, increasingly, cash. So long as these have been forthcoming, the management of their internal affairs has been a matter of indifference to townsmen and nomad alike, and they have been left to settle their own disputes, organise their own rituals and develop their own public works.

In the absence of outside interference the political structure of the village community was largely determined by kinship and operated through informal processes to maintain approved standards of behaviour. In larger settlements the status-ranking system was more complex and the significance of immediate bonds of kinship might be qualified by the operation of other criteria, such as descent (for example Sayyids, who claim descent from the Prophet) wealth, literacy or a reputation for holiness. Village leaders would usually be drawn from one or two traditionally prominent families. This tended to ensure stability and continuity; in its absence divisive factionalism could arise and, if carried to extremes, threaten the survival of the entire community. Competent leadership was essential to ensure the correct performance of activities essential to the continuation of the life of the community – settling disputes, organising special festivals and annual ceremonies, making decisions about the agricultural cycle and dealing with representatives of the outside world. Competence in this context implied neither the capacity to innovate nor even to coerce (in most instances) but rather to preserve traditional norms and knowledge and to ensure, by persuasion and example, that the wisdom they enshrined was acknowledged and acted upon. The successful village leader was one who could make tradition work. The model of the 'solid citizen' in village terms was one who would accept and support this mode of leadership, conform to tradition in every particular and behave in a totally predictable manner. Initiative, innovation and enterprise were not regarded as desirable qualities but as threats to the stability of the established order, an order whose capacity for self-preservation had evolved to cope with threats from predators and a harsh physical environment.

The significance of kinship and informal processes of control in village life is symbolised by the physical layout of many villages, just as their isolation is symbolised and maintained by the state of (or absence of) the roads. Houses and outbuildings rarely follow a regular plan of streets and squares, pathways and spaces are simply residual areas where no one has felt the need to build yet. The houses of various lineages tend to cluster together; 'newcomers', even those who have been in the village for a generation or more, tend to be, quite literally, outsiders. The central importance of the mosque in the life of the community, and where the village is large enough to support them, of the bath-house, coffee-house and shops, is reflected in its central location. In this sense the physical structure of the village symbolises the expression of its basic social pattern and needs.

Throughout the Middle East the village is undergoing a revolutionary transformation, sometimes consciously inspired by a revolutionary ideology, sometimes the unlooked-for outcome of the impact of improved technology and changing economic relationships. Even before the assertion of Arab nationalist ambitions the pace of change had begun to quicken. During the imperialist phase the penetration of the demands of a growing world economy encouraged landowners to press their tenants to plant cash-crops such as cotton, tying the fortunes of entire communities to movements of world prices. Growing urbanisation, improved communications and widening opportunities for non-agricultural employment (for example in building and transport) encouraged wholesale migration of young men from the villages, some of which became virtually dependent on their remittances for survival (especially in Turkey and the Levant).

Since the Second World War the pace of change has both quickened and taken on a new character – planned and purposive, comprehensive and cumulative – as newly independent governments have pledged themselves to the economic and social transformation of their societies. The nomad must be settled, the city must be modernised, the village must be integrated into the life of the nation. The practical outcome of the attempt to realise these objectives is the emergence of new tensions at the village level. Development demands new competences and thus creates new statuses; the pharmacist is paid more, and can do more, than the holy man; as the community comes to see him as one who knows more he may in time be perceived as one who is worth more. Naturally these transformations will be resisted by the current holders of positions of power and prestige (unless they can somehow define a role for themselves within the new order) – the more so as their conceptions of 'law and order' and 'public welfare' simply do not coincide with those of the bureaucrats and their agents, the teacher, the policeman and the agricultural 'expert'. These intruders threaten a way of life sanctioned by the unchallengeable past, and with it the values and virtues it seeks to uphold. As a wandering holy man told an American anthropologist in Southern Iraq, 'We want to preserve the way of life which God ordained for us, while you wish to destroy what is known to be good and bring about something which you hope will be better but which is usually worse.'

Development may not only be consciously resisted, it may also be retarded where it is superficially welcomed. Villagers are usually quick to appreciate its material promise, seen in terms of access to health services, electricity and consumer goods which are currently the coveted status symbols of the village elite. They are slower to appreciate the changes which accompany these longed-for benefits – increasing interference by government and its agencies (usually in the person of outsiders), more regular work patterns (possibly threatening valued leisure time, festivals, etcetera), the erosion of traditional patterns of authority and deference (especially within the family), the alienation between generations which education and urban life can bring about. The desire to gain the benefits of development without paying its price must produce frustration and disillusionment, which may lead either to violence or apathy.

Nothing illustrates better the collision of modernity and tradition than the uneasy co-existence of two types of school within the same community, each embodying a different conception of the good man and the good society. On the one hand there is the Qur'anic school, often housed in the mosque, its equipment a few battered texts and well-scratched slates, where rows of pupils chant memorised slabs of the Holy Book under the stern eye of an aged master. On the other is the newly built government school, with its shining new furniture and equipment, its emphasis on understanding rather than memorisation and its enthusiastic young (and often female) teachers. Both seek to inculcate loyalty but aim to direct it along divergent paths.

A city is essentially a complex of significant concentrations – of people, of wealth, of power and of information. Its size and range of functions, the grandeur of its buildings and the fact that news, specialised personnel and high-quality products flow from it to the countryside, rather than vice versa, are what distinguish it from the large village and the small town.

The functions of the city are reflected in the specialised occupations and buildings which define its character:

manufacture	– artisans	bazaar &
trade & commerce	– merchants & moneylenders	market place
government	– administrators & judges	palace & courts
religion	– ulema	mosques &
education	– students	colleges

The most powerful and prestigious members of these various specialised social categories together constitute the urban elite; literacy and landownership are usually prerequisites for admission into this circle. Traditionally members of the group have minimised their everyday contacts with the urban masses, dealing with them through intermediaries such as maids, clerks, bailiffs and managers or members of ethnic minorities who, being socially marginal, can move among both the elite and the mass because they are accepted by neither. Their aloofness is symbolised by the architecture of their homes which look inward to a courtyard and preserve their privacy with high wall, strong gates and small windows.

The complex and continuing network of linkages which bind the city to its hinterland has been admirably summarised by Paul W. English:

> The city is the major market place for everything the villagers produce . . . If his daughter is to be wed or his social position demands that a celebration be held, the peasant asks his landlord or weaving contractor for an advance, and failing that will have recourse to the moneylenders of the bazaar. And debt is a binding tie; many debtors live in villages, most creditors in the city. If a villager has broken the law or the army threatens to induct him, his last appeal will always be to the most powerful urbanite he or his family knows. (*City and Village in Iran*)[3]

This traditional pattern of exchanges has been both extended and intensified in the course of the present century. And the structure of the city, both physical and social, is likewise in process of transformation. The improvement in communications by land, sea and air has promoted its physical expansion and enhanced its international contacts, thus changing the character of its local culture.

New buildings — banks, hospitals, drugstores and filling-stations — signify the emergence of new occupational categories, a new counter-elite, Western-educated, young, restless and ambitious, impatient of tradition and eager for change. Old associations such as the craft guild and mystic brotherhood have decayed, and new ones, the trade union and the Rotary Club, have begun to emerge. The widening of boulevards and the creation of parks, squares and other open spaces through encroachment on private property signifies the assertion of novel civic priorities, just as the gradual dissolution of ethnic quarters and the rapid growth of Western-style suburbs and shanty towns symbolise the adoption of new principles of organising social space in regard to residence. Race and religion are becoming less significant than income and life-style in determining the character of residential areas.

Nevertheless, the process of homogenisation has far to go. The anonymity which is characteristic of life in Western cities is modified by the persistence of contacts and ties based on kinship and sectarianism. Even the sophisticated townsman will try to deal with the government bureaucracy through a well-placed kinsman rather than the appropriate functionary. Businesses, even large factories, are still referred to by the name of the proprietor rather than the trading-name, and may be listed in the telephone directory in the same way. The discerning observer can see the forcing-house of modernity as being at the same time a showcase of tradition.

The traditional Islamic city was the central component in a complex pattern of economic, social and political relationships involving townsmen, nomads and villagers. In the city (A) lived the wealthy, the literate and the decision-makers, skilled craftsmen and the religious leaders. The central position of the mosque, the palace and the bazaar symbolised their importance. Around this core were ranged the residential suburbs and, along the outer edges of the city, the cemeteries, a sacred collar which effectively restrained expansion until modern times. The services of the town were

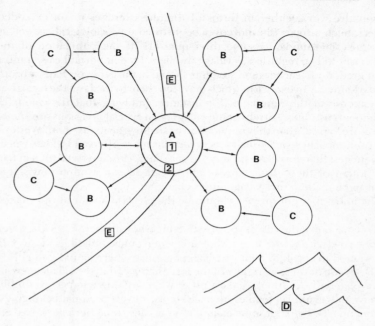

available to the villager (B), at a price, which was paid in grain, hides, vegetables and livestock. He could also exchange the products of his labour for such goods as tea, sugar, leather and metal wares, which could be traded with the nomads (C), who stood at the other end of the chain of exchanges, bargaining the increase of their flocks in return for the necessities of life.

The influence of the city – whether measured by its capacity to collect taxes, influence prices or change opinions – tended to diminish in direct proportion to distance, except along caravan routes (E). The nomads were, therefore, able to withdraw their allegiance for as long as they could manage to survive in the desert without the goods and services it provided. Between many cities there existed large areas of no-man's-land (D), usually harsh and often mountainous, the refuge of the bandit and the heretic who acknowledged no master.

In the twentieth century this classic pattern of interdependence has been disrupted and, in many places, quite extinguished. Air and motor transport enable the political authorities to extend their power into the desert and the mountains whilst at the same time rendering the camel redundant as a beast of burden, and thus undermining the nomad's economic *raison d'être*. Meanwhile, rapid urbanisation and increased labour mobility has tended to blur the ancient distinctions between townsman and peasant.

The study of a Middle Eastern village could make a very suitable topic for lower secondary pupils (eleven to fourteen) of average and below average ability, as it can provide considerable scope for simple descriptive and imaginative work, either in terms of discrete exercises or an extended project. Such a focus can moreover be justified on sociological, as well as pedagogical grounds, as some three-quarters of the population of the region can still be regarded as village dwellers. One important caveat must be entered. Both teachers and students should beware the (perhaps subconscious) tendency to exoticism which may lead them to focus on the bizarre at the expense of the mundane (for instance, implying that the colourful traditional costumes worn by some villagers on special occasions are somehow more 'typical' than the combination of shabby garments –both Western and traditional in style – which are, in fact, far more often and widely worn) or to suggest that the village is far more of a static, 'closed system' than in fact it is. Either of these distortions would negate the most important single point to be made – that village life is changing.

The initial focus of interest should be the physical layout of the village, thus:

(i) Draw a map of the village you are studying (showing houses, fields, water supply, roads, café, mosque, school and other public buildings, if any). If you wanted to speak to a lot of villagers at once where would you go?

(ii) Draw two or three examples of the sort of houses that the villagers live in (show plan and elevation). Make a list of what you might expect to find in each room (furniture, textiles, utensils, tools, stoves, personal belongings, ornaments). Draw/paint some examples of textiles, tools, jewellery, baskets or pottery.

(iii) Make a list of what you might expect to find on the shelves of the village store (e.g. sugar, spices, batteries, kerosene, tobacco, coffee, matches). What do these items tell you about the villagers' way of life? Describe the sort of meetings that take place in (a) the village mosque (b) the café. Describe a day in the life of a field labourer's household or a week in the life of the village. Which would be the most interesting day to visit the village?

Because a village is a human community and not just an assemblage of buildings or a pattern of activities, imaginative work should be employed to contribute an empathetic dimension, e.g.:

(iv) What sort of the things would (a) men talk about at the café (e.g. crop prices, politics, new farming methods, building or irrigation projects), (b) women talk about at the well (e.g. family and friends, marriages, illnesses, home tasks). Write an imaginary conversation between a group of male or female villagers. (Should show attitudes, for example deference to age, as well as topics of interest. Proverbs could usefully be introduced here.)

(v) Describe a weekly market in a nearby town (showing awareness of the range of goods exchanged, availability of services (scribe, faith-healer), opportunities for exchange of news and entertainment, meeting of townsmen, villagers and nomads. Explain the part played by the following people in the life of the community: (a) imam, (b) barber, (c) carpenter, (d) mason, (e) undertaker, (f) shopkeeper.

The exercise could be concluded by evaluative and analytical work:

(vi) What would you say were the advantages and disadvantages of living in a Middle Eastern village compared with living (a) in a Middle Eastern city, (b) in your community?

(vii) Describe some of the ways in which the village has begun to change (introduction of new crops, schools, radio, health programmes, new consumer goods and building materials). In what ways has it remained the same (e.g. seasonality of economic life). This could be presented as the reminiscences of an old man.

(viii) What changes would you like to see brought about in the village? (e.g. diet, hygiene) What sort of difficulties would you expect to face in trying to change things? (e.g. shortages of funds, technical personnel, social conservatism) Pupils could role-play a confrontation.

This exercise could, of course, easily be made more sophisticated by considering such factors as:

Land tenures and land reform. The pressure of population on land. Migration and remittances.

Kinship patterns and sex roles. The importance of males as revealed by differential socialisation of boys and girls, symbolism of marriage rituals (procession to groom's house), significance of patriarchal family authority, patrilocal residence and patrilateral marriage as the preferred ideal, the importance of lineages in giving mutual aid and protection and in maintaining social distances, the impact on life-chances of the sex ratio and birth order of families and the operation of Islamic inheritance laws, patterns of avoidance and segregation. These abstract concepts could perhaps best be conveyed through role-playing.

Social cohesion and control. Patterns of rivalry and loyalty within the village, causes of disputes (water-rights, boundaries, family honour), the work of the village government (law and order, record-keeping, settlement of disputes, liaison with central government). Village cohesion as accentuated by presence of government officials or disputes with other villages.

The study could be extended by taking into account various dimensions for comparison, such as examining the way of life in an Indian or African (or medieval English) village (to distinguish those aspects which are derived from the Islamic culture from those which are basic features of village life anywhere), or considering the differences between life in a Middle Eastern village and life in a Middle Eastern city (for example by focusing on the problems of adjustment facing new migrants).

Further topics for discussion and research

1 Do you agree that 'the future of the area as a whole lies in the wise management, not of its oil, but of its water'?

2 Show how far the following generalisations apply to the Middle East:
(a) 'The absolute amounts of any resource are far less important than its accessibility and distribution.'

(b) 'Land takes on new values with changing technology.'

(c) 'The most destructive of all natural forces is man.'

3   Put yourself in the position of Minister of Planning in a Middle Eastern country of your choice. Describe the objectives you would hope to achieve over the next: (a) year; (b) three years; (c) ten years. Outline the methods you would employ to achieve these objectives. Compare your plans with the policies currently pursued by the country of your choice.

4   Show how the discovery and exploitation of oil affected the economic life and organisation of any one Middle Eastern country. The following aspects may be considered: urbanisation; employment of foreign nationals; improvement in transport facilities; growth of imported manufactures; extension of health welfare and education services; foreign investment; industrial development.

5   What effect do you think each of the following might have on the life of a village: (a) the kerosine lamp, (b) the bicycle, (c) the transistor radio, (d) the wrist watch, (e) the telephone, (f) electricity, (g) main drainage, (h) a paved road, (i) a bus service, (j) television.
Imagine you have been away from your village for five years. Describe what changes you see on your return.

6   You are a young man returning to your native village after five years in the city. What would you tell each of the following to persuade them that city life was better: (a) your father, (b) your mother, (c) your brother, (d) your sister?

7   'The city is the hub of Middle Eastern civilisation.' Do you agree? Compare the ways in which any *one* of the following has affected the nomads, the villagers and the townsman: (a) the motor truck, (b) the radio, (c) electricity.

Sources

1 Van Nieuwenhuijze, *Sociology of the Middle East* (E.J. Brill, 1971), pp.167–8.

2 G. Lenski, *Human Societies* (McGraw Hill, 1970).

3 Paul W. English, *City and Village in Iran* (University of Wisconsin Press, 1966), chapter 4.

Further reading

For pupils

Roderic Dutton and John B. Free, *Arab Village* (A & C Black, 1980). Superbly illustrated simple account of life in an Omani fishing community, with the accent on change.

Fidelity Lancaster, *A Closer Look at the Bedouin* (Hamish Hamilton, 1978). Brightly illustrated information book, showing the influence of the changing seasons and the importance of camels, tents, water, feasts and celebrations and weaving. Terse text may be too difficult for some readers (e.g. 'The Bedouin are Muslim but they usually hold themselves aloof from the religious dogmatism of the towns').

Ailsa and Alan Scarsbrook, *Pakistani Village* (A. & C. Black, 1979). Superb colour photographs and simple but informative text. Very useful.

For teachers

Jean Duvignaud, *Change at Shebika: Report from a North African Village* (Allen Lane, 1970). Chronicles the impact of change on a remote Tunisian village. Useful on the effects of government policies, the relations between farmers and nomads and the conflicts which change produces.

Hani Fakhouri, *Kafr El-Elow: An Egyptian Village in Transition* (Holt, Rinehart & Winston). Detailed case study of a village on the edge of a major industrial growth area. Useful chapters on kinship, religion and education in the village.

Shirley Kay, *The Bedouin* (David & Charles, 1978). Readable survey with the emphasis on the impact of modernisation.

Joe E. Pierce, *Life in a Turkish Village* (Holt, Rinehart & Winston, 1964). Detailed case-study written around the life of a boy growing up in the village. Especially useful on how Islam and folklore permeate everyday life.

Unni Wikan, *Life Among the Poor in Cairo* (Tavistock Publications, 1980). First hand account of daily life and personal relationships with the emphasis on women.

For a survey of the relevant literature see John Gulick, *The Middle East: An Anthropological Perspective* (Goodyear Publishing, 1976), especially chapter 3 and its bibliography; and Dale F. Eickelman, *The Middle East: An Anthropological Approach* (Prentice-Hall, 1981).

Richard Tames, 'Islam and political education' in Robert Jackson (ed.), *Approaching World Religions* (John Murray, 1982), considers the contribution that the study of Islam can make to pupils' understanding of political concepts.

For geographical aspects see the following:

The Middle East and North Africa. A detailed survey of political and economic conditions, country by country, published annually by Europa Publications.

W.B. Fisher, *The Middle East* (Methuen, 7th edn, 1978). Comprehensive (600 pages) and rather more up-to-date; although unillustrated it has many maps.

Peter R. Odell, *Oil and World Power: A Geographical Interpretation* (Pelican, 6th edn, 1981). Sets the problems in a global context.

Useful papers on urbanisation can be found in V.F. Costello, *Urbanization in the Middle East* (Cambridge University Press, 1977) and G.H. Blake and R.I. Lawless (eds), *The Changing Middle Eastern City* (Croom Helm, 1980).

Two well-illustrated and well-produced books which pupils are likely to find particularly acceptable are Falco Quilici, *The Great Deserts* (Collins, 1969), and Martin Simons, *Deserts: The Problem of Water in Arid Lands* (OUP, 1968). On the diffusion of foodstuffs see *What We Eat: The Origins and Travels of Foods Round the World* by Lois S. Johnson (Bailey Bros & Swinfen, 1972). See also Xavier de Planhol, 'The geographical setting', *Cambridge History of Islam*, vol. II, part VIII.

Sterling Publishing Company Inc. of New York publish a *Visual Geography Series* of inexpensive illustrated hardback volumes, each of which is devoted to a general survey of a country, its geography, history, economy and peoples. This series is available in Britain and relevant titles include: *Afghanistan, Egypt, Iran, Iraq, Jordan, Kuwait, Lebanon, Morocco, Pakistan, Saudi Arabia, Senegal, Turkey.* Another attractive children's series is published by Macdonald. Profusely illustrated in colour, these give a discursive view of the past and present of particular countries. Relevant titles include: *Turkey, Egypt, Nigeria, India.*

The mosque

The mosque is, quite literally, of central importance to the Muslim community. It is central in the sense that in Muslim countries mosques are usually to be found in the physical centre of cities. And it is central in the sense that for Muslims it provides the focus for community life. Pupils should be encouraged to recognise that before Muhammad no such institution as the mosque existed, and the first mosque is held by Muslims to have been an extension of the Prophet's own house, built with his own hands from the simplest materials. The mosque represents the physical embodiment of a view of the relationship between Creator and created. As a setting for ritual, as well as an expression of belief, it might usefully be compared with the sacred buildings of other religions. (This is a theme favoured by some CSE syllabuses and textbooks.) The plainness and 'emptiness' of the mosque reflect the aniconism of the Prophet's teaching and the use of calligraphy in decoration reflects not only this but also Islam's acknowledgment of man's forgetfulness. The *mihrab* in the *qibla* wall signalises the significance of the Ka'ba, and the absence of pews both the submissiveness and the equality of believers.

Study of the mosque can obviously be related to drawing and model-making activities. As this topic does not involve representations of living things it would be a suitable one for Muslim children.

Gardens – a metaphorical approach to Islam

The Qur'an is rich in metaphor, an aspect of literary style which survives even the most brutal translation. And one of the most recurrent metaphors is that of a garden. This might therefore provide a focus for a discursive exploration of Islam, either at secondary or at primary level. Some aspects for exploration might be:

(i) The Qur'anic vision of Paradise as a garden. (See especially Suras 55 and 68.) Our word 'paradise' comes from the Persian word for an enclosed garden. Parallels with the biblical Eden? Milton?

(ii) The environmental setting. The attraction of a garden to desert-dwellers and nomads.

(iii) Historic gardens created by the Mughals, Ottomans and Safavids. Persian traditions and influence. Their conception of a palace as a series of pavilions amid gardens. The inspiration for Xanadu?

(iv) The garden in poetry and literature – as a metaphor of human beauty; as a setting for dramatic episodes; as a complex metaphor of a man's relation to God in Sufi poetry.

(v) The garden in carpets and tiles and textiles.

(vi) The social functions of the garden as a setting for picnics, holidays, teaching, meditation.

(vii) The garden as a total aesthetic experience, involving all five senses. (Think this through and find examples of each using the evidence of poetry and miniature paintings.)

(viii) The geometry and techniques of garden design. Similarities and differences compared with Western or Chinese gardens (symmetry; use of water; no circular ponds; birds and animals; shade and reflections; mounds and terraces; pruning).

Activities and discussion topics for primary level:

(i) Make drawings of actual or imagined Islamic gardens. Stylised representations of gardens in carpets could be used. This subject avoids problems which might arise with Muslim children drawing people or animals.

(ii) Make a collage of a garden carpet using coloured paper. This could be made full-size (say 9′ × 4′) and hung on the classroom wall.

(iii) Make a miniature garden to illustrate an Islamic theme such as charity, honesty, kindness to animals.

(v) Many books written by Muslims for small children refer to a colourful, growing garden as evidence of God's creativity and the harmony of his universe. Teachers could use this as a means of 'extending the child's sense of awe and wonder'.

(vi) Babur, the Mughal emperor, had names for his favourite gardens – 'Garden of the New Year', 'White Garden'. Think of some other suitable names.

Activities and discussion topics for secondary levels:

(i) Why has the metaphor of the garden been so popular in Islamic culture?

(ii) Find and compare examples of the garden and associated metaphors in Islamic literature. Can you detect any similarities with other literatures (for example the flower as a symbol of fleeting, earthly existence)?

(iii) Find some descriptions of gardens in the accounts of European travellers of the sixteenth and seventeenth centuries.

(iv) Do Muslims believe that Paradise is an actual place or that the Qur'anic descriptions of it are purely metaphorical?
Can such beliefs be reconciled with Islam's claim to accept the findings of Western science?

(v) Do you accept the 'Architect of Order' argument as evidence of the existence of God?

(vi) Islam and the ecological crisis. What is man's responsibility to the garden? Stewardship and the good life. (OPEC – making the desert bloom – oil and water do mix!)

Further reading

See especially Richard Yeomans' chapter 'Religious education through art' in Robert Jackson (ed.), *Perspectives on World Religions* (School of Oriental & African Studies, 1978).

Helen and Richard Leacroft, *The Buildings of Early Islam* (Hodder & Stoughton, 1976), contains some very imaginative 'cut-away' views of mosques and other religious buildings and would be very useful for pupils.

The following are all sumptuously illustrated: Sylvia Crowe and Sheila Haywood, *The Gardens of Mughal India* (Thames & Hudson, 1972); Jonas Lehrman, *Earthly Paradise: Garden and Courtyard in Islam* (Thames & Hudson, 1980); Elizabeth B. Moynihan, *Paradise as a Garden in Persia and Mughal India* (Scolar Press, 1979).

Integrated and Combined Studies

The following topics are offered as examples in which various areas of the curriculum may be integrated or combined.

An Islamic country

History

State of the country before Islam – political organisation; beliefs; economic activities; social organisation; major areas of settlement and centres of culture; priorities and achievements of cultural life; contacts with other areas and cultures; evidence for the above.

Impact of Islam on the above: (i) within 5 years, (ii) within 50 years, (iii) within 500 years.

Impact of the West on the above: direct/indirect, material/non-material.

Geography

Territorial identity – where does the country end? core/periphery; frontiers; disputes.

Resources – nature, extent and distribution; impact of technology on.

Ecology – relationship between climate, flora, fauna and human settlement patterns; impact of human activity on.

Society

Population – size and rate of growth, factors affecting; distribution and mobility (especially rural/urban); age structure and its implications.

Social stratification – changing sources of wealth, status and power; who has access to these?; how far do they coincide; elites and masses and the openness of society.

Social change and social conflict – focus of change (technology and ideology); agencies of change (the State and its derivatives: law, army, education, welfare services; but also foreign businesses, aid agencies, etc.); resistance to change (sources and forms).

An Islamic Open Day

The mounting of a classroom exhibition is often used as the climax and ultimate objective of a term's work. It can provide both a focus for enthusiasm and satisfying visible evidence of achievement. The same exercise, it is suggested, could be organised on a much larger scale, involving staff and students from every department and discipline. Needless to say, teachers proposing to undertake such a Herculean labour will need heroic qualities of tact and endurance to match their ambition. The following notes suggest some modes of involvement for various departments:

RE – The Qur'an (compared with the Bible?) Exhibition of Qur'ans, rosary, prayer-rug, etc. Cassette recording of Muslim/Christian dialogue, Muslim prayers. Tape/slide presentation of the 'Pillars of the Faith'. Co-ordination of exhibition programme as a whole.

Art – Calligraphy, ceramics, mosques. Examples of practical work (such as clay or plaster carvings of Kufic writing) and drawings. Collections of posters and postcards relating to the above. Acting as a service department helping others to realise their work in visual terms.

Drama/English – Wallcharts showing English words derived from Arabic. Writing and acting of short plays (including shadow plays). Selection and reading of translated poetry.

Languages – Wallcharts explaining basic aspects of Arabic language, alphabet, etc. (Urdu and other languages could be added).

History – Cassette recordings of eyewitness accounts. Tape and slide presentations of historic incidents, lives of famous Muslims etc.

Geography – Exhibitions of maps and wallcharts showing physical environment of the Muslim world, work of Muslim explorers and cartographers, traditional modes and routes of travel and their modernisation.

Science – Wallcharts and practical experiments and demonstrations showing Muslim contributions to optics, chemistry, medicine, botany, etc.

Mathematics – Wall-displays and puzzles relating to Muslim achievements in mathematics, astronomy, etc.

Craft – Practical examples of Islamic design in metal, leather, wood, etcetera. Acting as service department to others.

Home Economics – Practical examples of Muslim foods. Display of costume, textile design and interior decoration.

Music – Cassette recordings of selected examples of music from the Muslim world. Wallcharts showing Arab theories of music, notation, etc. Making of simple instruments.

Social Studies – Exhibition and/or tape/slide presentation relating to the Muslim family, education, Islamic law.

The open day could obviously be given a sharper focus by relating it to a single country. This could have obvious advantages in areas where Muslims from a particular country are living. Care should obviously be taken, however, to ensure that no Muslim minority is ignored.

Appendices

1 Glossary

There is no generally agreed system for transliterating Arabic into English and this may account for the many variant forms in which Arabic words are found. The following glossary is *not* intended as a pronunciation guide but as an indication of the meanings of some of the words more commonly found in texts on Islam. (Common variant forms are given in brackets.) There are no capitals in Arabic but it is conventional to use them for proper names (e.g. Hanafi) and for some words, such as Qur'an, Allah and Shi'ite.

abd servant or slave – often as part of a name

adala good character, a prerequisite for acting as a witness before a qadi or holding public office

adhan 'announcement' – the call to prayer

ahl tribe, people (Hebrew *ohel* – tent)

ahl al-bayt 'the people of the house' – the family of the Prophet

ahl al-Kitab 'the people of the book' – i.e. Jews and Christians, who possess books of revelation

aja barbarian, non-Arabic speaking (used of Persians)

al-Alim 'he who knows' (see 'ulama)

Allah God

aman safety, protection, pardon, quarter, safe-conduct

amir prince, governor, commander, a local ruler (Emir)

amir al-muminin 'commander of the faithful' – originally a title of the caliph; later assumed by other rulers

amsar military camp founded for Muslim warriors in non-Arab lands

ansar 'helpers' – the first converts in Medina; later used to denote all those who helped the Prophet in his campaigns

'aql intellect

arkan al-din the five pillars of the faith, the basic duties of a Muslim

aya 'sign' – verse of the Qur'an

badawi Arabian nomads (Bedouin)

balagh the content of Muhammad's preaching

baraka 'blessing': the air of sanctity possessed by holy men. More loosely used to denote special powers

bay'a recognition of authority,

proclamation of a ruler or heir apparent

bismillah   abbreviation of 'bismillah al-rahman, al-rahim' – 'in the name of God, the merciful, the compassionate' – a standard invocation used by Muslims before any significant act, task or journey. (basmala)

bid'a   'innovation' – the opposite of sunna: a belief or practice without divine sanction, heresy

da'i   'summoner', a propagandist or missionary

dar al-harb   'house of war' – territories beyond the rule of Islam

dar al-Islam   'house of peace' – lands under Muslim rule

dervish   member of a Sufi religious order (darwish)

dhikr   'remembering' mentioning – recitation of the names of God, a central feature of Sufi ritual. Each order has its distinctive dhikr (zikr)

dhimmi   'people of the convenant' – Jews or Christians living under Muslim rule; these protected classes were allowed to practise their religion in return for payment of a poll-tax but forbidden to exercise full civil rights

dinar   a gold coin

dirhem   a silver coin

diwan   list, register, administrative department, ministry, (also used to denote the collected works of a poet)

diyya   blood money

faqir   a person in physical or spiritual need: a mendicant holy man or mystic

al-Fatiha   the opening chapter of the Qur'an

fatwa   legal ruling made by an expert scholar

fiqh   'intelligence', 'knowledge' – hence Islamic jurisprudence

fitnah   persecution, conspiracy

fitrah   the original nature of man and things

ghaflah   negligence or forgetfulness of God, the root of most sins and the major obstacle to spiritual self-realisation

ghazwa   a razzia or raid; 'ghazi' came to denote a warrior in a jihad or on the borders of the dar al-Islam

ghiyar   compulsory mark, usually a coloured patch, worn by dhimmi as a sign of their status

ghulam   male slave, bodyguard, apprentice, servant, attendant

hadd   'limit, frontier' – the punishments for offences specified in the Qur'an (e.g. drinking wine, fornication)

hadith   'saying', 'statement', a record of something said or done by the Prophet

hajj   the pilgrimage to Mecca

hajji   a person who has performed the hajj

halal   'permitted' (i.e. an act conforming to the sunna)

Hanafi   school of law founded by Abu Hanifa (d. A.H. 180)

Hanbali   school of law founded by Ahmad ibn Hanbal (d. A.H. 241)

hanif   term used to denote a monotheist in pre-Islamic Arabia

haqiqah   ultimate reality

haram   'sacred' – sanctuary, holy territory: term used to denote the environs of Mecca, Medina and Jerusalem

haram   an action forbidden by shari'a law

hijra   the Prophet's departure from Mecca to Medina; variously translated as 'flight', 'emigration', 'exodus' and 'breaking of ties'. The Islamic calendar dates from this era (Hegira)

hikmah wisdom

'ibadah worship

'id al-adha 'feast of the sacrifices', major festival of the Muslim calendar, celebrated on the 10th Dhul-Hijja, the day on which pilgrims make their sacrifices in the valley of Mina (eid ul-Adha; id al kahr)

'id al-fitr 'feast at the breaking', festival to mark the end of the fast Ramadan (eid-ul-fitr)

ihram state of ritual purity assumed by pilgrims about to undertake the rites of hajj

ijma' consensus – agreed opinion on a legal matter

ijtihad 'effort' 'reflection' an individual judgement on a legal matter

'ilm 'knowledge' in respect of theology

imam 'he who stands at the front' – leader of prayers in a mosque

iman 'faith', 'belief'

al Insan al Kamil the perfect man (i.e. Muhammad)

'irfan gnosis, divine knowledge

Islam 'submitting' (i.e. oneself to God): also 'peace'

isnad the chain of transmitters of a tradition (hadith) about the Prophet

jahiliya 'age of ignorance' (i.e. period of Arabian history before Islam)

jihad 'struggle': term used to denote both war in defence of the faith and the effort to overcome one's imperfections to become a better Muslim

jinn a being created of fire

jizya poll-tax paid by dhimmi

ka'ba 'cube', the central shrine of Islam in Mecca

kafir unbeliever

kalam 'speech', academic theology

khalifa 'successor', title assumed by temporal heads of the Muslim community after the death of the Prophet (caliph)

khan caliph – ruler, king (Turkic) – also a caravanserai

khatib preacher

khutba sermon delivered in mosque at congregational prayer on Fridays

kiswa black cloth covering the ka'ba

kufr unbelief, wilful ignorance

madhab 'way', a school of law (e.g. hanbali etc.)

madrasa a maintained college for theological instruction

mahdi 'the guided one'; in Sunni Islam he will appear before the end of the world to aid the final victory of Islam; in Shi'a Islam the hidden imam

majlis assembly

makruh an act disapproved of by shari'a but not forbidden

maktab school for teaching the Qur'an

mala'ika angels

Maliki school of law founded by Malik ibn Anas (d. A.H. 179)

manasik al hajj 'ceremonies of the pilgrimage'

masjid 'a place of prostration', a mosque

math the substance of a tradition

mawali 'freed slaves' term used to denote non-Arab converts in the early centuries of Islam: they established their status within the Muslim community by accepting a 'client' relationship with existing Arab tribes

mihrab recess in mosque wall denoting direction of prayer

millet Turkish form of 'milla' (rite); used to denote a protected community

minbar pulpit from which the khutba is delivered

mu'adhdhin person who gives the call to prayer (muezzin)

mu'amalah Islamic law relating to transactions

mufti a jurisconsult, lawyer who gives expert opinions rather than actually conducts cases

muhajinun Meccan converts who went to Medina at the time of the Hijra

muhtasib censor of supervisory official appointed by the caliph as a guardian of public morals and commercial ethics

mujtahid one who exercises ijtihad

mu'minun 'the Faithful'

murid follower of the shaikh of a Sufi order

murshid spiritual guide or leader of a Sufi order

mushrik an idolator (see shirk)

Muslim a follower of Islam

Muslimun 'the obedient' (i.e. Muslims)

musta'riba 'Arabised', 'would-be Arabs'. Term used to denote converts to Islam in Spain (Mozarabs)

nabi 'prophet'

nafs the individual psyche

niya 'intention', conscious declaration preceding any ritual act

qadar the decree of God

qadi judge (kadi)

qanun an administrative decree (as opposed to a revealed law): adopted from Greek 'canon'

qibla the direction of prayer

qiyama 'arising', resurrection of the body on the Day of Judgement

qiyas 'analogy', in jurisprudence

Qur'an 'recitation', the sacred book of Islam (Koran)

rabb Lord, the most frequent title of Allah in the Qur'an

rak'a complete cycle of prescribed ritual movements performed during prayer

ra'is head, chief (e.g. of a diwan)

Ramadan ninth month of the Muslim calendar: a period of dawn to dusk fasting

rashidun term used to denote the first four, 'rightly guided' caliphs (Abu Bakr, Umar, Uthman, Ali)

rasul apostle, someone sent to a particular group, messenger

rawi tribal band

ra'y opinion, speculation on a legal matter

riba usury

ribat 'a place where horses are tied' Sufi monastery, often fortified

ridda apostasy

ruh the spirit of the individual

sadaqa alms given voluntarily

sahaba 'companions' of the Prophet, those who saw him in person

saluh 'sound' used to denote an accredited hadith

salat a ritual prayer, observed five times a day

saum a fast

Shafi'i school of law founded by al-Shafi'i. (d. A.H. 204)

shahada the profession of faith – La ilaha illa'llah, Muhammadur rasul Allah. There is no God but God (and) Muhammad is the Prophet of God

shaikh 'old man', title of respect used to denote tribal leader, Sufi master or a learned man

sharif 'noble' (plural *ashraf*) title

given to heads of prominent families; later restricted to kinsmen of the Prophet and their descendants, for whom the term 'sayyid' was also used

shari'a 'highway', revealed sacred law, the commands which guide man in the 'straight path'

Shi'a 'party', 'fashion', generic name for historic subdivision of the Muslim community: members of the various Shi'a traditions differ with regard to details of doctrine and ritual

shirk the association of any person, force or phenomenon with God, thus compromising the oneness of Allah

sira the traditional biography of the Prophet

Sufi an Islamic mystic

sultan 'power', a ruler

sunna 'custom', 'practice', the words and deeds of the Prophet

sura a chapter of the Qur'an

tafsir Qur'anic commentary and exegesis

tajalli the theophany of God's names and qualities

taqiya 'fear', dispensation from the requirements of religion under duress

tariqa 'road', 'path', 'way', spiritual observances of a particular Sufi order

tasawwuf the inner, mystic dimension of Islam, Sufism

tawhid the Oneness of God

ta'wil 'to take something back to its origin', the esoteric interpretation of the Qur'an

'ulama 'the learned', men professionally concerned with the interpretation of Qur'an and hadith; in effect they often spoke for the entire community in matters of faith and law

umma the community of Muslims

ummi illiterate (i.e. Muhammad). (His illiteracy is regarded by some Muslims as proof of the Divine origin of the Qur'an. A parallel is seen with Mary's virginity vis-à-vis the birth of Jesus, both being regarded as the untouched vehicles of God's purpose)

umra the 'lesser pilgrimage', undertaken at Mecca outside the mouth of Dhul-Hijja

'urf general custom

wahy revelation

wali saint

waqf property left as a pious bequest, the rents or profits of which were devoted to some charitable purpose

wazir minister of state (vizier)

wudu ablution performed before prayer

zahir the external manifestation of God

zakat alms tax

zanj East Africa; black slaves

zawiya Sufi monastery

zulm wrong-doing, false dealing

Glossaries can be found in the following:

B. Lewis, *Islam* (especially good on historical, political and administrative terms).

M. Rogers, *The Spread of Islam* (especially useful for architectural terms and dynasties).

S.H. Nasr, *Ideals and Realities of Islam* (especially for terms relating to mysticism).

K. Cragg, *The House of Islam* and *The Event of the Qur'an* (both very good).

P. Jeffries, *Migrants and Refugees* (contains useful list of Urdu equivalents of Arabic terms).

M. Rodinson, *Mohammed* (concentrates on historic characters and ethnic groups in seventh-century Arabia).

2   Museum List

Where relevant, the particular feature of the major collections is indicated. It is advisable to make enquiries before a visit; in many cases the exhibits from the Muslim World may be in reserve collections or not normally on public display.

Major collections

Cambridge, Fitzwilliam Museum especially carpets, pottery

Edinburgh, Royal Scottish Museum metalwork, armour, pottery and costume

Glasgow, Burrell Collection, Camphill Museum carpets, pottery metalwork – Museum and Art Gallery weapons.

London, British Museum and King's Library comprehensive collection – Science Museum scientific instruments – Tower of London, New Armouries weapons, armour – Victoria and Albert Museum comprehensive collection, notable for carpets

Manchester Museum special collection of bows, weapons, armour – Museum of the History of Science scientific instruments

Sheffield Art Gallery pottery, paintings (Persia and Indian Sub-continent)

Smaller collections

Aberdeen, University of Aberdeen Anthropological Museum some pottery

Bath, Victoria Art Gallery ceramics and some illuminated pages from manuscripts

Batley, Bagshaw Museum some ceramics mainly of Multan (Pakistan)

Birmingham, City Museum and Art Gallery various

Bradford, City Art Gallery uncatalogued collection from Indian subcontinent, available for loan by schools

Bristol, City Museum and Art Gallery various exhibitions

Cardiff, the Castle contains examples of 'Moorish' architecture

Durham, Gulbenkian Museum of Oriental Art. University of Durham- various

Ipswich Museums carpets, weapons and domestic items

Leeds, Department of Semitic Studies Museum, University of Leeds- manuscripts

London, Horniman Museum musical instruments – the Most Venerable Order of St John of Jerusalem Museum some armour and coins especially from the Holy Land – National Army Museum mostly in store, especially from India – Wallace Collection arms and armour – Royal Artillery Museum, Rotunda Woolwich various weapons and armour

Maidenhead, The Henry Reitlinger Bequest basically ceramic, a 'Persian Room'

Merseyside County Museums, Departments of Antiquities and Ethnology mainly in store, manuscripts, pottery, metalwork, domestic items

Oxford, Pitt Rivers Museum various examples of Muslim craftsmanship and some weapons – Ashendean Museum various

Sandhurst, Royal Military Academy mainly Indian

Stoke-on-Trent, City Museum and Art Gallery good collection especially of Persian ceramics

Swansea – Museum of the Royal Institution of South Wales pottery (Egypt)

3 The Shorter Encyclopaedia of Islam

The *Shorter Encyclopaedia of Islam* edited by H.A.R. Gibb and J.H. Kramers was republished in 1974 by E.J. Brill of Leiden. Its 671 pages include all the articles in the first edition and Supplement of the great *Encyclopaedia of Islam*, plus a number of new articles. Bibliographies have also been updated. The 'Shorter' is probably the most comprehensive and authoritative work of reference available in one volume at the present time. Newcomers to Islamic studies may, however, find the arrangement of entries rather confusing at first as articles are organised under Arabic headings; thus mosques are dealt with in the article 'Masdjid'. Some entries are also broader in scope than their titles might immediately suggest; thus the entry 'Madrasa' (a type of Islamic college usually associated with the Seljuk vizier Nizam-al-Mulk) in fact covers the entire history of Islamic education from earliest times to the 1920s. A 'Register of Subjects' (pp. 663–5) enables the reader to trace some topics and is especially useful where these involve a large number of biographical entries (e.g. Companions of the Prophet, Mystics, Reformers).

The following list is a personal selection of entries which might be useful to the teacher but whose subject-matter is not readily apparent to the non-specialist:

Abd slavery

Ahl al-Kitab position of Christians and Jews in Islam – see also Dhimma

Allah Islamic doctrine of the nature of God – see also Kalam, Khalk, Nur, Shirk, Tasbih, Thanawiya

Bai' Commerce

Djahannam hell

Djahiliya pre-Islamic Arabia

Djanna Paradise

Djihad holy war

Djinaza funerals

Djizya poll-tax

Djuma Friday service

Fikh   Islamic law – see also Idjma, 'Ilm, Kadi, Kiyas, Shari'a, Usul

Hadjdj   Pilgrimage to Mecca – see also Ihram, Umra

Hama'il   talismans – see also Sihr

Iblis   the devil – see also Shaitan
Iman   faith
Indjil   the Gospels

Khalifa   the Caliphate
Khamr   wine – see also Nabidh
Khatia   sin
Khitan   circumcision
Khutba   sermon
al-Kiyama   Resurrection – see also Shafa'a
al-Kuds   Jerusalem
al-Kuran   the Koran, Qur'an

al-Madina   Medina
Madrasa   education
Mahr   dowry
Mala'ika   angels
Masdjid   mosques
Mawlid   festival of the Prophet's birthday
Mi'radj   the Prophet's ascent to Heaven

Mirath   inheritance – see also Wasiya
Murtadd   apostasy

Nafs   soul
Nasara   Christians
Nikah   marriage – see also 'Urs

Riba   usury

Sadjdjada   prayer carpets
Salat   ritual prayer
Sawm   fasting
Shahid   martyrs
Sharif   descendants of the Prophet
Subha   rosary

Ta'am   food
Talak   divorce
Tarika   mysticism – see also Tasawwuf and footnote – cross references
Tarikh   chronology, calendars

Wahy   revelation
Wakf   charitable endowments
Wali   saints

Yahud   the Jews
Yatim   orphans

Zakat   alms

Other key articles include Hadith, Imam, Islam, Ka'ba, Mecca, Muhammad, Shari'a, Shi'a (see also Sab'iya, Ta'ziya), Sunna, Turban, Umma.

4   The peoples of Islam

Muslim communities and individuals can be found in almost every country. The table opposite indicates only those nations whose total population includes a Muslim presence of 2 per cent or above. A few countries may not appear due to the lack of accurate up-to-date census information regarding religious affiliation.

5   Admiral to zenith: Arabic loan-words in English

The number of Arabic loan-words in English is not particularly extensive (a list of about 300 is given as an appendix in W.M. Watt's *The Influence of Islam on Medieval Europe* Edinburgh University Press, 1972). But the character of those

Country	Total population	% of Muslims	Country	Total population	% of Muslims
Afghanistan	14,702,000	99	Maldives	144,000	100
Albania	2,626,000	70	Mali	6,350,000	90
Algeria	18,249,000	99	Mauritania	1,558,000	100
Bahrain	365,000	100	Mauritius	933,000	16
Bangladesh	88,092,000	83	Mongolia	1,639,000	4
Benin	3,379,000	12	Morocco	19,751,000	99
Brunei	199,000	60	Mozambique	10,108,000	11
Bulgaria	8,892,000	13	Nepal	14,028,000	5
Burma	31,800,000	4	Niger	5,133,000	80
Burundi	4,314,000	2	Nigeria	74,604,000	47
Cameroon	8,168,000	17	Oman	565,000	100
Central African	2,418,000	8	Pakistan	80,171,000	97
Republic			Peoples' Republic	1,017,477,000	3
Chad	4,523,000	50	of China		
Comoros	323,000	95	Philippines	46,893,000	4
Cyprus	614,000	18	Qatar	167,000	100
Djibouti	314,000	94	Saudi Arabia	8,103,000	100
Egypt	40,958,000	94	Senegal	5,519,000	80
Ethiopia	31,743,000	45	Sierra Leone	3,351,000	30
Fiji	621,000	8	Singapore	2,361,000	15
Gambia	584,000	85	Somalia	3,469,000	100
Ghana	11,741,000	12	South Africa	28,094,000	20
Greece	9,100,000	2	Sri Lanka	14,502,000	6
Guinea	5,276,000	75	Sudan	20,941,000	73
Guinea-Bissau	634,000	30	Surinam	98,000	20
Guyana	824,000	9	Syria	8,395,000	88
India	669,785,000	11	Tanzania	17,358,000	
Indonesia	148,085,000	90	mainland		30
Iran	37,582,000	98	Zanzibar		98
Iraq	12,907,000	90	Thailand	46,350,000	4
Israel	3,663,000	11	Togo	2,528,000	5
Ivory Coast	7,465,000	22	Trinidad & Tobago	1,136,000	6
Jordan	3,055,000	92	Tunisia	6,412,000	5
Kenya	15,364,000	7	Turkey	44,236,000	99
Kuwait	1,278,000	99	Uganda	13,225,000	10
Lebanon	2,943,000	44	USSR	263,818,000	16
Liberia	1,789,000	15	United Arab Emirates	862,000	96
Libya	2,873,000	97	Upper Volta	6,656,000	20
Madagascar	8,358,000	7	Western Sahara Region	75,000	100
Malawi	5,861,000	5	Yemen (Aden)	1,781,000	100
Malaysia			Yemen (Sana)	5,125,000	100
mainland	11,068,000	53	Yugoslavia	22,174,000	12
Sabah	990,000	38			
Sarawak	1,222,000	23			

Sources: *US State Department Fact Book*, 1979. *The Muslim Peoples, A World Ethnographic Survey*, Richard W. Weekes, 1978. US State Department Country Offices. The Embassy of Nepal.

words and the categories into which they may broadly be classified are indicative of the nature of the cultural and commercial relationships which existed between Europe and Islam in medieval and early modern times.

War   admiral (literally prince of a (transport) fleet); arsenal; assassin; musket

Trade & travel   cable; camel; cheque (written agreement); monsoon; safari (to travel); tariff

Architecture & furnishing   adobe (at-tub = brick); alcove (al-qubba = dome); balcony; baroque (uneven sand); divan (originally a sort of throne for an official); frieze; mattress (where something is thrown); sofa

Science & mathematics   alchemy; alcohol (al-kuhl = the distillation); algebra; alkali; almanac; amalgam: average; benzine (Javanese incense); calibre (model); drug; zero

Textiles   blouse; chiffon; cotton; gauze; mohair; muslin; satin

Food & drink   apricot; artichoke; aubergine; banana; candy (thickened sugar-cane juice); carafe; caraway; coffee; damson; date; ginger; lemon; marzipan; orange; rice; saccharin; sherbet (drink); spinach; sugar; syrup

Miscellaneous   albatross; baboon (lucky); checkmate (the king is dead); giraffe; guitar; lute; mummy (wax); racket (palm of the hand); talc

6   The Muslim calendar

Islam has its own calendar, which dates from the Hegira (Hijra) when the Prophet and his companions left Mecca for Medina (16 July 622). The year 1400 AH (Anno Hegirae) began at sunset on 19 November 1979.

The Muslim calendar was inaugurated by the second Caliph, Umar, who was faced with the practical problems of administering a rapidly expanding empire in which correspondence over long distances had to be accurately dated.

The Qur'an (10:5) decrees the use of lunar months and the Islamic year is therefore out of phase with the Gregorian calendar, which is based on the solar year. The lunar year is roughly 11 days shorter than the solar year and its months have, by convention, 29 and 30 days alternately. In relation to the Western system of reckoning, therefore, the Muslim calendar moves 'backward' each year, which means that Muslim festivals fall at different times of the Western year and bear no fixed relation to the seasons.

To calculate conversions from one calendar to the other, the rule of thumb is that a Western (i.e. Gregorian) century equals 103 years according to the Muslim calendar. The year 1300 corresponded with 700 AH. A more exact formula is that where G = Gregorian year and H = Hijra year

$$G = H + 622 - \frac{H}{33} \qquad H = G - 622 + \frac{G-622}{32}$$

Alternatively one can look up the dates in G.S.P. Freeman-Grenville's *The Muslim and Christian Calendars* (Rex Collings, 2nd edn 1977) which enables one to convert dates from the Hijra to 2000.

7 Examination syllabuses

Although CSE and O level examinations may well be replaced in the fairly near future, it is likely that when new syllabuses and examinations are designed they will draw on the accumulated experience of examining at these levels. The following lists of syllabuses indicate which Boards offer a study of Islam as part of the multi-faith section of their RE syllabuses.

CSE (Mode 1)

Associated Lancashire Schools Examining Board (Religious Knowledge)
East Anglian Examination Board, Northern and Southern syllabuses (Religious Studies)
East Midland Regional Examinations Board (Religious Studies)
London Regional Examination Board (Religious Studies)
North Regional Examination Board (Religious Studies)
North West Regional Examinations Board (Religious Education, Syllabus B)
Southern Regional Examinations Board (Religious Studies)
South East Regional Examinations Board (Religious Studies)
South Western Examinations Board (Religious Education)
West Midlands Examinations Board (Religious Education)
West Yorkshire and Lindsey Regional Examining Board (Religious Education)

GCE O level

University of Cambridge Local Examinations Syndicate (Religious Studies)
University of London (Religious Studies)
Associated Examining Board (Syllabus 2, Multi-Faith)
West African Examinations Council (Islamic Religious Knowledge)

GCE A/O level

University of London (Religious Approaches to Modern Life and Thought)

GCE A level

Associated Examining Board (Religious Studies)
Joint Matriculation Board (Religious Studies)
University of London (Religious Studies)

Oxford & Cambridge Schools Examination Board (Religious Studies)
Welsh Joint Education Committee (Religious Studies)
West African Examinations Council (Islamic Religious Studies)

The following selection of current syllabuses is intended both as a guide to what is available and as a help to teachers wishing to devise their own courses. They are reproduced with the kind permission of the respective Boards.

East Anglian Examinations Board: CSE Religious Studies (1982 and 1983)

Two Mode I examinations are available, the Northern syllabus and the Southern syllabus.

The Northern syllabus is assessed on the basis of two 2-hour papers, each carrying 50% of the marks, plus an optional project of approximately 1,000 words. For Paper 1 candidates must choose one of three options relating to Christianity; for Paper 2 candidates must choose one of four options, one of which is 'Multi-Faith World'. In this section candidates are required to study three of the following: Hinduism, Buddhism, Judaism, Christianity, Islam, Sikhism and Humanism. The selection must include Christianity, studied as a world religion.

Each belief system is to be dealt with under the following headings: (a) origins, (b) teachings, (c) sacred books, (d) festivals, (e) worship and holy places, (f) way of life, (g) some outstanding personalities.

With respect to Islam these are interpreted as follows: (a) Life of Muhammad. (b) One God (Allah), Five Pillars, Life after death, Charity and good works towards the poor, oppressed and orphaned. (c) Qur'an. (d) Ramadan and Id-ul-Fitr, Id-ul-Adha, Id-milad-un-Nabi. (e) Mosque, Friday, Prayer five times a day. (f) Home and family, position of women in society, Birth, Marriage, Dietary laws. (g) Al-Ghazali, Saladin.

The Southern syllabus is assessed on the basis of one 2½-hour paper and an optional project. Candidates must study two of five sections. Section C (World Religions) requires a study of two of the following: Hinduism, Judaism, Christianity, Islam, Sikhism. Islam is covered as follows:

1   The origins of Islam (a) Arabia before Islam: an examination of the social and religious background of Arabia before Muhammad. This area should include tribalism, idolatry and social injustices, e.g. slaves, the status of women, widows and orphans. (b) The prophethood of Muhammad: an outline of the life of Muhammad with special attention given to the significant moments in his life. This area should include the call, persecution, the Hijra, the return to Mecca and the main themes of his teaching.

2   The beliefs of Islam (a) The importance of the name Islam: submission. (b) The importance of the concept *tawhid*: the essential unity of Islam and all aspects of life. (c) The origin and authority of the Qur'an. (d) The nature and significance of each of the five pillars. (e) Life after death. This section should include the Qur'anic descriptions of the Day of Judgement, heaven and hell, and the significance of this teaching for a Muslim.

3 Life in an Islamic community (a) The mosque: its design, contents and uses within the community. (b) The festivals of Id-ul-Adha and Id-ul-Fitr: the reason for each celebration, the way it is celebrated and its significance. (c) The ceremonies associated with the rites of initiation, marriage and death. (d) The role and status of women. (e) Food customs: fasting and *halal*.

Section E (Religion – A Thematic Approach is organised in three parts: (1) Religion in tribal cultures. (2) The expression of religion in language, acts and objects. (3) Faith and behaviour.

Part 2 specifically mentions (a) The stories of religion, including the birth story of Muhammad. (b) Worship – regular worship by Muslims, and pilgrimage in Islam. (c) Sacred objects and buildings – the mosque (design, function, furniture and sacred objects).

Part 3 requires a study of moral codes and decision-making. Specific mention is made of 'the Five Pillars of Wisdom' (*sic*).

North Regional Examination Board: CSE Religious Studies (1983)

The Mode I examination consists of two written papers (80% of the final grade) and a teacher's assessment of pupil work (20%). Paper 1 (1¾ hours, 60 marks) is compulsory and requires a study of a Synoptic Gospel and other relevant Biblical passages, incorporating life situation themes. Paper 2 (1¼ hours, 40 marks) contains three options, of which candidates must choose one. The syllabus for Option C, World Religions: Islam, is as follows:

1 A knowledge of the life and times of Muhammad, and of the nature and influence of the Qur'an. (a) The Arabian setting – social conditions – religious practices and influences. (b) The career of the Prophet – Muhammad as a moral reformer and statesman – as the model for Muslims (Hadith). (c) The revelation of the Qur'an – what is revelation? What is prophecy? (d) The place of the Qur'an in Islamic art and daily life.

2 A knowledge of the practices and beliefs of the Muslim as summarised in the Five Pillars of Faith. (a) The Muslim conception of God. (b) Prayer – ablution – purpose of prayer – manner of prayer. (c) Charity – a Muslim's obligation to his fellows. (d) Fasting – the development of spiritual qualities. (e) Hajj – conditions for pilgrimage – the rites – equality of races in Islam.

Questions will be concerned with the importance of practice rather than of belief.

3 A knowledge and understanding of the importance of Family Life in Islam. (a) The status of women before Muhammad – his teachings on women. (b) The traditional role of women in Muslim society – their rights in law and practice – divorce and inheritance. (c) Family Life – authority in the family – growing up as a Muslim. (d) Forces for change – education, work and nationalism.

4 A knowledge of the importance of Islam as a world religion. (a) A sketch of Islam's expansion, in particular the part played by Islamic culture in Western civilisation. (b) Distribution of Muslims today – the challenge of change, with particular reference to Muslims in Britain. (c) A case study of *one* country with a strong Islamic tradition, e.g. Saudi Arabia, Turkey, Pakistan, Iran, Egypt etc.

Associated Examining Board: GCE O Level Religious Studies (155), Syllabus 2 (Multi-Faith) (1983)

The examination consists of one paper of $2\frac{1}{2}$ hours carrying 75% of the marks and a project of 3,000 to 4,000 words carrying 25%. Candidates will study at least three of the following: Christianity, Hinduism, Islam, Judaism, Sikhism.

The project is to concentrate on one particular religious area selected from the following: the family, birth, ceremonies of initiation, marriage, death. The study will be based on one religion only, and may incorporate first-hand experience in an appropriate community.

The syllabus is organised thematically as follows:

1 *Sacred places and places of pilgrimage* Buildings used for worship. The significance of their architecture, basic design, characteristic features, furniture and furnishings, symbolic decoration. The role of the buildings both officially in the religion and in the life of the individual adherent. The nature of pilgrimage and the role of famous pilgrimage centres.

2 *Worship and festivals* The basic form of congregational worship. The significance of the main activities, e.g. place of the scriptures, prayers, teaching. The role of both officials and laity in public worship.
Private or individual worship. Its nature, frequency, time, place, associated rituals.
The major festivals. Their origin and their meaning in the religion today. Their place in the religion's calendar. The way in which they are celebrated. The significance of the activities. The role of the family in the celebration.

3 *Sacred Writings* (a) Scriptures. (b) Writings which are accorded a place of honour in the religion but which are not technically Scriptures. Their origin and development. The kinds of literature contained in them. The languages of the original writings. Problems of translation, e.g. the non-equivalence of words and phrases in other languages and cultures, the attitude of Muslims to the Arabic of the Qur'an. The role of the sacred writings within the religion, in public worship and in private use. The nature of the authority of the sacred writings in the religion.

Welsh Joint Education Committee: GCE A Level Religious Studies (1982)

Candidates are required to attempt two of three 3-hour papers: New Testament, Old Testament, Religion in a Changing World (A3). For A3, candidates select 1 of 4 topics. Option 4, an Introduction to Some World Religions, requires candidates to study either Judaism or Islam, together with either Hinduism or Buddhism, answering two questions on each of the religions studied.

Islam is covered as follows:

A (i) Pre-Islamic Arabia, its cultural, economic and religious climate (e.g. trade routes and influence of tribal beliefs, Jinns, Zoroastrianism, Judaism and Christianity).

(ii) Muhammad in Mecca, noting the distinctive features of Mecca.

(iii) Muhammad in Medina and the Hegira, the establishment of community laws.

(iv) The first four caliphs.

(v) The expansion and decline of Islam 750-1500CE (to include the advance across North Africa to Spain; through Asia Minor to the Balkans; through Iraq to India).

(vi) The Mongol invasion.

(vii) The Medieval Empires of Islam.

(viii) Divisions and sects in Islam: Sunni, Shi'a, Sufis. Attention should be given to the following notable characters: Al Ghazali, Al Ashari, Rumi, Muhammad Iqbal.

(ix) Modern Islam – its spread into Africa and Asia; and its influence in Saudi Arabia, Turkey, Pakistan and Britain.

B The mosque. The basic architecture and the significant variations in the major Islamic countries. Mosques in Britain. Special consideration should be given to the place of prayer at the mosque, notably the Friday midday prayer, call to prayer, muezzin and imam, ablutions.

C The five pillars of Islam, the six essential beliefs. The prophet in Islam. Feasts and Festivals, Hajj, Ramadan, Eid-ul-adha, Eid-ul-Fitr, the Day of Hijra, the Birthday of the Prophet Muhammad, the night of power, the night journey.

D The Qur'an.

(i) The growth of the Qur'an and establishing the canon.

(ii) A study of the text – Sura 1, 74, 96, 97.

(iii) The teaching of the Qur'an on Revelation, Judgement, Doctrine of God, Society. The Medinan and the Meccan surahs should be noted.

(iv) Ijaz, Imam, Ijma, Hadith, Shari'a, Sunna.

E Muslim cultural growth. In mathematics, astronomy, medicine, art and technology, in the 10th and 11th centuries; and recently in Muslim resurgence due to political awareness and oil.

F (i) Religion and the home, place of women, marriage and divorce, food and drink, eating customs, dress, the life cycle.

(ii) Religion and the State, Zakat, brotherhood of all Muslims, Jihad, usury and the use of money, law and order, education, politics and religion in Pakistan, Saudi Arabia, Turkey.

G   Muslims in Britain.
   (i) Mosques and prayer rooms.
  (ii) Methods of adapting to the British life style.

8   Schools radio and television

BBC Radio

The following programmes have all been broadcast on BBC Radio 4. Many Teachers' Centres stock copies of the programmes, which can be either borrowed or copied for use in schools. Most of the programmes are repeated from time to time and it is worth checking the annual list of programmes published by the BBC. The series *Quest* is aimed at 9–11 year olds, *Religious Education* 12–15 year olds and *Religion and Life* sixth form. The dates listed below indicate when programmes were first broadcast:

Islam – *Quest,* 19 November 1975;
Coventry's Square Mile (radiovision) – *Religion and Life*, 9 March 1976 (seven frames on Islam); Festivals – Islam – *Religious Education,* 19 March 1976; The Story of the Prophet – *Religious Education,* 25 February 1977; Islam Today – *Religious Education,* 11 March 1977; East Comes West – Muslims in the British Isles – *Quest*, 8 November 1978; Learning from other Faiths – Judaism and Islam – *Religious Education,* 22 June 1979; Muslim Communities in Britain – *Religion and Life*, 4 October 1979; Pilgrimage – Mecca – *Religious Education*, 12 October 1979; The Problem of Suffering – Islam – *Religious Education*, 9 May 1980; The Qur'an and the Prophet's Birthday – *Quest*, 3 February 1982; Sacred Books (radiovision) – *Quest* and *Religious Education*, 26 March 1982 (five frames on Islam).

Filmstrips for radiovision broadcasts (the radio programme provides commentary and sound effects) are available from BBC Publications, School Orders Section, 114 Bermondsey Street, London SE1 3TH.

ATV: Believe It Or Not

This series (networked nationally) includes a programme on Islam, suitable for upper middle and secondary pupils. Teachers' notes for the series, written by Peter Woodward and containing many ideas for lesson preparation and follow-up work, are available from regional ITV offices.

9   Audio-visual materials

Descriptions of audio-visual materials listed below are generally based on those of the distributors or producers. Prices are those quoted early 1981.

Slide sets and filmstrips

Anadia from Sudan   UNICEF. A set of approximately 30 slides on the life of 14-year-old Anadia, who lives in a Muslim Furawi village in West Sudan. £6.00.

Arabian Peninsula – The Impact of Oil   Encyclopaedia Britannica Films, available from Fergus Davidson Associates. Four filmstrips, £5.50 each, 4 records or cassettes, teachers' notes. Filmstrips: 1 Oil: Fuel for Change, 2 The New Arabs of the Peninsula, 3 Oil for Continuing Growth, 4 Where the Oil Money Goes. The filmstrips are an introduction to the ways in which the discovery of rich oil deposits are changing Arab countries. Aimed at secondary level.

Arabs in the Holy Land   Woodmansterne, Slide Centre. Slide set, £2.40. Scenes include men sitting in a café in Jerusalem, man riding a camel in the Judean Desert, shepherd girl leading her sheep, country woman carrying baskets on head, two sisters, man riding donkey near Bethlehem, shepherd boy, women and children, old man near Jerusalem.

The Art and History of Iran   Audio-Visual Productions. 24 colour slides, £6.40. Includes Naghsh-e-Rustam, Pasargadal, Persepolis, the Royal Mosque at Isfahan.

Basic Maps of the World   Slide Centre. Individual slides, 35p each. Maps available include 6853 Jordan, 6583 Arabia, 6584 Iran, 6638 Iraq, 6851 Lebanon, 6664 Syria, 16446 South-East Asia, 16449 Morocco, 6637 Eqypt and Sudan. Features include capitals, main towns, rivers, roads, railways, surrounding countries and oceans.

Coventry's Square Mile   BBC Publications. Filmstrip plus radio-vision notes including the full transcript of the radio broadcast, £4.00. Tape of broadcast commentary available from Theatre Projects Services, 11–13 Neals Yard, Monmouth Street, London WC2H 9JG. Explores the variety of religious life in a square mile north of Coventry City centre.

East Comes West   1972. Educational Productions. 43-frame filmstrip, colour, teachers' notes, £4.05. An introduction to the way of life in the Hindu, Muslim, and Sikh communities in Yorkshire.

Egypt   Audio-Visual Productions. 20-frame filmstrip, colour, teachers' notes, 1973, £4.05. The filmstrip mainly deals with geography, but a picture of a mosque and several pictures of Muslim women are included.

Egypt: Town Life   Gateway. Thirty-nine frame filmstrip, colour, teachers' notes, £4.20. Several pictures of mosques and some explanation of Muslim worship and customs. Aimed at 9 to 13-year-olds.

Egypt: Village Life   Gateway. 30-frame filmstrip, colour, teachers' notes, £4.20. General view of village life. Several pictures of Muslim women. Aimed at 9 to 13-year-olds.

Encounter with Islam   1969. BBC Publications. 28-frame filmstrip, colour, teachers' notes, £4.00. Tape of original broadcast commentary available from Theatre Projects Services, 11–13 Neals Yard, Monmouth Street, London WC2H 9JG. Covers religious beliefs, the Five Pillars and the life of Muhammad, and the spread of Islam. Broadcast includes Arabic recitation and music. Teachers' notes include transcript of original broadcast.

Eyes on the Arab World   Edward Patterson Associates. Set of 4 filmstrips, 4 cassettes, 3 books, duplicating masters, £49.00.

Families of the Dry Muslim World   Encyclopaedia Britannica, available from Fergus Davidson Associates. Five filmstrips (averaging 70 frames each), colour, with sound cassettes, teachers' notes, £10.50 each. The filmstrip series includes: Village Life in Pakistan, Oil Worker of Kuwait, Co-operative Farming in Iran, A Berber Village in Morocco, and Nomads of Morocco. The differing lifestyles of peoples of the Muslim world are depicted. Each film includes the daily life of one family – ranging from a farmer in Pakistan to an oil company foreman in Kuwait.

Family of Bangladesh   Encyclopaedia Britannica 'Families of Asia' series. Available from Fergus Davidson Associates. 75-frame filmstrip, colour, sound cassette, £5.50. Way of life in Bangladesh viewed through a single family with children.

Family of Jordan   Encyclopaedia Britannica 'Families Around the World' series, available from Fergus Davidson Associates. 47-frame filmstrip, colour, £5.50. Using actual families and real situations, this series offers views of how people live in widely differing countries. Each filmstrip is narrated in caption by a child of the country, who introduces his family and helps explain what is seen. Jordan is the only Muslim country covered.

Focus on Egypt   Slide Centre. With cassette commentary and teachers' booklet. Available as a filmstrip, £8.50, or slide set, £10.50. Covers developments in education, agriculture and industry and the changes they are bringing. Illustrations provide insight into the daily life of Egypt today.

Iran   Rank Audio-Visual. 2 filmstrips. Part 1, 33 frames; Part 2, 34 frames. Colour. £4.00 each. Part 1 covers landmarks in Iran's ancient history and Part 2 covers modern Iran. (Made before the fall of the Shah's government.) Aimed at age 11 plus.

Iraq   Rank Audio-Visual. 30-frame filmstrip, colour, £4.00. Covers geography and ancient history, as well as modern developments in the field of petroleum. Agricultural activities also shown. Aimed at age 10 plus.

Islam   1972. Educational Productions. 25-frame filmstrip, colour, teachers' notes, £4.05. Covers obligations of Islam, prayer, Muslim places of interest, and other topics.

Islam   1967. Hulton, National Audio Visual Library. 37-frame filmstrip, colour, teachers' notes, £2.90. Covers the places of worship and the religious practices of Muslims.

Islam   Concordia Films, National Audio/Visual Library. 61-frame filmstrip, colour, teachers' notes, 14-minute cassette commentary, £5.19. The filmstrip follows Abdul and his parents on a pilgrimage to the Mosque of Omar (Dome of the Rock). Scenes shown include the ceremonial washing place, mosaics and designs of Muslim art, and the mosque museum. Feasting during Ramadan, the five 'religious duties' of Islam and the six essential beliefs or articles of faith are covered.

Islam Islamic Texts Society. 3 colour slide sets. To be made available through Longman, Autumn 1982. The slide sets were prepared by Faard Gouverneur, a Muslim, who through them describes his own faith. They include: *The Doctrine and Practice of Islam,* 111 slides; *The Historic Spread of Islam,* 113 slides; *Islam, Arts and Sciences,* 47 slides.

Islam Leicestershire Education Authority. 24 colour slides, teachers' notes. The slides show a Friday service at a Leicester mosque and Muslim families at home. The notes describe in detail each part of the prayer service and Islamic practices at home.

Islam Time-Life World's Great Religions series, 1957, available from Edward Patterson. One 54-frame filmstrip, colour, teachers' notes, £6.00. One filmstrip, notes and cassette, £12. Two filmstrips, the second 53-frames, colour, notes, 2 cassettes, 6 reprints, duplicating masters, £36. Individual reprints with numerous pictures, 65p each. Pictures covering mosques, the Qur'an, prayer, pilgrimage, customs. Part One provides a general introduction to Islam and Part Two looks at ceremonies, festivals and customs. Several British educationalists who have reviewed these filmstrips have been somewhat critical of their content.

Islam Visual Education Service, The Divinity School, Yale University. 112 slides and notes. Price in the range of £40.

Islam and Europe Gateway. 2 filmstrips, colour, with 2 cassettes. The two filmstrips are: *Islam: The Faith* and *Islam: History and Influence in Europe.* The first is a 32-frame general introduction to the faith and the second a 38-frame exploration of Islam's contributions to, and influences upon, European culture.

Islam: Mosques, Minarets, Domes, Mihrab, Mimbar 1977. Hugh Baddeley. Slide Centre. 40 frames, colour, with teachers' notes. Available as a filmstrip, £4.50 or slide set £6.00. A variety of mosques in various parts of the world are shown and features of Islamic worship portrayed.

Islam (Muslim Influences in India) Ann and Bury Peerless. Several sets of approximately 10–12 colour slides each with teachers' notes. These include: *The Muslim Festival of Id-ul-Fitr at Fatehpur Silri,* £4.00; *Mughal Cities: Delhi* £3.00; *Agra: Forts, Palaces and Mosques* £10.00; *The Taj Mahal* £3.00; *The Tomb of Akbar* £3.00; *Fatehpur Sikri* £3.00; *Tomb of Itimad-ud-Daulah* £6.00; *Babur Nama* £3.00; *Akbar Nama* £3.00; *Later Mughal Emperors* £3.00; *Mughal Court Scenes* £3.00.

Islamic Calligraphy and Illumination British Museum. 18 colour slides, £4.20. Notes by Martin Lings.

The Islamic Tradition Argus Communications. Teaching pack with 2 filmstrips, teachers' notes, 2 cassettes, £20. Each of the two filmstrips, *Islam* and *The Hajj,* available separately at £8.50. The filmstrip *Islam* provides an introduction to the faith covering the life of Muhammad, the Five Pillars, and the expansion of Islam, as well as family life and social practices.

The Hajj follows an American Muslim on his Hajj, providing a detailed look at this one aspect of Islam.

Lebanon   Educational Productions, 'Everyday Life' series. Colour filmstrip, £4.05.

Life Among the Arabs   Longman/Common Ground, Slide Centre. Available as a filmstrip, £4.50; or slide set, £6.00. Colour, accompanying teachers' notes. Includes a map showing languages and climate and scenes of general life such as villages, Bedouin tents, street scenes, donkeys, camels, irrigation, etc.

Life of a Malayan Family   1974. Hugh Baddeley, 'Families of Other Lands' series, Slide Centre. Available as filmstrip, £4.50; or slide set, £6.00. 34 frames, colour, teachers' notes. Optional cassette commentary, £3.50. A look at family life, with some material on worship and ablutions.

Life of a Nomad People   Gateway. Two filmstrips, *Life in Camp* (45 frames) and *Travel and Trade* (47 frames), colour, £8.20. An intimate view of the Kuchis of Afghanistan. Shows their customs, clothing, food, pastimes, articles of trade. Some pictures of sheep raising and the camel caravan as it moves to their winter valley home. Aimed at upper primary and above.

The Middle East   Educational Productions. A set of 4 colour filmstrips, £15.00; available individually at £4.05. The filmstrips are *The Physical Landscape*, *Social Contrasts, Settlements,* and *Farming*.

Moors in Spain   Visual Productions. Filmstrip with handbook, £3.20.

Morocco and its Neighbours   BBC, 'People of Many Lands' series. Slide Centre. Available as a filmstrip, £4.80; or slide set, £6.30. Covers the life and work of a number of communities in north-west Africa, with views of their surroundings.

Moslem Jerusalem   Woodmansterne, Slide Centre. Set of nine colour slides, £2.40. Includes Dome of the Rock from Mount of Olives, Gate of the Chain seen through Scale Gate, Dome of the Rock and El Aqsa Mosque, Dome of the Rock interiors, Muslims at prayer, El Aqsa Mosque – north front, El Aqsa Mosque – interior, El Aqsa mosque from Mount of Olives.

Muhammad and the World of Islam   Longman/Common Ground, Slide Centre. Set of 12 colour slides with notes, £3.55. Covers the main points of Muhammad's teaching and the spread of Islam. Slides include the Ka'ba, before the Battle of Badr, the Qur'an, the Friday Mosque in Isfahan, the Aqsa Mosque in Jerusalem, the Citadel in Cairo, Anamur castle, ships and sailors, farming scene c. 1200, a glass mosque lamp, an Iznik tile, the combat of Humay and Humayun.

Muhammad: the Last Prophet   Fergus Davidson Associates. Filmstrip with cassette, £5.00. 'Men Who Made History' series. Cartoon-type drawings. Muhammad portrayed as a historical figure.

New Developments in the Sahara   Longman/Common Ground, Slide Centre. Available as a filmstrip, £4.50; or slide set, £6.00. Includes a map of the area and pictures of people of the desert, settlements and cases, irrigation and crops, oil and natural gas facilities, air, road and rail transport, new towns.

North Africa   Hugh Baddeley, Slide Centre. Available as a filmstrip, £4.50; or slide set, £6.00. Covers Morocco to Egypt, including desert, irrigation, cultivation, oases, crafts, oil wells, and power stations.

Northern Nigeria Hulton. Colour filmstrip, £2.90. Survey of Northern Nigeria, describing occupations, homes, religions and scenery.

Oil in the Middle East Longman/Common Ground, Slide Centre. Available as a filmstrip, £4.25; or as a slide set, £5.75. Pictures include filling station, map of area, geologist taking rock samples, and surveying, drilling rig in action, diagram of typical oilfield, process plant, oil refinery, workers' houses, docks and transport, petro-chemical industry and other associated industries.

Pakistan A series of 4 kits covering Society and Culture, People and Places, Time and Change, and Arts, Crafts and Daily Life. Educational Media International.

Society and Culture in Pakistan. Kit with 40 slides, notes and other teaching resources. £17.50. A study of people in Pakistan, including the Islamic religion with its widespread influence on society; education in a developing country, sport and leisure.

People and Places in Pakistan Kit with 40 slides, notes and other teaching resources, £17.50. A geographical study including a perceptual approach to experiencing climate, an investigation of the role of water and the Indus River in this arid country, village life as perceived by Pakistanis and by foreign observers, urban life in old and new cities, and food in Pakistan, including some tested recipes.

Time and Change in Pakistan Kit with 40 slides, notes and other teaching resources, £17.50. A chronological study beginning with the ancient civilisation of Mohenjodaro, moving to Gandhara with its fusion of Buddhism and Hellenism, on to the coming of the Muslims and the Mughal dynasty, the colonial period, the independence movement and Pakistan in the modern world.

Arts and Crafts and Daily Life in Pakistan Kit with 40 slides, notes and other teaching resources, £17.50. The arts and crafts of Pakistan are an integral part of daily life, whether it is a highly painted delivery truck, the carved sides of a river boat, or the colourful costumes from different areas. An introduction to music, costumes, house design and traditional crafts in Pakistan.

Persian Miniatures, the Early Period British Museum. Slide set, £2.80.
Persian Miniatures, the Middle Period British Museum. Slide set, £2.80.
Persian Miniatures, the Later Period British Museum. Slide set, £2.80.

Patterns in the Arab World Longman/Common Ground, Slide Centre. Available as a filmstrip, £4.50; or slide set, £6.00. Complements Longman's *Patterns in Geography,* Book 2, but can be used independently. Covers the physical geography of desert landscapes, oases, and population distribution, the Nile and water control, the effects of man's intervention, oil and the resultant changes in the standard of living.

The Persian Gulf 1971. Visual Publications. 43-frame filmstrip, colour, cassette, handbook, £6.50. By explorer and composer David Fanshawe. Looks at the lands and people of the Persian Gulf – an area of extraordinary contrasts and contradictions.

Prayer in Islam (Salaat)   Slide Centre, National Audio/Visual Aids Library. 12 slides, £3.60. Slides show different positions taken during prayer at various times of the day by members of the Muslim faith. Notes in English and Arabic.

The Religions of Africa   Concordia Films. 35mm filmstrip, colour. Islam in Africa covered in one section of the filmstrip.

Religions of the World   Gateway. A filmstrip set consisting of 6 filmstrips plus 3 records or 6 cassettes, £65.40. Includes Many People, Many Faiths; Hinduism; Buddhism; Judaism; Christianity; and Islam.

Rites of Hajj.   Slide Centre, National Audio/Visual Aids Library. 12 colour slides, £3.60. Illustrates the rites undertaken by Muslim pilgrims on the journey to and on arrival in Mecca. Notes in English and Arabic.

The Sahara's Southern Fringe   Educational Media International. 24 slides, notes and cassette, £6.45. The pictures provide resource material for a study of the way the Hausa and Fulani people have adapted their life to a semi-arid region on the margin of a great desert.

Seeing Northern Africa   Gateway. A filmstrip set consisting of 4 filmstrips plus 2 records or 4 cassettes, £43.20. Includes Land and People, History and Culture, Agriculture and Fishing, Industry and Commerce.

Shirir of Bangladesh   UNICEF. A wallet of material with some 30 slides on the life of Shishir, a 15-year-old Muslim boy. £6.00.

Tunisia   Educational Productions, 'Everyday Life' series. Colour filmstrip, £4.05.

Tunisia   Hulton. Colour filmstrip, £2.90. A general look at Tunisia with scenes of towns, villages, general topography, people and occupations.

Tunisia   Rank Audio-Visual. 37-frame filmstrip, colour, £4.00. Details of the people and economy covered. Carthage and Tunis contrasted. Aimed at age 11 plus.

Turkey and Iran   Edward Patterson Associates, 'Living in Other Lands' series. 2 filmstrips, 1 cassette, £15.00.

The Turkish Pottery of Iznik   British Museum. Slide set, £2.80.

Village Life in Northern Nigeria   Longman/Common Ground, Slide Centre. Available as a filmstrip, £4.50; or slide set, £6.00. Pictures include building a village house, drawing water from a well, the different work of men and women, village crops, cotton growing, inter-village trade, town transport, streets and markets in towns, agricultural show.

The way of Islam   Church Missionary Society, 1975. 67-frame filmstrip, colour, with either cassette or open reel tape, teachers' notes, £5.00. An introduction to the beliefs of Islam and the Muslim way of life, with illustrations from various parts of the world.

Western Africa   Hugh Baddeley, Slide Centre. Available as a filmstrip, £4.50; or slide set, £6.00. Covers Nigeria, Cameroons, Gabon, etcetera. Includes topography, village markets, agriculture, industries, timber, cocoa, coffee and rubber.

Yemen Opens the Way to Change   UNICEF. Set of 30 colour slides. A look at everyday life in Yemen, with an emphasis on changes that are improving the standard of living.

Films and Video Tapes

Akbar 1967. High Commission of India. 16mm, colour, 15 minutes, lent free of charge. The life of the great Muslim Emperor Akbar, illustrated by sixteenth-century paintings.

The Arab Experience 1979. Concord Films. Set of 3 films, 16mm, colour, each film 50 minutes, hire fee £16.60 each. Anthony Thomas, who later made the controversial *Death of a Princess,* made this trilogy for Yorkshire Television, in which he examines the vast and many-hued Arab world. The films are: *Legacy of Faisal, Egypt, In search of an Identity,* for which the pilgrimage to the Holy City of Mecca was filmed by an all-Muslim crew.

Architecture of Pakistan Embassy of Pakistan. 16mm, 20 minutes, lent free of charge. Covers monuments from the Indus Valley civilisation of 2000 BC to the present day. Many Islamic buildings included.

Centres of Islamic Studies High Commission of India. Colour, 20 minutes, lent free of charge. A look at India's Islamic centres.

Changing Middle East Edward Patterson Associates. Colour, 27 minutes, hire fee £7.25.

The Chess Players Connoisseur Films. Colour, 128 minutes, hire fee £40.00. Hindi dialogue, English subtitles, some 50 per cent of dialogue in English. Highly acclaimed feature film directed by Satyajit Ray. The scene is Lucknow in 1856. The British Resident, General Outram, to complete British domination of the subcontinent, is manoeuvring the Muslim Nawab of Oudh into surrendering his throne. Two wealthy citizens, descendants of Moghul warriors, pass their days playing chess – indifferent to the historic contest that threatens to plunge their State into war.

Country of Islam Naitonal Audio/Visual Library. 16mm, colour, 17 minutes, hire fee £13.51 including postage and VAT. A study of Arab life, through the eyes of a Moroccan boy who leaves his village to start school in a town. We see people at prayer in the mosque, home life of both the poor and wealthy, life in village and town, a hydro-electric and irrigation scheme under construction. The commentary, in the voice of a Morrocan, conveys with much sympathy the point of view and philosophy of Islamic people.

The Dervishes of Kurdistan Concord Films. Colour, 50 minutes, hire fee £15.20. By director Brian Moser for Granada television's 'Disappearing World' series. Explores the way of life of a community of Kurds resident in Iran near the border with Iraq. What distinguishes this particular community is that its members are Qadiri Dervishes – followers of an unusual Islamic mystical cult.

Dr Mohamed Iqbal High Commission of India. Colour, 15 minutes, lent free of charge. A film about one of the subcontinent's most famous Muslim writers, who was both poet and philosopher.

Egypt: the Struggle for Stability Rank Audio Visual. 16mm, colour, 27 minutes, 2-day hire fee £14.00. Explores the contrasts and conflicts of modern Egypt – a land of both water wheels and massive hydroelectric power facilities; a country with great potential in its natural resources yet a level of poverty among the worst in the world. Age range 11 plus.

Egyptian Family (Modern) Edward Patterson Associates. Colour, 17 minutes, hire fee £6.00. Emphasises the changes that have taken place over the last century.

Faces of Change Concord Films. A series of films exploring the effects of Western society on traditional values in various Third World countries. The only Muslim country covered is Afghanistan. Films include: 1 *Afghan Nomads: The Maldar*, colour, 21 minutes, hire fee £6.40. 2 *Afghan Village*, colour, 45 minutes, hire fee £12.60. 3 *Afghan Women*, colour, 17 minutes, hire fee £5.20. 4 *Naim and Jabar* (a film on the hopes, fears and aspirations of two adolescent Afghan boys), colour, 50 minutes, hire fee £15.20. 5 *Wheat Cycle*, colour, 16 minutes, hire fee £5.00.

Festival in Kano Gateway. 16mm, black and white, 30 minutes, hire fee £7.40. Provides a detailed picture of the varied inhabitants of the city of Kano, in northern Nigeria, one of the oldest cities south of the Sahara. The majority of the population are Muslim, and the film was shot during the month of Ramadan. It ends with scenes of the Salla Festival, marking the end of the fast.

Four Centuries Ago 1961. High Commission of India. 16mm, colour, 20 minutes, lent free of charge. A film about the architectural beauty of the world-famous monuments at Agra and Fatehpur Sikri.

Four Religions 1960. National Film Board of Canada, Concord Films. 16mm, black and white, 60 minutes, hire fee £11.20. The 15-minute section on Islam can be hired separately for £4.00.

Garm Hava Contemporary Films. Colour, 120 minutes. Film in Hindi with English subtitles. A feature film that tells the story of a Muslim joint family living in the city of Agra at the time of the partition of India.

High Above the Dust High Commission of India. Colour, 20 minutes, lent free of charge. A look at Indo-Islamic architecture.

Indian Muslims and Their Religious Observances 1973. High Commission of India. 16mm, colour, 20 minutes, lent free of charge.

International Congress on Allama Iqbal Embassy of Pakistan. 16mm, colour, 25 minutes, lent free of charge. Covers the life and work of Mohamed Iqbal, Muslim poet and philosopher.

Islam National Film Board of Canada, from the series 'Four Religions'. Concord Films Council. 16mm, black and white, 19 minutes, hire fee £4.00. This film explores the life and teachings of Muhammad and the practice of Islam today. Shrines of holy men and heroes are shown.

Islam in Bolton 1976. Open University Programme, available from Guild Sound & Vision. 16mm film or video cassette, colour, 23 minutes, hire fee 2 days £15.50; 5 days £18.00. Examines the relationship between management and Muslim workers at Taylor's, a towel weaving factory in Horwich near Bolton, Lancs.

Jerusalem and its Contributions Boulton-Hawker Films, National Visual Aids Library. Colour, 17 minutes, hire fee £13.51 including postage and VAT. Covers Jerusalem's importance and its contributions to the history, religion, and present-day life of the Middle East. Looks at the roles of the three great religions: Judaism, Christianity and Islam. Age range 11 years and older.

Jhadoo Chowdhari, a Tongawallah from Delhi   1968. Gateway, 'Faces of India' series. 16mm, colour, 28 minutes, hire fee per day £8.90. A look at the way of life of an Indian Muslim who owns a fleet of horse-drawn carriages. Sympathetically treated. Includes scenes of the Muslim festival of Id, the Sikh celebration of the birthday of Guru Gobind Singh, and preparations for a Hindu wedding.

Koran Reading Contest   Malaysian High Commission.

Life in the Sahara   1954. Encyclopaedia Britannica Films, available from National Audio-Visual Aids Library or Scottish Central Film Library. 16mm, colour, 15 minutes. Chronicles patterns of life in the desert and contrasts nomadic life-styles with Arab and Berber settlements. This 1954 release provides a record of the time before the extensive mineral exploitations of the Saharan region.

Love and Remembrance   1966. High Commission of India. 16mm, 5 minutes, lent free of charge. A short film on the Taj Mahal.

Major Religions of the World – Development and Rituals   Encyclopaedia Britannica Films, available from National Visual Aids Library and Scottish Central Film Library. 16mm, colour, 20 minutes. Survey of the origins, rituals and symbols of Hinduism, Buddhism, Judaism, Christianity, and Islam.

Man and his World   Educational Media International. A series of family or community case studies produced by the Institut Fur Film und Bild, Germany, with English versions prepared by the Visual Education Centre, Toronto. Each of the films has a minimum of commentary, making them usable in a wide range of subject areas and with students of different ages. Teacher's guides with themes for discussion, questions and activities are available free on request. Films include: *Egyptian Villagers,* 14 minutes; *Oasis in the Sahara*, 16 minutes; *River People of Chad,* 20 minutes.

Mecca, the Forbidden City   Patria Films. 16mm, colour, 50 minutes. Covers the rites of Hajj.

The Middle East   1973. Encyclopaedia Britannica. 16mm, colour. An introduction to the way of life in the largely Muslim Middle East. Covers rural life, nomads and city dwellers.

Mirza Ghalib   1969. High Commission of India. 16mm, black and white, 15 minutes, lent free of charge. A film about one of India's most famous Muslim poets. Ghalib lived in the nineteenth century, and his life is told through paintings and illustrations of the period.

The Moghuls   1968. High Commission of India. 16mm, 11 minutes, lent free of charge. A look at the culture and beauty left by the Moghuls, who came to India as invaders and remained to love the country and build great courts, tombs, and palaces.

Moslems in Spain   Edward Patterson Associates. Colour, 32 minutes, hire fee £8.00. A juxtaposition of monuments from the past and scenes from life today to emphasise Spain's exotic heritage.

A Mosque in the Park   Film Forum, Concord Films, Knight Films. 16mm, colour, 50 minutes, hire fee ranging from £10.00 to £15.20. An insider's view of the Muslim community in Britain, showing the way of life of four families – two in London and two in Manchester. The film is not a discourse on Islam, but it does aim to be an authentic picture of the human situation in which four Muslim families from different parts of India and Pakistan try to come to terms with the English environment and succeed in evolving a way of life which preserves their own heritage without 'opting out' of English culture in their adopted country.

The Mosque – Prayer in its Setting 1979. Open University Programme, available from Guild Sound & Vision. Available as 16mm film or video cassette, colour, 24 minutes, hire fee: 2 days £15.50; 5 days £18.00.

Mughal India ILEA Learning Materials Service, also available through the Central Film Library. Video cassette only, black and white, 30 minutes. Looks at the Mughal Empire, the period when Muslim power was at its height in India. Tells the story of the Mughal Emperors through miniature paintings and architecture from the period of their rules.

Muslim India ILEA Learning Materials Service, also available through the Central Film Library. Video cassette only, black and white, 20 minutes, purchase price £35–£45 depending on system; hire fee for a full term £15–£19. Looks at Islam and its impact on Africa, trade routes across the Sahara and Indian Ocean, the growth of cities. Age range 12–14 years.

A Muslim Festival 1965. High Commission of India. 16mm, 9 minutes, lent free of charge. Two important Muslim festivals are shown, Id-ul-Fitr and Id-ul-Zuha. Both are observed as national holidays in India.

The New North Africa Boulton-Hawker Films Ltd, National Audio-Visual Aids Library. Colour, 16 minutes, £13.51 including postage and VAT. The film focuses mainly on Tunisia, one of the smallest but most progressive North African countries. Looks at the combination of modern European influences and traditional Arab ways.

A Nomad Family in West Africa 1976, from the 3-part series on Upper Volta 'After the Drought'. Concord Films. Colour, 30 minutes, hire fee £8.20. The life of a family in an almost self-sufficient Tuareg settlement. Includes instruction of children in the Qur'an and religious observances as well as many other details of settlement life.

Oasis Encyclopaedia Britannica Films, available from National Audio-Visual Aids Library and Scottish Central Film Library. 16mm, colour, 11 minutes. Life at a Libyan desert oasis. Shows the symbolic importance the date palm holds for oasis dwellers, problems of irrigation, daily life, the crowded market place.

Oh, for the Wings of a Dove Concord Films, Birmingham Council of Christian Churches. Colour, 30 minutes, hire fee £8.20. The life of a Pakistani family in Britain. The mother is widowed, her son and daughter are aged 15 and 13. Both find tension between their family culture and their outside environment difficult to reconcile at times.

Pakistan, Land and its People Embassy of Pakistan. 16mm, colour, 35 minutes, lent free of charge.

A Passage to England 1972. Concord Films, Film Forum, Knight Films. Colour, 50 minutes, hire fee approximately £10.00. About an attractive and intelligent Pakistani student who finds herself between two cultures – unable to fit in with either. Educated in England, she finds her parents wish her to return to Pakistan for an 'arranged marriage'.

The Pathans Concord Films. Video cassette only, colour, 45 minutes: Philips 1500VCR or U-Matic, L14. From the Granada 'Disappearing World' series. Looks at life of the Pathans living in Pakistan, close to the Afghanistan border. Explores the life of this community bound by a common language, a common heritage, and the powerful unifying spirit of Islam.

Pilgrimage 1979. Open University Programme, available from Guild Sound & Vision. 16mm film or videocassette, colour, 24 minutes, hire fee: 2 days £15.50; 5 days £18.00. Looks at a group of Muslims from Manchester going on the greatest of all pilgrimages, the Hajj, to Mecca. We witness their farewell prayers and those of the community and hear the pilgrims hopes and aspirations for the journey. Finally, on their return home they tell of their reactions to their devotions.

Prayer Breathes Life into Souls Muslim Information Service. 16mm, 25 minutes. Covers Islamic beliefs and religious and social practices.

Punjabi Village 1969. Concord Films. 16mm, black and white, 40 minutes, hire fee £5.80. A study of life in a Muslim village in the Punjab, in Pakistan. A village wedding is shown.

Rana Educational Media International. 16mm, colour, 15 minutes. Story of Rana, a young Muslim girl living in a crowded section of old Delhi. The custom of wearing veils and marriage by arrangement are examined.

Religion and Civilisation Edward Patterson Associates. A series available both in 16mm film and video cassette format. Colour, each film 29 minutes, hire fee for 16mm films £2.25 each. This series exploring religious traditions is being prepared with the cooperation of a team of teachers. Only two titles were available early 1981: *Origins* – which focuses on clues of the world's earliest religions and the light they shed on prehistoric life; and *Symbols* – a look at the symbolic nature of religious practice (prayers, festivals, places of worship, etc.).

The Road to Arafat Guild of Sound and Vision. A look at the way of life of the Islamic peoples. There are also scenes of the countryside and many buildings of architectural interest.

Saudi Arabia: the Oil Revolution Rank Audio Visual. 16mm, colour, 25 minutes, 2-day hire fee £14.00. An overview of Saudi Arabia which probes the internal tensions of this kingdom in transition since the oil boom of the mid-1960s. Glimpses of the lives of individuals of all classes reveal the unsettling effects of the sudden influx of vast oil revenue upon a traditional society.

The Sheep Must Live 1973. Knight Films. 16mm, colour, 30 minutes, hire fee £15.00. The story of the Bakhtiari migration in Iran. This film is a short version of a longer documentary first shown by the 'World About Us' series on BBC and much acclaimed.

Tabaski   Embassy of Senegal. Annual festival of Eid-el-Kebir.

Taj – a Muslim   1972. ILEA Educational Television, 'Exploring World Faiths' series. Also available from the Central Film Library. Video cassette only. A Muslim social worker talks of her faith and the experience of being a Muslim in England.

Taj Mahal   1959. High Commission of India. 16mm, colour, 12 minutes, lent free of charge. About the world famous Taj Mahal, built between 1630 and 1648 by Shah Jehan as an immortal tribute to the memory of his beloved wife, Mumtaz Mahal.

Three Families – Jerusalem   1979. Open University Programme, available from Guild Sound & Vision. Available as 16mm film or videocassette, colour, 24 minutes, hire fee: 2 days £15.50; 5 days £18.00. Visits three families who live within a mile of each other in Jerusalem – one Jewish, one Christian and one Muslim – and observes the devotions practised in the home. Family members talk briefly on what their religion means to them.

Turkey   'Families of the World' series. Educational Media International. Colour, 19 minutes. Presents a timeless vignette of Turkish village life. Girls work at weaving or embroidery and father and mother farm. A trip to Istanbul offers a respite from the normal daily routine.

Turkey, Nation in Transition   Edward Patterson Associates. Colour, 27 minutes, hire fee £7.25. Uses both animation and locally shot footage. Authentic Turkish music.

The United Arab Emirates – a New Oil Nation   1976. Educational Media International. 16mm, colour, 14 minutes. Once the region of Arab Bedouin and traders, the United Arab Emirates has become a nation of wealth and international importance due to the discovery of oil. Significant changes contrasted with ancient practices.

An Urban Family in West Africa   1976, from the 3-part series on Upper Volta 'After the Drought', Concord Films. Colour, 30 minutes, hire fee £8.20. The life of a comparatively well-off family living in Ouagadougou, capital of Upper Volta. Includes Muslim religious practices as well as other aspects of everyday life.

Visit us in Bangladesh   1972. Oxfam. 16mm, colour, 21 minutes, hire fee £2.60. Illustrates the daily life of a relatively prosperous family in a Bangladesh village. The film has a sound track but no commentary. Suitable for any age group from 7 upwards. Has been used very effectively in stimulating discussion.

The Way They Live There: An Egyptian Village   Gateway. Videocassette only, 17 minutes. VHS £35.00; Betamax £35.00; VCR £40.00; U-Matic £40.00. Looks at life in a village at the edge of the Nile delta. Shows the crops and animals on which the village depends and the importance of irrigation in agriculture under semi-desert conditions. Also shows the kind of life led by boys and girls in an Egyptian village. Age range upper primary, secondary.

Women of Pakistan   Embassy of Pakistan. 16mm, black and white, 15 minutes, lent free of charge.

Yemen   'Families of the World' series. Educational Media International.

Colour, 18 minutes. The sharp contrasts of the changing roles of young people is highlighted against a traditional Arab background.

Posters, Teaching Packs, and other materials   (Teaching packs in which slides or filmstrips are a major component are listed under 'Slides and Filmstrips')

Algeria – Country and People   1973. OXFAM, 52p. Resource wallet.

The Bedouin   Pictorial Charts Educational Trust, £2.60. 4 small wall charts. The life and customs of the Bedouin people.

Families of the World, OXFAM, 81p. Colour wallcharts, 16″ x 23″, set of 8. Several Muslim countries included, e.g. Morocco, Indonesia.

Hajj   Minaret House Publications. A portfolio of material. Black and White.

Heritage of Islam   Pictorial Charts Educational Trust, £2.60. Set of 4 charts (15″ x 20″). The four charts cover: Islamic Decorative Arts, The Five Pillars of Islam, The Spread of Islam, The Arab Contribution to Science.

ILEA Poster Maps   Within ILEA £2.00, non-ILEA £3.00. Seven large black and white maps of Asia and Africa.

Islamic Calendar   UK Islamic Mission. The mission publishes this calendar and is willing to make it available to schools.

Islamic Jigsaw Puzzles   Muslim Information Service, 65p each, £3.50 set of six. Six different puzzle designs (28cm x 20cm) each of one of Islam's holy shrines.

Mughal Painting Portfolios   Independent Publishing Co, approx. £4.25 per portfolio. Several sets of reproductions of Mughal paintings from India.

Muslim World Map   Muslim Information Service, £1.95. Colour, 100cm. x 40cm. Shows distribution of Muslims throughout the world, with inset photographs of Muslim shrines. The reverse side provides information on the world of Islam and Islamic customs.

My Neighbour's Religion   Pictorial Charts Educational Trust, £2.60. Large wall chart. Intended to promote a wider understanding of the rich variety of faiths in Britain. Covers Hindu, Muslim, Sikh, Christian, Jewish and Buddhist religions.

The Ninety Names of God   Minaret House. Poster.

A Muslim Testimony   Open University Publications, £7.00 for both. Audiotape only. 20 minutes. A Sikh Testimony on same tape, also 20 minutes. Not sold separately. Statements from different Muslim countries, such as Iran, Egypt, Saudi Arabia, etcetera, on what Islam, the Qur'an, the 'Shari'a' and the Five Pillars of Islam mean to the speakers.

Photographs from Bangladesh   1981. Learning Materials Centre, ILEA price £3.00, non-ILEA £4.75. 20 black and white photographs (297 x 210mm), teachers' notes. Various aspects of everyday life in Bangladesh. Several photographs deal specifically with religious themes – the Star Mosque in Dacca, a village mosque, an imam, a wedding ceremony. The teachers' notes contain a section on Islam in Bangladesh.

Postcards   A wide variety of postcards with Islamic themes – mosques, calligraphy, miniature paintings – are available from the British Museum, the Victoria and Albert Museum and the Muslim Educational Trust.

Prayer models   Muslim Information Service, £20.00 for set of nine. Each approx. 68cm x 68cm, colour. Large, colour, cardboard models illustrating the full range of movements of *salah* (prayer).

Prayer poster   Muslim Information Service, £1.25. Colour, 70cm x 50cm. The poster includes 21 colour photographs providing a step-by-step guide to the Islamic rituals of *wudhu* (ablution) and *salah* (prayer).

The Qur'an   Minaret House. Poster.

Qur'anic stickers, tapes of the recitation of the Qur'an, prayer mats and other items   Muslim Information Centre. The Muslim Information Centre makes available a number of items such as those listed above. Contact the Centre for further details.

The World of Islam   Jackdaw no. 143, Jonathan Cape, £1.95. Wallet of materials (Out of print but available at many resources centres.) A wide variety of visual materials, including many examples from Islam's rich artistic heritage.

World Families   Centre for World Development Education. Posters (16″ x 23″) include Nigeria, Morocco and Indonesia. Aimed at middle school level.

World Religions and Philosophies   Pictorial Charts Educational Trust, £2.60. Large wall chart. Covers the historical development of the world's great religions.

10   Addresses of Audio-visual Suppliers

Argus Film Library Ltd, 15 Beaconsfield Rd, London NW10 2LE; *Audio-Visual Productions,* Hocker Hill House, Chepstow, Gwent NP6 5ER; *BBC Publications,* School Orders Section, 144–152 Bermondsey St, London SE1 3TH; *Birmingham Council of Churches,* Central Hall, Corporation St, Birmingham B4 6QW; *Boulton-Hawker Films,* Hadleigh, Ipswich, Suffolk IP7 5BG; *Central Film Library,* Bromyard Ave, Acton, London W3 7JB; *Centre for World Development Education,* 128 Buckingham Palace Rd, London SW1W 9SH; *Church Missionary Society,* 157 Waterloo Rd, London SE1; *Concord Films Council Ltd,* 201 Felixstowe Rd, Ipswich, Suffolk IP3 9BJ; *Concordia Films,* Viking Way, Bar Hill Village, Cambridge CB3 8EL; *Connoisseur Films,* 167 Oxford St, London W1R 2DX; *Contemporary Films,* 55 Greek St, London W1V 6DB; *Educational Media International,* 25 Boileau Rd, London W5 3AL; *Educational Productions,* 10 Snow Hill, London EC1A 2EB; *Edward Patterson Associates,* 68 Copers Cope Rd, Beckenham, Kent; *Embassy of Pakistan,* (High Commissioner for Pakistan), 35 Lowndes Square, London SW1; *Fergus Davidson Associates Ltd,* 22 South Audley St, London W1Y 6ES; *Film Forum,* 56 Brewer St, London W13 3FA; *Gateway Educational Films,* Waverley Rd, Yate, Bristol BS17 5RB; *Guild Sound and Vision,* Woodston House, Oundle Rd, Peterborough PE2 9PZ; *High Commission of India,* India House, Aldwych, London WC2; *Hugh Baddeley,* 64 Moffats Lane, Brookmans Park, Hatfield, Herts AL9 7RU; *Hulton Educational Publications,*

Raans Rd, Amersham, Bucks HP6 5BR; *ILEA Learning Materials Centre*, Thakeray Road, London SW8 3BT; *Jackdaw Publications Ltd,* Jonathan Cape, 30 Bedford Square, London WC1B 3EL; *Leicestershire Education Authority,* County Hall, Glenfield, Leicester, LE3 8RF; *Longman Common Ground Filmstrips,* Promotional Services Dept, Pinnacles, Harlow, Essex CM20 2JE; *Minaret House Publications,* 9 Leslie Park Rd, Croydon, Surrey CRO 6TN; *Muslim Information Service,* 233 Seven Sisters Rd, London N4 2DA; *National Audio-Visual Aids Library,* Paxton Place, Gipsy Rd, London SE27 9SR; *Open University Publications,* 12 Cofferidge Close, Stony Stratford, Milton Keynes MK11 1BY; *Oxfam Education,* 274 Banbury Rd, Oxford OX2 7DZ; *Pendennis Pictures Corp.,* 10 Green St, London W1; *Ann & Bury Peerless,* 22 King's Avenue, Minnis Bay, Birchington-on-Sea, Kent CT7 9QL; *Pictorial Charts Educational Trust,* 27 Kirchen Rd, London W13 OUD; *Rank Audio-Visual,* PO Box 70, Great West Rd, Brentford, Mddx TW8 9HR; *Rickitt Encyclopaedia of Slides,* Portman House, 17 Brodrick Road, London SW17; *Slide Centre Ltd,* 143 Chatham Rd, London SW11 6SR; *UK Islamic Mission,* 146 Park Road, NW8; Unicef, 46–48 Osnaburgh St, London NW1 3PU; *Visual Education Service,* The Divinity School, Yale University, 409 Prospect St, New Haven, Connecticut, USA; *Visual Publications,* 197 Kensington High St, London W8 4BR.

11 Addresses of Muslim Organisations

The Centre for the Study of Islam and Christian-Muslim Relations, Selly Oak Colleges, Birmingham, B29 6LE.

The Centre's *Newsletter* appears in May and November. Other publications are: *Research Papers: Muslims in Europe* (four issues each year); *Abstracts: European Muslims and Christian–Muslim Relations* (twice yearly); *News of Muslims in Europe* (six issues each year). Subscriptions are available and trial copies will be sent on request.

The Institute of Ismaili Studies, 14–15 Great James Street, London WC1N 3DP. The emphasis of the Institute's work is primarily academic and educational and its programme of activities includes public lectures, conferences, seminars, teacher training courses and the publication of works on Islam. It has a permanent academic staff and a library of some 10,000 volumes.

The Islamic Centre, 2A Sutherland Street, Leicester LE2 1DS. The Islamic Centre, established in 1968, provides a number of educational services. Quarterly seminars and annual conferences on various aspects of Islam are held for the benefit and interest of the Muslim and host communities in Leicester. Classes in religious education for Muslim children and adults are held at the Centre, and classes in English and mathematics, taught by volunteers, are to be begun soon.

Recent publications of the Centre include *Imam Hussain, Come to Prayer* and *Prophet of Islam.* The Centre provides some materials free to schools. These include an English translation of the Holy Qur'an, the publication *Imam Hussain,* and other Islamic leaflets and books.

The Centre accepts visits by school groups and will provide speakers for schools and colleges for payment of travel expenses only. The Centre also offers a consultancy service for teachers. Correspondence and inquiries should be addressed to Mr M.H. Khan (Chairman) or Mr M.S. Raza.

The Islamic Cultural Centre, 146 Park Road (off Baker Street), London NW8. The Islamic Cultural Centre encourages schools, colleges and other education institutions to write and ask for the Centre's help and advice with regard to all aspects of Islam. Publications provided free of charge to schools include *Islam, an Introduction, Translation of the Glorious Qur'an, The Straight Path, Forty Hadith, Islam, Our Choice, Islam – The First and Final Religion, Family Life in Islam,* and *The Meaning of Islam.* Other recent publications that might be of interest to schools are *Islam in Focus, Islamic Pious Foundations in Jerusalem,* and *English Speaking Orientalists.*

The Centre accepts visits by school groups, but by arrangement only. It will provide speakers for schools and colleges for payment of travel expenses only, and is willing to offer consultancy work in some circumstances. Correspondence and inquiries should be addressed to Dr M.A. Badawi, Director.

The London Mosque (built by the Ahmadiyya Movement in Islam), 16 Gressenhall Road, London SW18. The London Mosque of the Ahmadiyya Movement in Islam is one of the UK's oldest Islamic institutions, founded in 1924. It provides several publications free to schools including *Islam: Its Message, Philosophy and Teachings of Islam,* and *What is Ahmadiyyat?* Other recent publications that might be of interest to schools – *Golden Deeds of Muslims, The Muslim Prayer Book, A Book of Religious Knowledge, Islam: My Religion,* and *Islamic Teachings.*

The Mosque accepts visits by school groups and provides speakers to schools and colleges free of charge. It will arrange classes for small groups on special request. Correspondence and inquiries should be addressed to Shaikh Mubarak Ahmad, Imam, London Mosque.

The Muslim Schools Trust, 78 Gillespie Road, London N5 ILN. The Muslim Schools Trust was organised to impart the teaching of the Qur'an to Muslim children in Britain. It has established ten weekend and twelve evening Qur'anic centres in nine cities including London and Birmingham. It has also started a series of publications on various aspects of Islam for Muslims living in the West and for non-Muslims. Further information is available from Mr Afzalur Rahman at the address above.

Muslim Women's Association, 63 Coombe Lane, London SW20 OBD. The Muslim Women's Association, founded in 1962, offers a consultancy service to schools and colleges, but does not accept school visits or provide speakers. Teachers might find its magazine *The Muslim Woman* useful in the classroom. Correspondence and inquiries should be directed to the above address or to 141 Norval Road, Wembley, Middlesex HAO 3SX.

Muslim Youth Association, 31 Draycott Place, London SW3. The Muslim Youth Association, founded in 1965, makes available a number of publications on general Islamic concepts. It will provide its journal, the *Islamic Echo,* to schools free of charge. Group visits to the Muslim Youth Association are not possible, but the Association will provide speakers for schools and colleges free of charge. Correspondence and inquiries should be directed to the Secretary at the address above.

Paigham-E-Islam Trust, Britain, 423 Stratford Road, Sparkhill, Birmingham, B11 4LB. The Paigham-E-Islam Trust, established in 1974, publishes the monthly magazine *Young Muslim, Birmingham,* which teachers might find interesting for classroom use. It also operates the Muslim Printers and Booksellers (from the same address), which stocks a large range of Islamic literature in English and Urdu, as well as educational books in Urdu and a number of texts in Bangla, Farsi and Arabic.

It does not accept visits by school groups but is willing to provide speakers free of charge in the Birmingham area. Correspondence and inquiries should be addressed to Mr Sayed Munawar Hussain Mashadi (Chairman).

The UK Islamic Mission, 202 North Gower Street, London NW1 2LY. The UK Islamic Mission, founded in 1962, has some forty centres scattered throughout Britain, which provide Islamic education for Muslim children, carry out welfare work to help needy Muslims in Britain, assist in solving problems of Muslims in Britain such as halal food for Muslim children and proper dress for Muslim girls in schools, offer information services for non-Muslims and provide access to a large number of books on Islam through branch libraries.

The Mission publishes an Islamic Calendar which has prayer time-tables for Muslims and beautiful specimens of Islamic architecture, calligraphy and verses of the Holy Qur'an. Another item that might be of interest to schools is the Mission's recent publication *Towards Understanding Islam.* Some publications on Islam are made available to schools free of charge.

The Mission accepts visits by school groups and provides speakers to schools and colleges free of charge. It will also provide consultancy services to teachers. Correspondence and inquiries should be addressed to Mr S.M.T. Wasti, General Secretary.

Union of Muslim Organisations of the UK and Eire, 30 Baker Street, London W1M 2DS. The Union of Muslim Organisations of the UK and Eire can provide consultancy services to teachers at present. It hopes to begin classes on Islam soon and to establish Muslim denominational schools, for boys and girls separately. Recent publications likely to be of interest to teachers include *Islamic Education and Single Sex Schools, Guidelines and Syllabus on Islamic Education, Call from the Minaret* and *The Prophet.*

Visits by school groups are not possible, but speakers are provided to schools and colleges for payment of travel expenses only. Correspondence and inquiries should be addressed to Dr Syed A. Pasha, General Secretary.

Index